NUMBER 101

Yale French Studies

Fragments of Revolution

Yale French Studies

Published with assistance from the foundation
  established in memory of James Wesley Cooper
  of the Class of 1865, Yale College.

Caroline Weber and Howard G. Lay, *Special editors
  for this issue*
Alyson Waters, *Managing editor*
Editorial board: Edwin Duval (Chair), Ora Avni, R.
  Howard Bloch, Peter Brooks, Mark Burde, Shoshana
  Felman, Catherine Labio, Christopher Miller, Susan
  Weiner
Editorial assistant: Joseph Mai
Editorial office: 82-90 Wall Street, Room 308
Mailing address: P.O. Box 208251, New Haven,
  Connecticut 06520-8251
Sales and subscription office:
Yale University Press, P.O. Box 209040
New Haven, Connecticut 06520-9040
Published twice annually by Yale University Press

Designed by James J. Johnson and set in Trump
  Medieval Roman by The Composing Room of
  Michigan, Inc. Printed in the United States of
  America by the Vail Ballou Press, Binghamton, N.Y.
ISSN 044-0078
ISBN for this issue 0-300-09238-5

For Ross Chambers

CAROLINE WEBER AND HOWARD G. LAY

Editors' Preface:
Fragments of Revolution

An allegorized calendar and a police facsimile of a home-made bomb;
a newspaper advertisement promising the regeneration of society and
an engraving documenting its destruction; a novelist's vision of a fecund maternal body and a poet's meditation on a little boy's corpse:
these are among the fragments of revolution passed down to us by a century of resistance, opposition, and repression. During the volatile period in French history that stretched from the end of the Old Regime to
the anarchist Terror of the early 1890s, a host of writers, artists, activists, and otherwise ordinary citizens devoted their efforts not so
much to interpreting the world—*pace* Marx's famous thesis on Feuerbach—as to changing it. The desired changes rarely occurred. But revolutionary discourse was nonetheless steeped in faith, in optimism,
and in the belief that boundless potential lay just on the other side of
even the most disheartening failures. This is Marx looking back at the
disappointments of 1848:

> The so-called revolutions of 1848 were but poor incidents—small frac-
> tures and fissures in the dry crust of European society. However, they
> denounced the abyss. Beneath the apparently solid surface, they be-
> trayed oceans of liquid matter, only needing expansion to rend into frag-
> ments continents of hard rock. Noisily and confusedly they proclaimed
> emancipation . . . i.e., the secret of the nineteenth century, and of the
> revolution[s] of that century.[1]

This is a suggestive passage, and it invites a double reflection. On the
one hand, it intimates that revolutionary activism contributed a *material* (if insufficient) disruption of dominant ideological structures; the

---

1. Karl Marx, "Speech on the Anniversary of the *People's Paper*," in David McLellan,
ed., *Karl Marx: Selected Writings* (Oxford: Oxford University Press, 1977), 338.

YFS 101, *Fragments of Revolution*, ed. Weber and Lay, © 2002 by Yale University.

"apparently solid surface" of the Old Regime, of the restored monarchy, and of bourgeois republicanism was scarred by "small fractures and fissures" that somehow promised to alter the very fabric of sociopolitical life. On the other hand, the richly metaphorical language ("dry crust," "liquid matter") in which Marx couches this ostensibly materialist point reveals another component at work in the interplay between "so-called revolutions" and society as a whole. To the extent that social relations are constituted by and through the mediations of language, the revolutionary interventions of the nineteenth century— and the fragments they left behind—can be understood to possess a markedly *figural* dimension, one that continues to generate a complex feedback loop of signification, interpretation, and at times, hermeneutic confusion.[2] "Noisily and confusedly they proclaimed emancipation": the sound and fury of revolutionary intransigence invariably signified *something*, even when it failed to effect a radical transformation of existing social hierarchies and symbolic networks. In a contemporary context, the on-going media blitz launched by last year's attacks on the World Trade Center and the Pentagon attests, for better or for worse, to the persistent mutability of signification and interpretation alike (and to a naggingly incongruous relationship between the two).[3] However much an incident seems—as the horrific events of 11 September still do—to defy explanation, our shared tendency is to keep talking.[4] We sift through the wreckage left in the wake of previously unimaginable developments, and we endeavor to make heads or tails of it all.

In an important sense, of course, the task of gathering and parsing the fragmentary detritus of life-changing events falls to those of us who

2. This point—developed at length by the likes of Jacques Derrida and Paul de Man— has in the field of revolutionary historiography found a convincing spokesman in Keith M. Baker. See the introduction to his edited collection, *The French Revolution and the Creation of Modern Political Culture* (London: Pergamon Press, 1987) I, xii, as well as his essay, "On the Problem of the Ideological Origins of the French Revolution," in Dominick LaCapra and Steven L. Kaplan, eds., *Modern European Intellectual History* (Ithaca and London: Cornell University Press, 1982), 198–99.

3. Of course it has not gone unnoticed that these acts of "brute violence" derived tremendous symbolic significance from their targets: the World Trade Center and the Pentagon as metonyms, respectively, for Western Capitalism and American military might.

4. The same phenomenon seems to be borne out by the recent proliferation of studies devoted to trauma in general and to the Holocaust in particular—the latter being, on an even greater scale than the recent "Attack on America," an occurrence for which, on the most obvious level, words are lacking (*les mots y manquent*, as Jacques Lacan would say).

work in the liberal arts, and who read and write in the related disciplines of art history, literary criticism, and history. As an attempt to address the questions that arise when representation stands face-to-face with broad-based sociopolitical change, *Fragments of Revolution* consists of contributions from all these fields. Unlike the last issue of *Yale French Studies* to address the interplay between aesthetics and revolutionary politics, *Literature and Revolution* (1967), the present volume benefits from the paradigm shift that the academy has undergone in recent years, one that has sanctioned seemingly "nonliterary" or "extraartistic" cultural phenomena as valid objects of research. The essays that comprise this collection focus on works both canonical and noncanonical, conventional and unconventional. Just as provocatively as the writings of Diderot, Balzac, and Baudelaire, for example, popular prints, newspaper advertisements, and even exploding flower pots serve as springboards for reflection on the difficult questions that attend the theory and practice of radical social transformation. In this regard, the methodological underpinnings of *Fragments of Revolution* owe a great deal to the kinds of scholarship that coalesce loosely under the rubric "cultural studies," and that tend to marshal a broad range of materials to the exploration of a single theme—all the while resisting the allure of history's various master narratives. A famous novel and an act of vandalism may both function as highly politicized modes of address, but the one does not necessarily imply or explain the other. Rather than merging into a unified account of a complex and multifaceted cultural moment, they stand as informative fragments of a bygone era, our access to which is determined almost entirely by artifacts. The title of this volume thus underscores not only the heterogeneity of the materials examined in the following pages, but also the necessarily incomplete or inconclusive nature of its findings.

It should be stressed, however, that the work put forward here parts company with "cultural studies" in one critical way, insofar as scholarship bearing that label sometimes insists on a cleavage between the *materiality* of historical and textual phenomena, and the *interpretability* thereof.[5] The essays in this collection problematize any such

5. In "Matérialisme and Révolution," Jean-Paul Sartre deplores a similar trend among orthodox "historical materialists" of the mid-twentieth century—writers who, he argues, misread or simplify Marx himself in their haste to dismiss thought and language as instruments of idealist mystification. See Jean-Paul Sartre, *Situations III* (Paris: Gallimard, 1949), 135–225. As is indicated by our reading, above, of Marx's richly figurative assessment of the events of 1848, and as Marshal Berman demonstrates at greater length

facile separation by highlighting the degree to which even the most iconoclastic or unspeakable of "material events" both derives from and yields to instances of mediation and exegesis.[6] While the Montagnard architects of the Reign of Terror, say, argued for a privileging of things over words and of a republican clean slate over royalist symbolism, they could not effect this sweeping agenda without themselves resorting to figural expression. Similarly, a century later, a terrorist bomb—placed on the window sill of a Parisian restaurant for no apparent reason and by no obvious culprit—unleashed an explosion of discursive activity in journalistic, legal, and political circles. By turns implicitly and explicitly, these two instances (and the others analyzed in this volume) demonstrate that the raw material of history insists on its own readability, ideological pressures to the contrary notwithstanding. We are by no means suggesting that the people and things impacted by violent political upheaval are devoid of any reality outside the realm of semiotic play and symbolic exchange. By the same token, we cannot in good faith claim to offer our readers unmediated access to the stuff of history. If, in keeping with Nabokov, we insist that we "have only words" at our disposal, this time when examining the turbulent age of French revolutions, this is a function not only of our own training as interpreters of cultural production, but more fundamentally of the profoundly mediated nature of the subject matter itself. In the vexed task of "proclaiming emancipation," the revolutionary fragments investigated in these articles partake of—and of course perpetuate—all the noise and confusion proper to the signifying process.

---

in *Adventures in Marxism* (London and New York: Verso, 1999), the philosopher's relationship to reading and interpretation was and is especially complex.

6. Detractors of deconstruction often overlook the fact that de Man himself rigorously labored to undo the apparent antimony between referential truth and figural language, particularly in his posthumously published collections, *The Resistance to Theory* (Minneapolis: University of Minnesota Press, 1993) and *Aesthetic Ideology*, ed. Andrzej Warminski (Minneapolis: University of Minnesota Press, 1996). See also Ernesto Laclau, "The Politics of Rhetoric," in Tom Cohen, Barbara Cohen, J. Hillis Miller, and Andrzej Warminski, eds., *Material Events: Paul de Man and the Afterlife of Theory* (Minneapolis: University of Minnesota Press, 2001), 229–53. In *For they know not what they do* (London and New York: Verso, 1991), Slavoj Žižek observes that "deconstructive" efforts like de Man's do not—as is commonly charged—lump history and rhetoric together in the name of *il n'y pas de hors-texte*, but rather work to demonstrate that "the establishment of truth as something which is prior to and independent of 'secondary' rhetorical effects and figures is [itself] founded upon a radical rhetorical gesture" (33–34).

We are grateful to our contributors for their perceptive analyses along these lines, as well as to the enormously talented Alyson Waters for her thoughtful, patient revisions of each piece. Finally, we wish to thank our readers for their interest in what is, for us, an endlessly compelling subject: the confrontation of language and matter, born of a utopian belief in a world made better by words and deeds alike.

I. Material Strategies

CAROLINE WEBER

Freedom's Missed Moment*

The time is out of joint.
　　—William Shakespeare, *Hamlet*

On 26 July 1794, the last day of his rule and his life, Maximilien Robespierre sounded a note of doom from the podium of the National Convention. Although he had led the Convention, the Montagnard party, the Committee of Public Safety, and by extension France itself for over a year, Robespierre felt the political tides turning against him and his self-proclaimed "despotism of liberty." Under his stewardship, violence had devastated the French polity. His chief means of establishing freedom—which to him meant a state cleansed of all royalist vestiges and counterrevolutionary impulses—was Terror, that "prompt, severe, and inflexible justice"[1] that sent countless citizens to the guillotine. Once revered as the very embodiment of republican virtue, Robespierre was now a marked man. Sensing that his days were numbered, he made an extraordinary speech about the failures, past and future, of his reign. "We shall perish," he informed his fellow *conventionnels,*

> for having failed to seize a moment that the history of men had marked
> for the founding of liberty; we shall surrender our fatherland to a cen-

*I would like to thank the members of the University of Pennsylvania French Cultural Studies seminar for their helpful comments on my work, and my research assistants, Dan Edelstein and Erin Kearney, for their invaluable contribution to the editing of this volume as a whole.

1. Maximilien Robespierre, "Sur les principes de morale politique qui doivent guider une république," in *Robespierre. Écrits*, ed. Claude Mazauric (Paris: Messidor/Éditions sociales, 1989), 300. Except when marked otherwise, all references to Robespierre's writings come from this abridged edition, which I prefer to the older *Oeuvres complètes* for reasons of availability and editorial clarity. All translations of the Montagnard's language are my own; many also appear in Caroline Weber, *Terror and Its Discontents: Suspect Words in the French Revolution* (Minneapolis: University of Minnesota Press, 2002 [forthcoming]).

YFS 101, *Fragments of Revolution,* ed. Weber and Lay, © 2002 by Yale University.

tury of calamities, and the maledictions of the people will attach to our memory.[2]

Read not only in light of Robespierre's final months but also from the privileged vantage point of history, these words seem prophetic to say the least. In addition to belying the liberty, equality, and fraternity pledged in 1789, his stringent measures of Terror also, for historians of later times, provided the model for many of the calamities that attended subsequent revolutionary activity: from the uprisings of nineteenth-century France to the purges of Stalinist Russia. Accordingly, Robespierre's own name has been subject to many a malediction since his rise and fall.[3] With his prospective evocation of the centuries to come, the Montagnard leader thus successfully predicted the future of his historical reception, even if he met with supreme failure in the summer of 1794.

Admittedly, Robespierre's primary task was a daunting one. "Those who tell you that the foundation of a Republic is easy are deceiving you," he remarked in his final speech (Robespierre 1840, 722). The "founding of liberty," in particular, was no mean feat, and a close examination of selected documents reveals that it may have been all but impossible according to the very terms in which the republican project was couched. It is therefore my aim in this paper not to engage in yet another discussion of how the Revolution, courtesy of the Montagnards, betrayed its own ends, but rather to suggest that such a betrayal may have been *constitutively* inevitable. Taking my cue from Robespierre's comment about the missed moment that heralded his government's demise, I shall focus on the vexed notions of temporality that he and his acolytes developed as an explicit part of their public policy. I shall show that their desire to wipe the slate clean and found a polity freed from its tyrannical, monarchical past put into play a back-and-forth between an ahistorical present and a curiously retroactive future. On the one hand, "real" history was consistently denied in favor of what Walter Benjamin has, in a different context, called the "time of the *now.*"[4] On the other

2. Robespierre, "Discours du 8 Thermidor An II," in *Oeuvres*, vol. 3, ed. Lapponeraye and Carrel (Paris: n.p., 1840), 730.

3. On the perception of the Terror as a model for Stalinism, see, in the French tradition, Albert Camus's eloquent *L'homme révolté* (Paris: Gallimard, 1951). On Robespierre's reception as a villain in nineteenth- and twentieth-century historiography, see Hilary Mantel, "What a man this is . . . ," in *The London Review of Books*, 22/7 (30 March 2000).

4. See Walter Benjamin, "Theses on the Philosophy of History," in *Illuminations*, ed. Hannah Arendt (New York: Shocken Books, 1969), trans. Harry Zohn, 254. Benjamin's

hand, a not yet existent history was repeatedly constructed and projected forward for the benefit of future generations. The result was that in their attempt to reconfigure time as a vital component of liberty, the architects of the First Republic repeatedly and invariably engaged in a logic of the *will have been*. It is perhaps insofar as this unrealizable future anteriority informed the effort to found freedom that the Revolution came to undermine its stated goals, to devour its own children.

My allusion to cannibalistic family dynamics—a popular trope during the Terror—is by no means incidental. For the link between temporal complexity and the instantiation of civic law finds a most helpful expression in *Totem and Taboo,* Sigmund Freud's account of a primordial and cannibalistic parricide. Of course, this text has already been invoked by numerous scholars of the Revolution to theorize the derivation of republican "fraternal" bonds from the murder of that paternal tyrant *par excellence,* Louis XVI.[5] These accounts fail, however, to identify what I take to be the most important parallelism between Freud's band of brothers and Robespierre's—and that is the unusual temporal mode that characterizes the laws and liberties that develop, in each case, in the wake of the parricide. This temporal mode, *nachträglichkeit* or "after effect," emphasizes the deferred nature of all civil obedience. For although the overthrow of a single tyrant is necessary to the establishment of a society based on reciprocal relations and equal rights, the sense of justice that underpins them never coincides with the primordial murder itself. At the moment of the *Urvater's* actual defeat, as narrated by Freud, the "liberating" awareness of law and morality that will soon dictate the brothers' behavior does not yet exist. Only through the subsequent intervention of the after effect do the brothers, "by deferred obedience to" the dead authority-figure, devise a self-legislating morality (à la Kant and Rousseau) that will retroactively become the foundation of their community.[6] The after effect operates, in short, as "the effaced signal of something which only takes on its value in the future, . . . in its integration into the history of the

---

German neologism, *Jeztzeit,* is according to his translator, explicitly intended to distinguish revolutionary "time filled by the presence of the now" from a more conventional "present" tense (*Gegenwart*).

5. See Lynn Hunt, *The Family Romance of the French Revolution* (Berkeley: University of California Press, 1992) and Jacques André, *La Révolution fratricide. Un essai psychanalytique sur le lien social* (Paris: PUF, 1993).

6. Sigmund Freud, *Totem and Taboo,* ed. and trans. James Strachey (New York and London: W. W. Norton, 1950), 145.

subject. Literally, it will only ever be a thing which . . . *will have been.*"[7] Under these conditions, time unfolds in the space of an irreconcilable disconnect: the space, we might say, between synchrony and diachrony. Or between what Slavoj Žižek has termed the "non-historical place" of the mythical parricide and the history that both follows from and retroactively posits this same point of "origin."[8]

My hypothesis is thus that if in their quest for liberty the French revolutionaries did indeed become, as one popular print from the era suggests (Figure 1), an "eater of kings," then they did so with considerable consequences for time itself. In the pages that follow, I will demonstrate how their supposedly radical break with the past ineluctably followed the contorted logic of the after effect—how retrospection and deferral inhered in even the most impassioned pleas for untainted republican immediacy. I shall take as the focus of my investigation two sets of materials from the period: the orations delivered by Robespierre and Saint-Just in late 1792, arguing for Louis XVI's execution, and the texts and images surrounding the adoption, in October 1793, of a new calendar designed to herald the "era of the Republic." In both cases, we shall see that there is a marked and irreconcilable tension between the notion of revolutionary time as absolute rupture on the one hand, and as a future-bound, retroactive positing of an origin on the other. We shall also be led to ask what this tension implies for the notions of liberty that such conceptions of time were meant to advance. For if, as my opening citation from Robespierre indicates, establishing freedom is ultimately a question of timing, of seizing a particular historical moment, then it follows that in "fail[ing] to seize the moment," one fails to seize liberty itself. Derived from a vexed and impossible temporality, the state, to modify our Shakespearean epigraph, is out of joint. Time is not on Robespierre's side.

SPECTERS OF FREEDOM

Let us turn then to that history-making parricide, the unprecedented execution of a king that began with Louis XVI's trial in the fall of 1792. In the wake of Louis's failure to prevent his palace guards from firing on a mob on 10 August, the radical Montagnard party pushed the Na-

7. Jacques Lacan, *Seminar I: Freud's Papers on Technique,* ed. Jacques-Alain Miller, trans. John Forrester and Sylvia Tomaselli (Cambridge: Cambridge University Press, 1988), 159; Lacan's italics.

8. Slavoj Žižek, *The Sublime Object of Ideology* (London and New York: Verso, 1989), 135.

Figure 1. Anon., *Le Peuple mangeur de Rois*, 1793. Engraving. Musée Carnavalet, Paris.

tional Convention to declare the monarch an enemy of the state and execute him before he could betray the French people any further. The Montagnards' opponents in this matter were the Girondins, who reminded everyone that according to the Constitution ratified a year beforehand, Louis XVI retained a degree of royal inviolability, complicating the question of whether he could be tried at all.[9] In light of this fact, the Girondins insisted that a careful parsing of the Constitution would have to precede any such measure as the king's outright execution. Now, as this relatively simplistic and necessarily abbreviated account of the debate is intended to demonstrate, the underlying issue was one of temporal politics—with the Montagnards advocating immediate action, over and against what they perceived to be the Girondins' legalistic deferrals and filibustering deliberations.[10] When Robespierre's future right-hand man, Louis Saint-Just, addressed the assembled legislators for the first time on 13 November, this was the precise opposition he articulated in his electrifying speech. "I have often noticed," he remarked,

> that false precautionary measures, delays, reservations, have often in this case been true acts of foolhardiness; and after the imprudent act that defers our moment for giving laws to the nation [*le moment de nous donner des lois*], the most deadly would be the one that would make us temporize with the king.[11]

Saint-Just's vocabulary explicitly denigrates the temporal units or "measures" that his opponents' hesitations and delays fritter away. For him the Girondins' strategy—their own pretensions to prudence notwithstanding—is downright imprudent, because it puts off "our moment for giving laws to the nation," the instantiation of the self-legislated (*"nous* donner des lois"*) freedom with which the Montagnards wish to

9. On the difficulties posed by the constitutional language regarding Louis's royal inviolability, see Michael Walzer, "The King and the Law," in *Regicide and Revolution* (Cambridge: Cambridge University Press, 1974), 35–46.

10. On the instantaneous temporality championed by the Montagnards, see Mona Ozouf, "La Révolution française et l'idée de l'homme nouveau," in *The Political Culture of the French Revolution*, vol. 2, ed. Colin Lucas (Oxford: Pergamon Press, 1988), 219–30. Ozouf's essay is a fine source of information on attitudes toward time in the revolutionary era; it does not, however, mention the new calendar, nor does it insist on the trial of the king as a particularly crucial showcasing of the Montagnards' radical approach to temporality.

11. Louis-Antoine de Saint-Just, *Discours et rapports*, ed. Albert Soboul (Paris: Messidor/Éditions sociales, 1988), 62; my translation.

replace monarchical rule. Insofar as they work against this goal, the Girondins' legalistic orchestrations are mere "temporizing" measures, designed to put off the inevitable triumph of republican right.

Despite this vituperation against his adversaries' deferrals, however, Saint-Just's own conception of time is itself caught in a deadlock. Like the "deferred obedience" adopted after the fact by Freud's parricidal horde, the code of behavior prescribed by the young Montagnard is paradoxically not experienced or even posited at the time of its articulation. Even in what he presents as the best-case scenario—instantaneous action and the refusal of all temporally mediating structures—Saint-Just's notion of self-imposed liberty is, from a temporal perspective, neither here nor there:

> Someday, people will be surprised that in the eighteenth century, things were less advanced than they were in Caesar's day: then, the tyrant was sacrificed in the middle of the Senate, with no other formalities than twenty-three blows of a dagger, and with no other law than the liberty of Rome. [63]

Ostensibly, Saint-Just is arguing here for an immediate governmental overthrow echoed semantically in the *coups* or dagger-blows of Caesar's assassins. The murder that he hypothetically proposes—opposed as it is to the "other formalities" of his opponents' platform—seems, as Maurice Blanchot has noted, to occur in a kind of radical present.[12] As a corollary to this temporal immediacy, the gesture also purports to escape all interference from the constitutionally-based ideas of legality championed by the Girondins. Upon closer inspection, however, we realize that this valorization of "no other law than the liberty of Rome" is itself profoundly mediated, and bears all the marks of the after effect. First, the emancipatory murder that Saint-Just describes occurs at a foundational moment of the Roman republic; the exemplary law of freedom thus invoked only reaches the speaker's compatriots after a delay of almost two thousand years. Second, even the moment at which the French revolutionaries do allegedly receive this liberating gospel is deferred: like Caesar's originary murder, it is at a great temporal remove

12. In reference to the "unmediated" temporal politics promoted by Saint-Just, as well as by his contemporary the Marquis de Sade, Blanchot describes "that time of between-times during which, between the former laws and the new laws, reigns the silence of the absence of laws." See Maurice Blanchot, "The Main Impropriety," trans. June Guicharnaud in *Yale French Studies* 39, *Literature and Revolution*, ed. Jacques Ehrmann (1967): 58.

from any revolutionary experience at the moment of enunciation "in the eighteenth century."[13] For, tellingly enough, Saint-Just relates not a contemporary emulation of Brutus and company, but rather the reaction that people will have at some unspecified future date, when looking back on the *conventionnels'* arguments over Louis's fate. "Someday, people will be surprised": he envisions a future act of retrospection, at which point the Revolution will or will not have realized the Montagnards' goals. In this manner, the moment of self-legislated independence is projected back into the past and forward into the future, while serving as the basis for discourse in a present with which it can never coincide. Such a wrinkle in time is not negligible, because the temporal parenthesis that Saint-Just opens up here encompasses the very law of republican freedom. Liberty, like the time zone (past and future) in which Saint-Just locates it and the men (past and future) with whom he associates it, partakes of the logic of *spectrality.* Bracketed between being and nothingness, "the specter desyncrhonizes time."[14] Freedom itself assumes the quality of a ghost.

The temporally and ontologically vexed—or "hauntological," to borrow an apt neologism from Derrida[15]—nature of Saint-Just's call for freedom also characterizes Robespierre's speeches on the same subject. Following fast upon his colleague's oration of 13 November, Robespierre addressed the Convention and treated his auditors to a long series of oppositions between past and future, with the present oddly located outside of time. In perhaps his most peculiar development of this temporal schema, Robespierre mentioned Louis XVI's ambiguous historical status as the ultimate grounds for the monarch's dismissal. "Louis," he declared, "has outlived [*a survécu à*] the royalty, and the royalty itself had outlived [*avait survécu au*] the superstitious prestige that once surrounded it" (207). According to this logic, the king is unfit to rule because he is no longer a man of the times: the fact of having outlived a system that has itself long since been outmoded makes him a misfit in the temporal register of the Revolution. Only by executing the king, Robespierre argues, will it be possible to place the necessary

13. Classical antiquity in general, and the Roman republic in particular, could themselves be said occupy a "hauntological" position in the Montagnards' vision of the state, in that they persistently haunt the political rhetoric of that party. As Jacques André observes in *La Révolution fratricide,* "the Revolution . . . permits Antiquity to remain so *present . . .* in the *res publica*" (164; my translation, André's italics).

14. Ernesto Laclau, *Emancipation(s)* (London and New York: Verso, 1996), 68.

15. Jacques Derrida, *Specters of Marx,* trans. Peggy Kamuf (New York and London: Routledge, 1994).

"incommensurable distance between what the king was [*ce qu'il fut*] and the dignity of a citizen" (Robespierre, 215)—between the monarch's past and the citizen's present. Like the Freudian *Urvater*, Louis would appear in this formulation to have been brutally suppressed: the very application of the literary *passé simple* to the king's existence practically fictionalizes the monarch, suggesting that he is not (or is no longer) real. Nevertheless, in Robespierre's schema as in Freud's, the repressed father figure returns, giving shape to the very system that requires his exclusion. Immediately after relegating the king to a no-man's land outside of republican space and time, Robespierre brings him back with the pithy phrase: "Louis was king [*fut roi*], and the republic is founded [*est fondée*]: the famous question that has been preoccupying you is decided by these words alone" (215). In this parallel structure, republican actuality is at the level of language haunted by the presence of the king, who is not exactly alive (because, again, confined to the fictional time of the *passé simple*) while not yet dead (because inscribed in the sentence all the same). Furthermore, and disconcertingly, it is through Robespierre's very positioning of him as a quasi-effaced, "hauntological" personage that Louis XVI functions just like the freedom that was supposed to supplant him. The "incommensurable distance" that Robespierre aims to place between the French king and the French citizen has collapsed in the zone of spectrality. And if the royal tyrant's cause can be confused with that of liberty, if the two polar opposites can contaminate or be confused with one another, then, in Robespierre's prescient words, "what is to become of the Revolution?" (215)

The prognosis was not a good one, and it was made worse by the fact that Robespierre continued doggedly to reiterate the lingering importance of the monarch in his own antimonarchical political system:

> I propose that from this very moment, you make a statute [*statuer*] about Louis's fate. . . . I ask that from this very moment the National Convention declare him a traitor to the French nation. I ask that as such he be made to stand as a great example to the entire world, in the very place where the generous martyrs of liberty perished on 10 August; and that this memorable event be consecrated by a monument destined to nourish in the hearts of the people a sense of their rights and a horror of tyrants, and in the hearts of tyrants, a salutary terror of the people's justice. [219]

In the few literary analyses that have been done of Robespierre's oratory, much has been made of its performative characteristics, and certainly the repetition of constructions such as "I ask" and "I propose" places this passage in that category.[16] Not surprisingly, both the aim and the effect of such performativity are to collapse the gap that traditionally separates speech from action; insofar as Robespierre's speech creates this rhetorical effect, it would appear to emulate the temporal immediacy of, say, Julius Caesar's sudden assassination. But this is far from being the case, given that Robespierre's series of urgent requests culminates in a call for the construction of a monument commemorating the execution that *will have been.* Already evoked homonymically in Robespierre's use of the verb *statuer,* the proposed statue itself derives from a prolepsis: in its very essence, it anticipates the gaze of future generations looking back on what will, by that time, have become a significant historical moment. Structured around a "great example" that can only be grasped after the fact, the revolutionary present is again placed within temporal parentheses. Worse yet, it is placed under erasure: for Louis's monument will stand on the site of, and thus in the place of, the "martyrs of liberty" slain by royal troops on 10 August. Although Robespierre's proposal was intended as a tribute to the revolutionary heroes of that day, it in fact ordered that these men's ghosts be joined and even overshadowed by the specter of their greatest nemesis. By introducing the king into the very temporal and ontological space occupied by the partisans of liberty, Robespierre again, and like Saint-Just, undermined his party's effort to eliminate the vestiges of monarchical power.

THE REPUBLICAN CALENDAR BETWEEN
SYMBOL AND ALLEGORY

Fast forward about a year, to the fall of 1793: the Montagnards have prevailed and Louis XVI is dead, but the work of overwriting France's royalist past with an untainted republican present has only just begun. Terror has become official public policy, and Robespierre's government is working to purge the state of "counter-revolutionary" elements. As a part of the purge, a special committee is formed in the Convention[17]

---

16. See Marc-Eli Blanchard, "The French Revolution: A Political Line or a Language Circle," in *Yale French Studies* 39, 64–78, as well as Marie-Hélène Huet, *Mourning Glory: The Will of the French Revolution* (Philadelphia: University of Pennsylvania Press, 1997).

17. This commission was a subcommittee of the Committee of Public Instruction, which itself reported to the Convention. Its principal mandate was to reform not only the French calendar but the French language, school system, and so on. The members of

and charged with the task of reconfiguring time itself—of erasing from the national consciousness all traces of the monarchical history. Finding that the best means to this end would involve doing away with the Gregorian calendar itself, this committee decides to create a new calendar based on purely patriotic symbolism. As Hannah Arendt has observed, this measure functioned to perpetuate the notion that with the Revolution, "the course of history suddenly beg[an] anew."[18] Accordingly, and in keeping with the Montagnard rhetoric of immediacy that dominated Louis's trial, many of the new calendars displayed an iconography of instantaneous destruction, figured by a lightning bolt decimating the Bastille and the royal "hydra of despotism" (Figure 2). Fabre d'Églantine–the *de facto* spokesperson for the special committee—jubilantly described the radical new present that the reformed calendar was to usher in:

> The regeneration of the French people [and] the establishment of the republic have led [*ont entraîné*] necessarily to the reform of the vulgar era. [After the fall of the monarchy,] we could no longer count [*nous ne pouvions plus compter*] the years when the kings oppressed us as a time when we were actually alive. The prejudices of the crown and the clergy, and the lies propagated by both, sullied every page of the calendar that we had been using.[19]

As in the Montagnards' call for regicide, Fabre's main concern in this speech is to eradicate the grave threat to freedom that prerevolutionary history represents. In order to efface the time, precisely, when the people were alive but were not free, Fabre proposes to purge the calendar of its absolutist associations with monarchy and clergy. Only in this way, he declares, can the nation's ideological principles of freedom and equality be solidified. Very much in the manner of Robespierre, Fabre drives his point home through a deft manipulation of verb tenses. Using the *imparfait* to narrate the recent process of calendar reform (*"nous ne pouvions plus compter"*), he appears to locate the process in a more distant past than the one implied by his initial *passé composé*

---

this special commission came from a variety of backgrounds, from astronomy to literature. Although Fabre, himself a playwright, proved the poetic and theoretical mastermind behind the new calendar, the commission was chaired by a *conventionnel* named Gilbert Romme, and is thus still occasionally referred to as the "Romme commission."

18. Hannah Arendt, *On Revolution* (London and New York: Penguin Books, 1990 [1963]), 28.

19. Fabre d'Églantine, *Oeuvres politiques*, ed. Charles Vellay (Paris: Éditions Fasquelle, 1914), 173–74.

Figure 2. Anon., *Un calendrier révolutionnaire, An II*. Engraving.
Bibliothèque nationale, Paris.

("la régénération . . . et l'établissement . . . ont entraîné . . ."). If, however, Fabre's speech effects an apparent distancing of the age of Louis
XVI, the same cannot be said of the republican calendar itself. The first
and most glaring problem with the temporal "regeneration" in question consists in the new calendar's peculiarly retroactive nature. For although the Convention approved it on 24 October 1793, it posited 22

September 1792, the date on which the republic was first officially declared, as its point of departure. The course of history—*pace* Arendt—
indeed began anew at this point, but it began in what the republicans
dubbed Year II of Liberty, defined with respect to a Year I (September
1792–1793) that itself never occurred by that name except in retro-
spect. Yet again, the founding moment of the new state was suspended
in its immediacy and deferred until a group of future citizens—namely,
the calendar reformers, *conventionnels*, and citizens of 1793—could
apprehend it as having taken place. The "reform of the vulgar era" and
the institution of the "new" one occurred under the sign of the after effect.[20]

The convoluted temporality instantiated by the calendar becomes
even more apparent when we examine the representations that commonly attended its temporal reconfigurations. These representations
can be divided, crudely, into two categories: discursive (nomenclature, dating systems, etc.), and visual (the calendar as material object,
adorned with various images). Fabre d'Églantine made a key contribution to the first group by inventing new names of the month based on
the seasonal qualities specific to each one. Bemusedly commenting on
this substitution, Thomas Carlyle would later quip: "*Vendémiaire, Brumaire, Frimaire,* or as one might say, in mixed English, Vintagearious,
Fogarious, Frostarious: these are our three autumn months."[21] To justify this fanciful and innovative terminology, Fabre made the following remarks when presenting the calendar for a general vote in the Convention on 24 October:

> The people's longtime habit of using the Gregorian calendar has filled
> their memory with a considerable number of images that they have
> revered since time immemorial and that are to this day the source of
> their religious errors; and so it is necessary to replace these visions of
> ignorance with the realities of reason, and to replace the prestige of the
> church with the truth of nature. We cannot conceive of anything with-
> out the help of images: in the most abstract analysis, in the most meta-
> physical formulation, our understanding only makes sense of things
> through images, our memory only rests upon images. You must there-
> fore apply images to your calendar, if you want it to penetrate in its en-

20. Jacques André makes this point when he remarks in passing that the republican
calendar "n'ouvr[e] la nouvelle ère que dans l'après coup" (161), *l'après coup* being the
French translation of "after effect."

21. Thomas Carlyle, *The French Revolution*, vol. 2 (New York: A. L. Burt Company,
n.d.), 269.

tirety and with relative ease the people's understanding and to be etched into their memory. [174]

This argument for image-based representation recalls, once again, the diatribe against forms and formalities leveled by Saint-Just and Robespierre against the Girondins during Louis XVI's trial. For Fabre, as for his fellow Montagnards, the establishment of freedom could only be brought about through the removal of artifice, mediation, and delay from the conceptualization of republican time. Indeed, this position lies at the root of Fabre's opening invective against priests and religious holidays. In his view, the new calendar would, by suppressing the clerical associations of its predecessor, eradicate the lingering influence of Catholicism on the people of France. The striking parallelism between Fabre's rant against "the prestige of the church" and Robespierre's attack on "the superstitious prestige that once surrounded [the monarchy]" (207) is telling in this regard: it posits as a fact of language the close alliance between church and state that had formed the basis of pre-revolutionary despotism. Once liberated from the external, "tyrannical" authority of the clergy and the king, the people would be governed in true republican fashion—by themselves. Released from the bondage of Old Regime tutelage, they would henceforth take as their sole guide those innate qualities shared, according to Enlightenment ideology, by one and all: "the realities of reason" and "the truth of nature."

The natural connotations of the new month names were particularly vital to their political efficacy. Informing his colleagues in the Convention that they should look to the reformed calendar as an instrument of great public utility, Fabre went on to explain that the natural overtones of its month names should prove especially useful in the construction of the new polity.

> This should be a fortunate opportunity for you to seize, the opportunity to use the calendar, the most widely read of all books, to bring the people back to agriculture. Agriculture is the political foundation of a people like ourselves, whom the earth, the sky, and nature herself look upon with so much love and predilection. When at each instant of the year, of the month, of the *décade* [the new ten-day alternative to the week], and of the day, the mind and the gaze of the citizen settle upon an agricultural image, on one of nature's benefits, on an object of rural economy, you must not doubt but that this represents, for the nation, great progress toward the agricultural system, and that as a result every citizen conceives a great appreciation for the real and effective gifts [*présents*] of nature. [174–75]

Taking to its logical conclusion Fabre's panegyric of immediacy, this passage suggests that a calendar based on seasonal cycles eliminates the artificial mediating structures—like the Gregorian calendar—manipulated to nefarious ends under the Old Regime. The agricultural imagery of the new calendar is truly a "political element" insofar as it liberates the people from their former, externally imposed and hierarchically marked experience of time. The citizen here invoked by Fabre inhabits a pure present characterized by a changeless and unceasing communion with nature: "*at each instant* of the year, of the month, of the *décade,* and of the day," he or she will be led to contemplate the wonders of agriculture. Through the purportedly transparent mediation of the "agricultural image," the French people were, in Fabre's scheme, to achieve a life of radical synchrony—in sync with what psychoanalytic historian Jacques André has called "the *history-free* rhythm of nature, the time of nature, of the eternal return, of the return of the same" (161).

In aesthetic terms, this kind of effort to seek in nature a stable and timeless basis for one's representations—a veritable obsession in late eighteenth-century European poetics—can be understood as the adoption of symbolic diction. Unlike the allegorical diction with which it is often mistakenly confused, the symbol provides the speaking subject with the illusory sense of an absolute identification between himself and the outside world. ("This melancholy landscape 'symbolizes' the pain in my heart," the literary heroes of the day are wont to proclaim, "I am as one with my surroundings.") Because this identification represents the subject's "attempt to borrow from the outside world a . . . stability which [he] lack[s] within [him]self," Paul de Man explains that it likewise involves a singular approach to temporality:

> In the world of symbol it would be possible for the image to coincide with the substance, since the substance and its representation do not differ in their being but only in their extension: they are part and whole of the same set of categories. Their relationship is one of simultaneity, which, in truth, is spatial in kind, and in which the intervention of time is merely a matter of contingency, whereas in the world of allegory, time is the original constitutive category.[22]

This idea of a temporal and ontological simultaneity between image and substance also, of course, informs the rhetoric of immediacy and

22. Paul de Man, "The Rhetoric of Temporality," in *Blindness and Insight* (Minneapolis: University of Minnesota Press, 1983 [1971]), 207.

fusion that Fabre employs. He claims that his proposed new months coincide with the eternal constant that is nature—not only insofar as
they take the natural world as their sole organizing principle, but also
insofar as they bear "natural," *symbolic* names, names that require no
mediating thought or complicated abstraction to decipher. "Thermidor," for instance, is a "natural" term to apply to a hot summer month,
"the month of heat that is both solar and terrestrial, that sets the air on
fire in July and August" (Fabre 180). By aligning itself with nature,
Fabre's nomenclature would therefore seem to eliminate the interventions of both time and tyranny. No time is lost in consulting arcane eru-
dition ("January is derived from the Roman god Janus"); no autonomy
compromised in seeking an explanation from priests ("we call today
Saint Peter's day because . . .").[23] Of the clergy, Fabre complained
precisely that "their ministrations used to interfere between heaven
and ourselves" (175). Along with the *imparfait* of his verb tense in
this statement, the symbolic diction of his calendar instituted a new
time, a time when such interferences would no longer beset the French
people.

But this account of how symbolic diction informs Fabre's month
names does not tell the whole story. As I have already mentioned, symbol is easily mistaken for allegory, and Fabre's theorization of the relationship between time and nature in the new era displays, as if in spite
of itself, distinctly allegorical overtones alongside the symbolic ones.
And while we have encountered de Man's assertion that "time is the
originary constitutive category" of the allegorical mode, some additional elaboration may prove helpful as we set out to determine just
how time impinges on the radically untainted present promised by
Fabre's calendar. Once again, de Man's elegant essay on allegory and
time will point us in the right direction:

> [In allegory,] the relationship between signs necessarily contains a con-
> stitutive temporal element; it remains necessary, if there is to be alle-
> gory, that the allegorical sign refer to another sign that precedes it. The
> meaning constituted by the allegorical sign can then consist only in the

23. One contemporary Vaudeville play entitled *Un violin pour tout le monde* [A Violin for Everyone] mocked the calendar's substitution of animal, vegetable, and mineral
terms for the saints' names that had long organized the French experience of time and
even identity: "Imagine my extreme surprise/When, looking for Saint Nicodema,/
Whom I had been given as a patron,/I found that I am—a Turkey!" My translation; cited
in French by Henri Wleschinger, *Les Almanachs de la Révolution* (Paris: Librairie des Bib-
liophiles, 1884), 50.

repetition . . . of a previous sign with which it can never coincide, since
it is of the essence of this previous sign to be pure anteriority. [207]

The noncoincidence of signs described here can also, and more simply,
be understood as the foregrounded existence of mediation—something
that pervades Fabre's proposal even as he tries to avoid it. On perhaps
the most obvious level, the predominance of allegory over symbol in
Fabre's speech manifests itself in his choice of agriculture in particular, and not "nature" in general, as the reference point and model for
his new temporal configuration. Whereas symbol seems to offer a
nondifferentiated, nonhierarchical, and therefore liberating fusion between the subject and his environs, agriculture involves the submis-
sion of nature to man's designs. The farmer's toil is moreover inscribed
in what Fabre himself dubs a "rural economy," a system of substitutive
exchanges in which the monetary sign—as Robespierre and Saint-Just
frequently remarked in their contemporaneous debates about money—
only corresponds in an artificial and alienating way to the fruits of the
earth. An economy of this kind could only thwart the dream of transparency that underpinned virtually all public policy during the Terror.
In a specifically temporal dimension, the interjection of economics,
rural or otherwise, into the proposal for calendar reform undermines
this creation's illusion of simultaneity or timelessness, for both farm-
ing and economic exchange depend just as much on the "effective gifts"
as on the "real gifts of nature." The field that lies fallow in preparation
for sowing does not, by definition, coincide in time with the field that
bristles with new crops—the former stands in a relationship of "pure
anteriority" to the latter—but each is *sequentially* necessary if the agricultural enterprise is to work. Likewise, if I insisted above on the
alienation implicit in the farmer's supposedly exemplary commercial
transactions, I meant this in a temporal as well as an existential sense.
Because the purchase and sale of crops and livestock presupposes the
prior establishment of an external measure by which agricultural and
monetary value can be brought into relation, temporal immediacy or
the "purity" of the present go out the window along with freedom from
any external mediating principle. Allegory is temporal and ontological
mediation *par excellence,* and it places its unmistakable mark on this
passage in which Fabre tellingly refers to his own invention as a book.
    The problems raised by allegory are furthermore not restricted to
the verbal discourses that surround and compose the new calendar; its
visual representations also unwittingly destabilize the notions of syn-

chronic temporality that Fabre and his fellow committee members were trying to set forth. Perhaps the most striking example in this vein is a popular print from 1794 entitled "The Republican Calendar Vanquishing the Gregorian Calendar" (Figure 3). At first glimpse, this image appears to thematize the very defeat of monarchist hierarchies and mediating structures proclaimed by its anonymous creator's more prominent political counterparts. The print depicts the Gregorian calendar, figured by a host of scattered lists of religious holidays; the Catholic clergy, represented by a man in a bishop's mitre lying on the ground; and the royalty, personified by another man whose crown has all but fallen off his head. All these trappings of Old Regime ideological mystification are shown in the process of being trampled on one side by a group of pitchfork-wielding peasants, and on the other by a female figure dressed in classical garb and bearing a sort of wand. It is this latter figure, I believe, who complicates the otherwise transparent reading that the image seems to invite, for she bears no "natural," readily discernible relation to the calendar that the title alone sets her up to have—i.e., as the triumphant republican calendar. On the most basic level, the fact that we need to refer to the image's title in order to understand what is depicted reveals the visual representation's reliance on an allegorical series, not a symbolic coincidence or conflation, of signs. And of course the figure's flowing robes and feminine attributes—clichés of allegorical visual representation—only heighten her status as allegory. Her spatial positioning, moreover, is *before* a columned building engraved with Fabre's new month-names: from these markings as well as its own visible "title," "Temple de l'année dédiée aux lois et aux jours" [Temple of the Year Dedicated to Laws and Days], this edifice looks much like another allegorical representation of the republican calendar. And yet it does not coincide physically with the triumphant female figure. The woman and the building do not even exist in the same temporal register: the cloud of smoke that swirls around her suggests that she has just arrived on earth (an ethereal companion hovers above the ground, holding her hand as if preparing to draw her heavenward once more), whereas the Temple of the Year is clearly hewn from limestone and rooted to the spot. The effect of these spatial and temporal divisions between the republican calendar's two principal representations is further to underscore the allegorical mode that characterizes each of them individually. The woman and the temple form a series or even a sequence; to understand their meaning is no instantaneous business, but instead requires several stages of intepretive cross-referencing that

FRONTISPICE.

Figure 3. Anon., *Le calendrier révolutionnaire vainc le calendrier grégorien* [n.d.], Frontispiece for Louis-Sébastien Mercier, *Le Nouveau Paris*. Engraving. The Houghton Library, Harvard University.

negates the supposed temporal immediacy and representational transparency of their referent. It is, finally, ironic that the popular print's allegorical manipulations should be reserved for the figure(s) of the republican calendar, and not for those of the Gregorian calendar whose visual metaphors are so immediately comprehensible, so "symbolic."

I see another, similarly disjunctive or "allegorical" visual effect in the imagery that decorates a page of a republican calendar alluded to earlier in this essay (Figure 2). As in the case of the popular print, this material actualization of Fabre's proposal does not at first appear unusually rich in potentially problematic imagery. This particular page represents a fairly uninteresting assortment of proud, statuesque figures tricked out in Graeco-Roman draped fabric and Phrygian bonnets—themselves ubiquitous representations of freedom in both the art and the wardrobes of the day—which were veritable commonplaces of the newly booming calendar genre. Even the calendar's visual centerpiece, the hydra being struck by lightning, was a customary topos for monarchical and religious despotism in revolutionary discourse generally.[24] Given the interpretive mediation that all these allegorical figures require (e.g., a knowledge of ancient history, or a familiarity with the figurative language being used in reference to the monarchy in current newspapers and political speeches), they can certainly be said to undermine the "symbolic" temporality that Fabre ascribed to his calendar. What I find more interesting still, however, is the pair of tiny portraits, rendered in profile, that frame the central image of the hydra. The man shown on the right, with his pockmarked skin and hallmark turban, is Marat—as anyone familiar with David's famous painting of the politician, then or now, would realize. The man on the left, eminently dignified in a high collar and a powdered wig, is most likely Le Pelletier, the *conventionnel* who was assassinated by a royalist for having voted in favor of Louis XVI's execution in December 1792. Before I explain this qualifier "most likely," I should point out that here as in the speeches at that trial, the new republican present that the text seeks to establish is haunted by the presence of the dead. Figures like Marat and Le Pelletier live on in martyr portraits such as these, thereby reminding the republic that it too has blood on its hands—that its own history, no matter how brief, is nevertheless just that, a history with points of reference more contingent and more unjust than anything

24. For a discussion of the widespread revolutionary topos of the hydra, see Jacques André, 154.

contained in the more timeless and "natural" world with which the new polity would like to be wholly aligned. Even in the ostensibly pure present of the republican calendar, specters are afoot, bringing the un-welcome truth of the past to bear upon the "time of the now."

There remains, however, an even more provocative and unsettling problem with these martyr portraits, and that is the very problem of de-termining the subjects' identities to begin with. I have already hinted at this difficulty by noting that the figure on the left is "most likely" Le Pelletier. I made this inference because I know that he and Marat, considered exemplary martyrs to liberty, were two of the most popular artistic subjects in Year II, the year in which this calendar was made. But because these portraits' legibility requires reference to "an extra-neous principle that determines the point and the manner at and in which the relationship [between sign and referent] is articulated" (de Man, 209), and because that extraneous principle is, by definition, no-where available on the calendar page itself, Le Pelletier's identity is up for grabs. Such indeterminacy becomes all the more problematic when we recognize that the iconography associated and applied to (a possi-ble) "Le Pelletier"—the powdered wig and the starched, stiff-collared jacket—was also the same imagery that characterized Robespierre dur-ing this time (Figure 4). Under the Old Regime, dressing in this manner had been the norm in noble and even some bourgeois circles; with the Revolution, practically all right-thinking citizens shed these items in favor of looser, simpler, less "artificial" clothing meant to denote vir-tue and honesty. Robespierre alone, and inexplicably, retained his fancy wigs and collars. His potential confusion with Le Pelletier, an aristo-crat who had died before the vogue for republican simplicity caught on, is, in the context of Figure 2, disturbing at best. For when this calendar was published, probably in October or November 1793, Le Pelletier was dead but Robespierre was very much alive, still fighting the "counter-revolutionary" forces that had laid his *doppelgänger* low. At the very least, the "Le Pelletier" portrait loses some of its efficacy as an image of martyrdom if it could be thought to represent Robespierre instead. No martyr, that one . . . not yet.

Not yet: therein lies the final temporal twist. For although Robes-pierre still reigned supreme in the first months of Year II, he was over-thrown and guillotined before it was over, in Thermidor (July 1794)—the month that this very calendar page happens to represent. The bizarre future anteriority that we have been examining throughout this essay thus resurfaces one more time, with a vengeance. However

Figure 4. Anon., *Robespierre* [n.d.]. Graphite and white chalk on paper. Chateau de Versailles.

inadvertent on the part of the calendar's creator, the casting of Robespierre as a republican martyr while he is still alive seems to suggest that the Montagnard leader *will have died* for the polity he once ruled. It not only predicts the imminent occurrences of Thermidor Year II; more significantly, it projects the Montagnard leader himself forward in time, into the land of the living dead that is history. Reconsidered in this light, the quotation from Robespierre with which I began this essay becomes considerably less eerie. "We shall perish," he avowed with such unflappable certainty about the future. To come to this conclusion, it turns out, he had only to look as far as the republican calendar.

ERIKA NAGINSKI

The Object of Contempt*

> . . . no Divinity was more harmful to Savages than gold, which they certainly believed to be the Fetish of the Spanish. . . . The Barbarians of Cuba, knowing that a Castilian fleet was about to land on their island, decided they had to appease the Spanish god in order to be rid of him. They gathered all their gold in a basket. . . . They danced and sang around it according to religious custom, then threw it into the sea.
>
> —Charles de Brosses, 1760[1]

> I see everything in action and reaction; everything destroying its own original form; everything reconstituting itself into another form; vaporizations, dissolutions, combinations of all kinds, phenomena incompatible with the purported homogeneity of matter; from which I conclude that matter is heterogeneous . . . from all this is born movement or, rather, general fermentation in the universe.
>
> —Denis Diderot, c. 1770[2]

My subject is the image of destruction in revolutionary France. In particular, I shall focus on one image whose title *Moyen expéditif du peuple français pour démeubler un aristocrate* [Expeditious Means By Which the French People Move an Aristocrat Out of His Residence] (Fig. 1), announces with no small measure of relish what representation goes on to reenact for the viewer: the circumstances under which the fate of an aristocrat's private residence was sealed in the fall of 1790. However, if I risk initial digression by making the following claim, it

*I am deeply grateful to Howard Lay for his careful reading of this essay, as well as to Jacques de Caso, Tom Gretton, Darcy Grigsby, and Anne Wagner for helpful comments on earlier drafts. Thanks also go to attentive listeners at the Association of Art Historians Conference (University of Edinburgh, April 2000) and at "Iconoclasm: Contested Objects, Contested Terms," a conference organized by Richard Clay and Stacy Boldrick and hosted by the Henry Moore Institute in Leeds (July 2001). Unless otherwise indicated the translations are mine.
    1. Charles de Brosses, *Du culte des dieux fétiches* (Paris: 1760), 53.
    2. Denis Diderot, "Principes philosophiques sur la matière et le mouvement," *Oeuvres complètes* (Paris: Hermann, 1987), vol. 17, 18.

MOYEN EXPÉDITIF DU PEUPLE FRANÇAIS POUR DÉMEUB-
-LER UN ARISTOCRATE. 13 novembre 1790.

Figure 1. Anon., "Moyen expéditif du peuple français pour démeubler un aristocrate," *Révolutions de France et de Brabant* 52. Engraving. The Houghton Library, Harvard University.

is because I think it will offer a broader discursive context for describing that image and its interestingly methodical framing of destructive actions in the revolutionary public sphere. The claim is this: that the High Enlightenment recognized the potential agency of things and of the sensuous materials from which things are made—a fact that has some altogether peculiar implications for the way the power of objects came to be experienced. Consider, for a start, de Brosses's famous theorization of fetishism and the way it sets the stage for indigenous culture's ritual eradication of the enemy. Then compare it with Diderot's scientistic account, atheistic and anti-Cartesian, of matter's heterogeneity and of self-propelled forms continually authoring their own dissolution, permutation, and reassembly. In bringing the two together as epigraphs, my point is simply to stress that they posit the *tabula rasa* as a site of dynamic exchange. For de Brosses, primitive society wipes the slate clean by performing a counter-alchemical gesture, one whose latent carnivalesque aspect makes manifest the rejection of impending conquests and (so Marx would later surmise) of modern economics; the gold is cast into primordial depths in order "to be rid of" the system of commodity exchange it otherwise promises to deliver in the form of money.[3] Meanwhile, for Diderot, a cosmological phenomenon discloses its inner workings by means of the shimmering molecular flux of sempiternal fragmentation and condensation, of "everything destroying its own original form" so as to perpetuate the universe's "general fermentation." Despite different thematic points of departure, both of these examples mark the distinctive place the impulse to destroy retains in world-making events.

Hence these are accounts that can be seen to play their part in dramatizing a general shift away from seventeenth-century understandings of matter as essentially passive and subject to God's arbitrary judgment. The presumed dependence of material bodies on external forces was a premise that sat squarely at the center of Baroque theological doctrine, political philosophy, and scientific thought. To be sure, such a premise came to be contested more or less directly in contemporaneous alternative intellectual movements like Vitalism and Neo-Epicureanism. But as John Rogers, among others, has shown, a good part of its staying power was due to the way it cut across belief systems and

3. On Marx's citing of the passage and the extent to which his theories of commodity fetishism rest on Enlightenment formulations, see William Pietz, "Fetishism and Materialism: The Limits of Theory in Marx," in Emily Apter, William Pietz, eds., *Fetishism as Cultural Discourse* (Ithaca and London: Cornell University Press, 1993), 130–34.

explanatory realms as different as Calvinist providentialism or Hobbes-ian mechanistic explanations of agency.[4] The Enlightenment, by con-trast, gradually sought out a markedly less deterministic position. It evolved toward the possibility that matter was radically active, with power being construed as "substantively present in entities, thus defin-ing the entities' essence in terms of inherent activity."[5] Inherent ac-tivity, that is, *was* matter's substance—and destructive (as much as constructive) forces were a necessary part of its equation in a post-New-tonian world.

So whether the frame of reference is alchemy or chemistry, or the point of view the Cuban *barbare*'s or the French *philosophe*'s, the ap-pearance of erasure as an operative function highlights the material presence of absence in eighteenth-century epistemologies. From an an-thropology of ritual to a microphysics of motion: if substance and ab-sence are similarly brought together in such disparate spheres of knowl-edge production, it is because the pairing itself is repeatedly cast in terms of agency (social, scientific, or otherwise). So thought Philo in David Hume's *Dialogues Concerning Natural Religion* (1779): "This world, therefore, with all its events, even the most minute, has been before produced and destroyed, and will again be produced and de-stroyed, without any bounds or limitations."[6] The claim not only im-plies that matter moves ostensibly without God's volition (as Philo's interlocutor Demea despairingly points out). It also implies that mate-riality is inseparable from mutability, integrity indistinguishable from disintegration, thereby endowing things (even the most prosaic) with an intrinsic and troubling vitality.

How might these discursive parameters help to make sense of the image of destruction in revolutionary France? How does the idea of

4. John Rogers, *The Matter of Revolution: Science, Poetry, and Politics in the Age of Milton* (Ithaca and London: Cornell University Press, 1996), 8. On Neo-Epicureanism in this context, see Richard W. F. Kroll, *The Material Word: Literate Culture in the Restora-tion and Early Eighteenth Century* (Baltimore and London: Johns Hopkins University Press, 1991), 85–179.

5. P. M. Heimann and J. E. McGuire, "Newtonian Forces and Lockean Powers: Con-cepts of Matter in Eighteenth-Century Thought," *Historical Studies in the Physical Sci-ences* 3 (1971): 235–36. Herman and McGuire argue that the new explanation of matter and movement resulted from the epistemological intersection of eighteenth-century philosophical and natural scientific theories. See along these lines John W. Yolton, *Think-ing Matter: Materialism in Eighteenth-Century Britain* (Oxford: Basil Blackwell, 1984); and Simon Schaffer, "States of Mind: Enlightenment and Natural Philosophy," in G. S. Rousseau, ed., *The Languages of Psyche: Mind and Body in Enlightenment Thought* (Berke-ley: University of California Press, 1990), 233–90.

6. David Hume, *Dialogues Concerning Natural Religion* ([London]: 1779), 82.

matter's alterity—its innate forces and dispersive pressures—come to figure in the politically radical exercise of erasure? To begin with, pre-revolutionary valuations of matter's irruptive qualities routinely left their stamp on revolutionary rhetoric. Strong echoes of this aspect of High Enlightenment philosophical materialism are discernible in the yoking of destruction and renewal that persistently surfaced as leit-motif in legislative tracts, republican pamphlets, and artistic treatises during the 1790s. Indeed it is arguable that the yoking, by the simple fact of its ubiquity, is one of the more obvious ways in which language is made to fabricate (through repetition) a symbolics of violent collective action: "I am well aware," wrote artist and art dealer Jean-Baptiste-Pierre Lebrun in the year III, for example, "that during the storms that inevitably accompany great revolutions, the first moments must be devoted to setting down the first stones of the great edifice that will rise up in place of the one that is destroyed."[7] This was hardly an original formulation. The vision of a phoenix-like edifice emerging from the smoldering ashes of the past—the edifice in this instance being the Constitution of 22 August 1795—had an all-too-familiar ring, for this was the refrain tirelessly sounded to justify the revolution's mythic advent. But the pervasiveness of such clichés does not mean that what underlies them, a thematizing of erasure, should be dismissed as the in-consequential symptom of overused rhetorical mannerisms. To the contrary, when placed against eighteenth-century notions of fetishism (like de Brosses's) or of anarchic unrest at an infinitesimal level (like Diderot's), the thematizing moves beyond the conventions of ideolog-ically-inscribed discourse to reveal how the empirical world of things might have been perceived at Enlightenment's end.

Propulsion, dispersion, reassembly: I am saying that this is the net-work of forces—the recipe for ferment (inherited from materialist in-terpretations of absence and substance, destruction and production)—that asserts itself when people destroy objects of everyday life or works of art in revolutionary France. Where that network of forces is most tan-gible, interestingly enough, is in the *representation* of erasure: in wood-cuts recording pillage, in engravings depicting toppled royal statues, in etchings setting down the fragile silhouettes of mutilated cathedral fa-çades, or in drawings and paintings recapitulating significant histori-cal junctures like Bastille Day or the desecration of Saint Denis. This is not to suggest that images of destruction, including the one I go on

7. J. B. P. Lebrun, *Essai sur les moyens d'encourager la peinture, la sculpture, l'ar-chitecture et la gravure* (Paris: An III [1795]), 3.

to discuss in the next sections of this essay, are somehow tantamount to an objective record of events as these actually unfolded. The point of the exercise is different. It is to address a distinctive exegesis on negation that is paradoxically visual in nature (how does the representation of erasure work, exactly?), to compare it to its written counterparts, to track its figural resonance, and to decipher the conflicted response to things that it carefully rehearses: a response to things inspiring both desire and scorn; a response to things that, while they might have reified religion, culture, privilege, or the enemy, also bore within them the capacity to animate, destabilize, and transform those who touched them.

PROPULSION

Let me now turn to the image in question (Fig. 1). Although *Moyen expéditif du peuple français pour démeubler un aristocrate* is nothing more than a small anonymous engraving, it arouses considerable interest in its viewers for a number of reasons: first, because it serves as frontispiece to an issue of Camille Desmoulins's *Révolutions de France et de Brabant;*[8] second, because it offers a specific date (13 November 1790) as a clue for historically locating the scene it describes; and third, because it delivers its message with exquisitely incisive humor. But above all, what an image like *Moyen expéditif* does is to establish some clear guidelines for how to orchestrate the sack of an architectural space that, under prerevolutionary conditions, would have been deemed both imposing and impregnable

Begin, so the image instructs, by opening a window through which to display the domestic treasures you are about to hurl from the sanctuary of affluence: bed sheet after bed sheet, a cracked mirror in a gilt frame, or an overstuffed chair waiting to meet its embroidered twin down below. It is crucial that the display—which secures for these objects a framed and centralized location in pictorial space—allow for a brief moment of contemplation, for what thereby gets signaled to the outside world is an internal struggle between a desire to possess and an ethos of refusal. Your companions will accordingly be vulnerable to flashes of indecision. Can you detect, for instance, a note of regret in the young woman on the lower right who fingers, gingerly, the heavy drape made of finer material than the dress she wears? Or when hats

8. The radical slant of the journal's frontispieces is highlighted by Jack R. Censer, "The Political Engravings of the *Révolutions de France et de Brabant,* 1789 to 1791," *Eighteenth-Century Life* 5/4 (Summer 1979): 105–24.

come off in salute to the King's likeness on the second floor, derision mixed with a sense of wonder for the commanding dimensions of the state portrait? And in the middle of it all perhaps a tinge of longing for the lady in the oval frame held, for the first time, at arm's length? While individual encounters with luxury are successively captured in each window, ensuing propulsion ensures that debris from the everyday life of privilege will continue to accumulate in the courtyard: a commode beyond repair, a shattered window, a frying pan, an enema syringe there perhaps as an indecorous metaphor for purging France of its elite—and thrown in as junk along with the rest, a single bill of paper money.[9]

The image, to summarize, presents us with a visual compendium of things and outlines for us a methodical way of proceeding the simple gestural mechanics of which belie the complexity of the performance at hand. But before I address the pictorial terms of that complexity, it is necessary to recover the historical circumstances from which the performance itself arises. Whose private property is being transgressed, by whom, and why? Part of the answer emerges from the way the print names (in its title) and figures (through class and gender) *le peuple*. To do so at all calls attention to the thorny issue of authorship and accountability. In this respect, it seems important to observe that when the vandal appears in the annals of the French revolution, it is to take on the part of devoted patriot, naive judge, souvenir peddler, fanatical barbarian, blood-thirsty harpy, hardened criminal, duped participant, passive observer, hapless bystander, or accessory after the fact—an encyclopedic typology of human behavior, in short, that glosses over the real conundrum for participants and historians alike. For where transgressive deeds such as these are concerned, the historical record never manages cleanly to disentangle above from below, individuals from the crowd, official decisions from popular interventions, or a given set of political prejudices from retrospective verdicts on the ethics of collective action. Such schizophrenic doubleness of authoriality—and the oscillation between heroism and culpability it necessarily carries with it—might depend as much on the politics of the

9. Readers of Mikhail Bakhtin will, of course, recognize in excremental imagery such as the enema syringe one of many explorations, in French revolutionary caricature, of the Rabelaisian body and its symbolic purging. Somatic allusions to aristocratic excess or ecclesiastical greed harness such carnivalesque imagery in order to present revolution as the moral corrective to old regime degeneracy—and thereby insert that same imagery into what Peter Stallybrass and Allon White, in *The Politics and Poetics of Transgression* (Ithaca: Cornell University Press, 1986), have called "a generalized economy of transgression and of the recoding of high/low relations across the whole social structure" (19).

moment as on the bias a given historical account will later betray. But, as sociologically attentive analyses rightly observe, the doubleness is also a constitutive part of how vandalism and iconoclasm happened to unfold in the revolutionary public sphere.[10]

For the purposes of this essay, which reflects on the means to an end proposed by one exemplary representation of erasure, I simply want to point out that *Moyen expéditif* seems to insist on an episode coming from below. Whether or not this holds true for how things actually came to pass on 13 November 1790, the assumption that the people were primarily responsible has significant repercussions for the way the destruction of property comes to be *figured* here. For turn to press releases on the incident the print illustrates is to discover that when *le peuple* takes it upon itself to punish the object of its contempt, it is faced with not one but two options: either hunt someone down or lay his property to waste. These were the courses of action—according to one provincial sheet whose left-wing sympathies would have been aparent to its readership—open to those gathering in cafés and politi-cal clubs at the Palais-Royal to discuss the outcome of a highly publi-cized duel between Charles de Lameth and the Duc Armand de Cas-tries (Fig. 2).[11]

The two deputies were surely aware when they faced off in the Bois de Boulogne on 12 November 1790 that any personal differences of opinion would instantly be converted by the gallant sword play in which they chose to engage into a public skirmish pitting the earnest republicanism of the former against the disingenuous royalism of the latter. And if the political stakes of such a chivalric butting of heads were as obvious as Louis Prudhomme's *Révolutions de Paris* made them out to be, this was ostensibly because of what the weekly char-acterized as an insidious "plot formed to grant the king a military res-

10. Among those more recently to stress this point is Dario Gamboni, *The Destruc-tion of Art: Iconoclasm and Vandalism Since the French Revolution* (London: Reaktion Books, 1997), 31–39. A comprehensive bibliography would be far too voluminous to in-clude here, so I refer the reader to Bronislaw Baczko, *Comment sortir de la Terreur. Ther-midor et la Révolution* (Paris: Gallimard, 1989), 255–304; Édouard Pommier, *L'art de la liberté. Doctrines et débats de la Révolution française* (Paris: Gallimard, 1991); and Richard Wrigley, "Breaking the Code: Interpreting French Revolutionary Iconoclasm," in Alison Yarrington, Kevin Everest, eds., *Reflections of Revolution* (London: Routledge, 1993), 182–95.

11. *Journal de Versailles* 167 (15 Nov. 1790): 722. Pierre de Croze's late nineteenth-century account, "Un duel politique pendant la révolution. Castries et Lameth," *Le cor-respondant* 67 (25 June 1895): 1101–34, contains biographical details as well as an apol-ogy for aristocratic motives.

Figure 2. Anon., "Duel entre M. M. Charles de Lameth et de Castries," *Révolutions de Paris* 70 (6–13 November 1790). Engraving. The Houghton Library, Harvard University.

idence manned with 6,000 troops from the National Guard."[12] In order to preclude the project's veto by the Assembly, members of a royalist faction had apparently attempted to "assassinate without being compromised" no less than six "eloquent defenders of the people" by challenging each of them, more or less all at once, to a duel. It should be stressed that such a strategy, in which treachery posed as valor, was by then utterly controversial;[13] a duel fought three months earlier by the deputies Antoine Barnave and Jacques-Antoine-Marie de Cazalès was among those loudly denounced in any number of proposals to abolish a patrician manner of conflict resolution that, for the guardians of enlightened republicanism at least, bore all the reprehensible signs of "the ancient feudal system, its inimical influence, its intolerable violence."[14] As for the *affaire d'honneur* in the Bois de Boulogne, it had left the streets rife with rumors of a poisoned sword, de Lameth wounded more or less seriously, his aggressor on the run, and Parisians up in arms. But as the mass press makes clear, daily updates on the victim's condition did little to detract from the most memorable part of the story. Those café-goers and club members metamorphosed into the irritated multitude that, once gathered at the Tuileries, made its way to the rue de Varenne then ransacked without further ado the Hôtel de Castries. "Ah ça va bien. Punissons les aristocrates" [Hey all's okay. Let's punish the aristocrats]: if we are able to take the strophe gracing the image at face value, this is because throwing things out windows had emerged to win the day as the most efficacious expression of the people's judgment.[15] De Castries would go into hiding, as the *Annales patriotiques* wryly noted, "so as not to share the same fate as his furniture."[16]

12. *Révolutions de Paris* 70 (6–13 Nov. 1790): 249. For a municipal proclamation addressing the issue, see *Le moniteur universel* 317 (13 Nov. 1790): 355.

13. Jules Michelet, *Histoire de la Révolution française* (Paris: Gallimard-Pléiade, 1952), vol. 1, 472.

14. A. J. Alexander, "Lettre d'un Anglais à un Français sur le duel de M. C*** et de M. B***," *Le moniteur universel* 229 (17 Aug. 1790): 405. Among those to lobby for reform was Philippe-Antoine Grouvelle, *Projet d'adresse à l'Assemblée nationale sur le duel* (Paris: Imprimerie Nationale, 1790).

15. As the translation suggests, this is a clumsy transposition of the *Carillon national* whose intoxicating, often vengeful refrains—such as "Ah! ça ira, ça ira, ça ira, les aristocrates on les pendra!" [Hey! All's going to be okay. The aristocrats, we'll hang them!]— were a collective call to arms. See Michel Delon, Paul-Édouard Levayer, eds., *Chansonnier révolutionnaire* (Paris: Éditions Gallimard, 1989), 13; 52–55.

16. *Annales patriotiques* 409 (15 Nov. 1790): 667.

DISPERSION

Taken together, then, journalistic word and satirical image would seem to rest on common ground. Both are products of newspaper culture. And both highlight identical moments of social transgression by fixating on the same peculiar details of specific actions taken. Journalists were eager to report, for instance, that paintings were chewed to bits while a portrait of Louis XVI emerged unscathed (even inciting respect in the midst of chaos).[17] The print correspondingly notes the tipping of hats before the royal image in the upper left—and, along the edge of an ecclesiastical portrait laid to rest in the courtyard, telltale bite marks serving as evidence of cannibalism once removed. Shared also is anecdotal information about the kinds of objects destroyed, so that the impressive variety of domestic articles depicted in the print is reiterated with varying degrees of precision in lists the press made sure to publish: sometimes brevity was called for ("All the furniture, mirrors, and jewels were thrown out the window"[18]); otherwise a more comprehensive record of things chewed, shredded, crushed, or merely discarded was there to provide both theatrical punch and the requisite documentary proof with which to certify journalistic veracity.[19] Word and image thus can be understood on some level to be in close dialogue, disclosing with equal enthusiasm the idiosyncracies of violence and the pressing need to make lists. (It is surely worth noting that those lists included hand-crafted things—marble tables, elaborately carved furniture, rugs, tapestries, mirrors, chandeliers, paintings, beds, silverware, porcelain, a *piano forte,* a clock reportedly worth 1,000 *louis*—as well as money itself in the form of coins and bills. Might we not therefore speak of the ceremonious destruction of gold by de Brosses's Cuban savages as having found its modern incarnation in the Hôtel de Castries episode? In this respect, the rejected "assignat de 10000" in the picture's foreground plays a key role because it intimates that an ethos of refusal was aimed not only at the old order's system of privileges but

17. *Chronique de Paris* 318 (14 Nov. 1790): 1270. On Mirabeau's defense of the people's actions along these lines, see the *Journal de Paris* 319 (15 Nov. 1790): 1298.

18. *Le moniteur universel* 319 (15 Nov. 1790): 369.

19. Compare for example the detailed list offered to the international readership of the *Mercure historique et politique* 47 (20 Nov. 1790): 205, to what is inventoried in a provincial sheet like the *Courrier de Villeneuve-les-Avignon* 204 (21 Nov. 1790): 840. That the loss of the Vernets was particular regrettable is stressed by the *Journal de Paris* 318 (14 Nov. 1790): 1294.

also at the new order's arbitrary tabulations of exchange value. That this might be so seems all the more plausible given the fact that in the wake of the nationalization of ecclesiastical property on 2 November 1789, the general precariousness of fiscal conditions was continually being made apparent by the perennially disastrous depreciation of paper money.[20])

Mutually shared details such as these expressly contribute to a hagiography of *le peuple*, its virtues, and its excesses. They also give grounds for speculating more generally on an interesting confusion during this period between iconoclasm (aimed at images) and vandalism (aimed at things)—whereby the destruction of aristocratic privilege is accomplished by means of both simultaneously. What seals the two together is a communal repertoire of bodily gesticulations whose fast-paced rhythms and labor-intensive repetitiveness generate for their audience the fullest expression of spleen possible. This is suggested as much by the image's emphasis on looking, touching, grasping, holding, carrying, breaking, and then hurling as by the narrative references to stampeding, trampling, tearing, biting, throwing, smashing, or setting on fire. Only in this way, so one notably scathing letter to the editor of a royalist sheet argued, could erasure demonstrate its true cultural merit:

> It is clear, in fact, that nothing is better suited to inspire the emulation of artists of all kinds: for the precious paintings by Vernet, Greuze, etc., that patriotism tore to shreds; the chests of drawers and other works of cabinet-making and sculpture that were reduced to ashes; the gold- and silver-plated items, clocks, marbles, mirrors, porcelain, crystal, jewelry that were pulverized or made to disappear; the tapestries, rugs, and precious pieces of furniture that were thrown out the window or burned— all this may have seemed valuable to the artists who, back in the old days, made these masterpieces. But today they are perfectly worthless to the nation's young artists, whose talents are doubtless superior to those of our ancient masters just as our current legislation, administration, and civilization are, as everybody knows, superior to our past government and old customs. . . . [I]t would be extremely desirable, in fact

20. For the revolutionary government it would always be a question not only of how to expropriate but, perhaps more problematic, of how to assign monetary value in the first place in order to lessen the tax burden and restore faith in systems of credit. The ensuing debate over the forms currency should take is described, for example, by J. L. C. J. G. Trevilliers, *Assignats de deux espèces nouvelles, proposés pour être mis au lieu et place des assignats-monnoie ou des quittances de finances* (Paris: Roland, 1790), 59.

entirely fitting, for those who so zealously took on the Hôtel de Castries
henceforth to let patriotism inspire demolition from top to bottom.[21]

Obliterate the masterpiece. Neutralize culture. What better way to sum
up the revolutionary artist's patriotic code of conduct? The bitter sarcasm to be discerned here soars to new heights in the ensuing bid to let
demolition work its way not only from "top to bottom" but across the
entire horizontal expanse of the city: Why not raze *all* residential buildings in Paris? With the Hôtel de Castries as ground zero, the ultimate
dispersion of destructive energies would guarantee the capital's artistic rebirth through total annihilation. This was, after all, the age of "La
Destructiomanie."[22]

Briefly stated, erasure is the only art form revolution has to offer.
Yet there is more to be gleaned from this assertion than the angry mis-
sive just cited lets on. The wrathful calisthenics that erasure requires
to assert its presence in public space—the collective physiological release on which it depends to lay siege to the commodity culture of *ancien régime* luxury—is prompted (sanctioned, even) by matter's heterogeneity, its imminent combustion, its ontic volatility. Think back
to Diderot. If shattered objects occupy center stage in the Hôtel de Castries's courtyard, this means that an archaic world of impenetrable
spaces and inviolate things can be revealed for what it is: an illusory
scrim, a surface far too flimsy to keep matter's liberating energies in
check. It is as if a philosophical materialist doctrine in its High Enlightenment configuration—in which substance, movement, and disintegration coalesce to create the necessary preconditions for foment—had
served to reify, in the form of fragments and their making, revolutionary consciousness itself.

Or had served, more precisely, to represent the mechanisms of that
reification. We can push this idea further by taking into account the
way in which the print I have been discussing begins to pull away from
its verbal counterparts. Insofar as the latter are concerned, it is important to recognize that the colorful distortions and exaggerations
permeating written accounts in the mass press ultimately yield a bi-
furcated, hyperbolic, and transparently politicized representation of
popular actions. Either we witness willing contributors to the workings of justice who, by offering to be searched as they exit the de Cas-

21. *L'ami du Roi* 171 (17 Nov. 1790): 3–4.
22. *Les Sabats jacobites* XI (1791): 161.

tries residence, pledge in unison to uphold the moral dignity of their final ruling: Pierre-Jean Audouin's *Journal universel*, for instance, asserted that following voluntary inspection by the National Guard, the people proclaimed their goal was not to plunder but rather to prove, simply and forcefully, that counter-revolutionary efforts were in vain;[23] the *Révolutions de Paris*, in turn, applauded the joyful parade of unbuttoned vests, open shirt collars, and empty pockets.[24] Or, taken from another point of view, we are faced with unscrupulous marauders and frenzied women whose bestial instincts allow for pedestrian sins like greed and spite to fuel their criminality; hence the *Courrier français*'s allusion to "a band of thieves masquerading as the people"[25] was echoed by the observations of a columnist for *Le spectateur national* who noticed that "during popular uprisings, the extremists are always spurred on by women" to trespass, loot, and burn.[26] We are left, in other words, to contemplate those highly conventionalized substitutes for the popular body—one reporter's *brigand* was another's *soldat citoyen*—finding their place in the protean roster of the revolution's *dramatis personae*.

The recourse in writing to such stock-in-trade presences effectively works to arrest a more careful (less implacable) reflection on the semantic ambiguities brought into play both by the physical impulse to destroy and its accompanying revolutionary *état d'âme*. Such a reflection, however, is precisely what the visual field seems to invite. For despite the lilt of irony in its title, *Moyen expéditif* manages to exit the inflammatory rhetoric of newspaper culture by distancing itself from stereotyping altogether. What makes the distancing possible is a series of pictorial maneuvers that signposts a sustained meditation on destructive actions and their consequences. Consider for a start—and this is a key element in the image's downplaying of collective hysteria and its mythography—that the people are represented by a small group of individuals caught in the act: three women and seven men, all of whom are singled out by (or in two cases paired off in) private zones of contemplation. Our access to those quarantined regions is made possible by an architectonic grid—by those separate bands of rectangular and arched windows serializing, each time with slight variation, the

23. *Journal universel* 358 (15 Nov. 1790): 2859.
24. *Révolutions de Paris* (*op. cit.*): 250.
25. *Courrier français* 317 (14 Nov. 1790): 109.
26. "Variétés," *Le spectateur national* 349 (15 Nov. 1790): 674.

singular encounter between individual and thing. How these encounters translate into the temptation to possess, and thus are formulated to acknowledge the possibility for multiple outcomes, is a matter of the pictorial register's ability to make literal the idea of (narrative) suspense. Are all objects perfunctorily destroyed, or are some furtively kept after all? Do we really know whether the man holding the chair in the upper right is moving toward or away from the ledge? By the mere fact of dwelling on those charged moments when things hang in the balance, the tableau of vandalism's actors necessarily lingers on the options plural, on choice as an open visual signifier, on an image of the people that anticipates divergent, idiosyncratic responses (anger, desire, reverence, and so on). This brings us, finally, to the material things on which those responses hinge, and to the planned emphasis in the foreground on splintered objects whose size far exceeds the individuals who handled them just moments earlier. The absence of normative compositional logic here is too easily explained away as the charming side-effect of an ill-conceived (read unskilled or primitive) rendering of perspectival recession by an anonymous hand, the result of which might be the courtyard that tilts too steeply or a spatial transition between horizontal ground and vertical façade that is too abrupt. Disjunctions in proportion, scale, and orientation function instead to shift focus directly onto scattered fragments the presence of which is earmarked as much by a mutilated condition as by a violent transfer from sheltered domestic comfort to indecent public exposure.

Formal aspects such as these all testify to the image's capacity to work against the grain of narrower, more tendentious characterizations. Once freed from the rhetoric of caricature, ambiguity emerges. It begins in the articulation of an unconventionalized (because unresolved) image of *le peuple,* since the depiction of contemplation, hesitation, and decision-making invites us to insert the cognitive dimension, in all its ethical complexity, into the domain of collective action. This accomplished, we are left as a matter of course to ponder the psychological inner workings of revolutionary consciousness as it is showcased by the fragment and its making. For what is the fragment if not reified negation? What we have here, in essence, is the final material product of an oppositional social practice that openly dispenses with the concept of exchange value by means of a gesturally dictated subversion of any kind of official enumeration (in inventories) or appraisal (in *assignats*) of France's newly nationalized patrimony. Instead of nominalizing the object-signs of the past in a catalogue or on a wall, the throwing of objects through windows—the propulsion of things through apertures mediating inside and outside, private and public— serves to instigate a spatial metonymy of dispersion.

REASSEMBLY

Windows (like doors and mirrors), explains Henri Lefebvre in *The Production of Space*, are transitional objects or thresholds bearing a ritual significance.[27] In selecting descriptive terms like "transitional" and "threshold," Lefebvre is speaking directly to the capacity of architectural openings and reflective surfaces to breach the physical boundaries they demarcate (with frame, sill, ledge, balcony, or roofline). That is, they repeatedly negotiate exchange between interiority and exteriority by collapsing together different spatialities, bringing the room (and the objects it contains) to the street and vice versa. The concept of ritual adds another, more complicated dimension to this ongoing process of two-way transference. For Lefebvre, it is a means of shifting attention to the way thresholds can localize sacred precincts (temples, palaces, churches) and, by extension, can inaugurate life-defining rites of passage (the example he gives of such critical junctures is the moment of "graduating"). Thus his argument seeks to demonstrate how localizations themselves as they work to produce social spaces "derive not only from ideology but also from the symbolic properties of space, properties inherent to that space's practical occupation."[28] This inherent hybridity of space—cast in terms of both symbolics and practices—brings us back to the window as it figures in the Hôtel de Castries episode, and to the threshold's potential ritual function in social practice more broadly defined. What I mean to suggest with the help of Lefebvre's architectural model of mediation is that the image of erasure that has thus far held our attention presents us with a whole series of thresholds (of windows as passageways) the ultimate semantic effect of which readily inserts itself into an ever more far-reaching mode of collective response to the world of material things. For just as *Moyen expéditif* moves beyond the kinds of *ad hominem* views of the people on which the language of the press relies, it likewise sheds its immediate, circumstantial relationship to a specific event and becomes something else entirely.

27. Henri Lefebvre, *The Production of Space*, trans. Donald Nicholson-Smith (Oxford: Blackwell, 1997), 209–10.
    28. *Ibid.*, 210.

The spatial metonymy of dispersion this particular print sets in motion, in other words, is everywhere to be found in revolutionary images of destruction. A handful of examples will suffice to demonstrate its pervasiveness. The *Révolutions de Paris*'s version of 13 November 1790 (Fig. 3) includes the throwing of objects out windows as part of a public spectacle (actors and audiences included). Jean-Louis Prieur's depiction of Saint-Lazare's plundering at the dawn of revolution takes that same spectacle to the streets (Fig. 4). And in an engraving celebrating Bastille Day, the piles of debris encircling the building's foundation perceptibly metamorphose, with each stone cast from above, into uniformly pyramidal—and entirely monumental—shapes (Fig. 5). To be sure, these are all trenchant recapitulations of particular events. But they are also general blueprints for the changing symbolic relation between a certain class of people and a certain class of things. By laying bare the mechanisms of propulsion and dispersion, of matter and volatility, of repetitious collective gestures and the activation of the threshold, these examples attest to the formation of a central visual trope in the representation of erasure—a trope finding monumental expression in pyramids of debris. Hence representation's capacity to transform erasure itself into a kind of revolutionary rite of passage, one calling forth its very own commemorative procedures, as the following eyewitness account makes clear:

> The monument was erected at the entrance of *Franciade*, the old city of Saint-Denis, in the middle of the square. Every patriot was a worker. They made a verdant mountain or triumphant allegory to the mountain party of the Assembly. . . . At the heart of this mountain was a grotto formed of the debris of the tombs of the kings of France. The marbles that had once decorated these sepulchers were brought in great numbers to form this patriotic grotto's arches and pillars. I saw several sandstone figures of Kings set across pillars to serve as pediment. The most beautiful materials of this kind were used artlessly by free hands. This bizarre monument to liberty is perhaps the most philosophical lesson of its kind.[29]

29. "Surplus des objets d'art à conserver qui se trouvent dans la ci-devant abbaye de Saint-Denis . . . ," cited in Louis Courajod, *Alexandre Lenoir, son journal et le musée des monuments français* (Paris: Honoré Champion, 1878), vol. 1, xci. The monument was purportedly erected in honor of Jean-Paul Marat and Louis Michel Le Pelletier de Saint-Fargeau, and coincided with the national convention's decree of 14 November 1793 (24 brumaire an II) authorizing the transfer of Marat's remains to the Pantheon. See Lenoir's sketch of the monument, *1793. La montagne à St. Denis*, in which two busts of the revolutionary martyrs are set above the inscription "Ils furent les amis du people" [They were the friends of the people] (Musée du Louvre, cabinet des dessins).

EVENEMENT QUI A SUIVI LE DUEL ENTRE MM. CHARLES LAMETH ET CASTRIES LE 13. 9.ᵇʳᵉ 1790.

Le peuple irrité de touttes les agressions faites aux seuls Deputés patriotes, s'est mis sur le Champ en mouvement pour exercer sa juste vengeance sur le Sr Castries il a couru en force à son Hotel, et a tout brisé, tout cassé meubles, glaces, Lustr, argenterie, argent, billets de caisse touta été mis en piecer et jetté par les fenêtres

Bureau des Revolutions de Paris, rue des Marais N.º G. N.º 20.

Figure 3. Anon., "Le peuple irrité . . .," *Révolutions de Paris* 70 (6–13 November 1790).
Engraving. The Houghton Library, Harvard University.

Figure 4. Pierre-Gabriel Berthault after Jean-Louis Prieur, *Pillage de la maison Saint Lazare, le lundi 13 juillet 1789*, c. 1791. Engraving. The Houghton Library, Harvard University.

Démolition de la Bastille.

Figure 5. Le Campion, *Démolition de la Bastille,* c. 1789. Engraving. Musée Carnavalet, Paris.

We owe this narrative of iconoclasm's final outcome to an anonymous observer who, in mid-November 1793, went to Saint Denis with the express purpose of drawing up an inventory of works left behind by the *Commission des monuments* in the wake of the officially-sponsored dismantling of the royal necropolis' tombs. As for philosophical lessons, it was Jacques-Louis David who would have had the most to learn from artless hands and the pyramid of fragments they erected. The lesson was this: that the remnants of pillage might, after all, be brought into the realm of public art. Small wonder that his allegorical image of the people as Hercules should also have been destined to stand on "the truncated debris of [royal] statues, piled up any which way." "Such monuments are worthy of us," David went on to proclaim to the Convention, because "those who have adored liberty have always erected them; . . . they are there raised as pyramids and menace foolhardy kings who would dare to violate the land of free men."[30] These are memorable words. David, it seems, had determined that his monument could be made to pick up the pieces so as to order the world anew. In response to that short-lived moment of rhetorical optimism, the Ministry of the Interior requested that citizen Scellier, marble-cutter, present a "report on the status of the debris of the signs of conquered superstition for which he was responsible so that they might be readied to serve as pedestal for the colossal statue."[31]

It is all too tempting to end here by letting a fortuitous citation gleaned from the archives speak for itself, and therefore to confer upon David's astonishing pedestal the responsibility of bringing closure to

30. Jacques-Louis David, *Convention nationale. Discours prononcé par le citoyen David, dans la séance du 17 brumaire, l'an IIè de la République* (Paris: Imprimerie Nationale, nd [1793]), 2–3. The decree dated 17 November 1793 (27 brumaire an II) that David's proposal prompted specifies that his statue "shall be erected on the accumulated debris of the idols of tyranny and superstition," *Archives parlementaires* (Paris: P. DuPont, 1911), vol. 79, 373. On the larger cultural significance of David's Herculean image of the people, see Lynn Hunt, *Politics, Culture, and Class in the French Revolution* (Berkeley: University of California Press, 1984), 87–119.

31. Arch. nat. F[13] 202. See also Louis Tuetey, *Procès-verbaux de la commission temporaire des arts* (Paris: Imprimerie nationale, 1912–17), vol. 1, 45. The commission would later propose incorporating two statues from Fontainebleau—one representing Charlemagne and the other, Louis IX—into David's pedestal (Tuetey, vol. 1, 248). François-Joseph Scellier was the entrepreneur officially entrusted with "the demolition of monuments" who offered his services to the *Commission des monuments* for the transport, conservation, or disposal of works of art confiscated from ecclesiastical and royal establishments. For his various accounts and activities, see arch. nat. F[17] 1039^A and Louis Tuetey, "Procès-verbaux de la commission de monuments," *Nouvelles archives de l'art français. Troisième série* (1902–3), vols. 17–18.

the revolutionary cycle of destruction and construction I have been tracking. The temptation lies not so much in the succinctness with which get instantiated certain aspects of High Enlightenment materialism. Rather, it resides in the pleasure of letting the historical record establish some vividly formal grounds for representation's repeated attempts to recuperate, by means of a highly distinctive experience of the empirical world of things and of the violently contingent forces to which it is subjected, a system of signification credible enough to be called revolutionary. That the system of signification was indeed credible enough seems fairly clear if we are at all invested in discerning its legacy in any number of discursive situations: in Marxist historical materialism, say, in avant-garde subversion tactics, in Modernist strategies of negation, or, if we like, in the Heideggerian notion of *Destruktion*. But this should not detract us from the fact that the recuperation of that system is what makes the image of destruction a highly wrought proposition in the French revolutionary context. For the material nature of the acts that pictures and sculptures set out to record puts unrelenting pressure on the job of representation. It does so primarily because what gets recorded is not just a tangible event, but an event whose sheer negativity is inherently double-edged. On the one hand, erasure is fundamentally antirepresentational. It is about destroying objects and images. On the other hand, the actual overturning of a hierarchical set of circumstances—the reality of laying siege to aristocratic privilege or to the principle of private property by throwing things out windows—is an utterance, a mode of representation giving material value to an abstract concept like "the will of the people." Vandalism and iconoclasm, then, are strangely paradoxical and powerful gestures. And perhaps the best way of assessing representation's ensuing conundrum is this: a print such as *Moyen expéditif* is depicting an act of rote destruction that *all by itself* wants to suggest that representation is, in effect, extraneous. The question as a result is how the image goes on to handle its own uselessness, how it fictionalizes erasure as a matter of deep deliberation—and, by extension, how anonymous prints, collectively made pyramids, and allegorical images of the people allow representation to fight back as an Apollonian register of interpretation invoking form to diffuse the annihilation with which it is faced.

JEANNENE M. PRZYBLYSKI

Revolution at a Standstill: Photography and the Paris Commune of 1871*

> Revolution is a drama perhaps more than a history, and its pathos is
> a condition as imperious as its authenticity.
>
> —Auguste Blanqui

"Angelus Novus"[1]

Look at them. Heads peering over piles of paving stones, smiling for
the camera or squinting down the barrel of a gun (Fig. 1). They stand
bathed in the flat light of late winter, suspended between the fact of
photographic stillness and the promise of fighting in the streets. It
hardly needs saying that in March of 1871 Paris itself was no less between states—half taken apart, half put back together. Even in
Ménilmontant, far from the boulevard/showcases under construction
in the city center, the effects of the official modernization projects begun under the Second Empire are detectable in the new gaslamps and
iron-corseted saplings receding in the distance. Baron von Haussmann's street furniture was a sign of the times, but so equally was its
use in building barricades, the one in this photograph strengthened by
the interlocking fanshapes of the pavement grills designed to protect
the roots of new trees. Who was in command of the forces of progress,
of destruction, of regeneration? These were not easy questions to answer during the *année terrible* spanning the fall of the Second Empire
and the revolutionary uprising known as the Commune. One man

*I owe special thanks to Vanessa Schwartz for her comments on an earlier draft of this
essay. Research was enabled by a National Endowment for the Humanities Summer
Stipend and a J. Paul Getty Postdoctoral Fellowship in the History of Art and the Humanities.
1. See Walter Benjamin, "Theses on the Philosophy of History," in *Illuminations: Essays and Reflections* (New York: Verso, 1969), 257, for Benjamin's reading of Paul Klee's
Angelus Novus.

YFS 101, *Fragments of Revolution*, ed. Weber and Lay, © 2002 by Yale University.

standing atop the barricade catches my eye. Baton raised to signal his troops (or to cue the photographer), he is held against the blank whiteness, transfixed, illuminated. A defiant insurgent? A playful poseur? An angel about to ascend to heaven? I look at this man and wonder what he expected to see when he faced the camera? When the shutter closed, did he feel history's force like a storm rushing against his angel-wings?

*   *   *   *

If you believe the newspapers, Parisians hardly could have avoided looking at the photographs made on the Commune's barricades. There also appears to have been little doubt as to their significance. Contemporary accounts had them cluttering the windows of engraving and stationary stores, displayed proudly over the mantelpieces of homes in the *faubourgs*—and falling into the hands of the police. Photographs like the one made on the boulevard de Puebla in March, it was widely reported, were used to identify those insurgents left at large in the wake of the Commune's suppression in May. "All of the arrests being made at the moment," Adrien Huart chuckled in *Le charivari*, "are owing to collodion."[2] Maxime du Camp declared that the lessons of this windfall of unintentional wanted posters were not lost on the authorities; the police went into the photography business not long after the Commune fell.[3]

By and large modern scholars of the medium have fitted these photographs into a similar narrative, identifying the Commune as an important milestone along the path of photography's progressive refinement as a tool of social oversight and regulation.[4] The barricade photographs were supplemented by numerous images of Communard notables gathered by the police into albums to identify those revolutionaries still on the lam. Hundreds more *carte de visite* portraits made

2. Adrien Huart, "Chronique du jour," *Le charivari* (21 July 1871); 4; my translation.
3. Maxime Du Camp, *Les convulsions de Paris* (Paris: Hachette, 1881), vol. 2, 235; my translation.
4. See, for example, Gen Doy, "The Camera Against the Paris Commune," in *Photography/Politics: One*, ed. Terry Dennett and Jo Spence (London: Comedia Publishing Group, 1979), 17; Donald English, *Political Uses of Photography in the Third French Republic* (Ann Arbor, MI: UMI Research Press, 1984), 69–70; André Rouillé, "Les images photographiques du monde du travail sous le Second Empire," *Actes de la recherche en sciences sociales* 54 (September 1984), 41. On the development of police photography in France see Christian Phéline, *L'image accusatrice* (Paris: Cahiers de la photographie, 1985) and Allan Sekula, "The Body and the Archive," *October* 39 (Winter 1986): 1–64.

Figure 1. Anonymous, *Barricades, boulevard de Puebla (rue des Pyrénées), 20th arrondissement, March 1871.* Photograph. Bibliothèque nationale, Paris.

in the prison camps at Versailles were added to this rudimentary archive of *malfaiteurs*. In 1874, amid continuing anxieties about recidivism, Prefect Léon Renault announced the creation of a *Service photographique de la Préfecture,* charged with the task of photographing all suspected criminals detained in Paris (the Commune stood squarely behind these anxieties: not only had its repression swelled the prison population to nearly ungovernable proportions, but the burning of the Hôtel de Ville during the Commune's last days had destroyed much of the city's civil record, making it difficult for the police to trace anyone born before 1859). In 1883 a police functionary named Alphonse Bertillon successfully identified a repeat offender via an anthropometrical system combining photography and statistical data; he would spend the next decade refining and promoting the process of criminal identification that came to be eponymically dubbed *bertillonage.* By the turn of the century, the technology of the mugshot had become a mainstay of the police and prison systems. And so it goes, we might sigh. I-could-have-told-you-so. Photography's relation to revolution is ever the same, and far more apt to serve the interests of those in the business of putting down popular uprisings than those who embrace them.

And yet . . . I find it hard to turn away from these images. I am held by their visual richness—the details of dress and physiognomy that would have been useful to the authorities, but also their hokey posturing and their cataloguing of the ad-hoc technics of barricade-building. I am touched by their combination of formal gravity and *plein air* informality, taken with their hybrid crossing of historical document and street theater. The barricade photographs offer a rare and precious vision of the living density of the Parisian street when you'd least expect it: right in the midst of Haussmannization. None of the dark and desolate alleyways slated for demolition that were so often pictured in the official photographic record; not only fighting men and women crowd the barricades, but children and sometimes even dogs perch amid the *pavés,* and rubberneckers crowd in at the sides or lean their heads out of unshuttered windows. But also none of the unstable and fugitive "impressions" typical of avant-garde versions of Parisian boulevard culture. The barricade photographs are not adequately described as alienated, disenchanted, ephemeral—in a word, "modern." Rather, their vividness is excessive rather than strategic, concrete rather than illusory, rooted in a deep familiarity with *this* street and a willingness to stand ground *right here.* They trouble the disciplinary narrative by their refusal of other more predominant visions of urban modernization and modernity.[5]

Or, perhaps the very terms of this refusal brought the disciplinary machinery crashing down around the Communards' heads—intransigence before the disciplinary paradigm as much as utility to it, photographically speaking. Reclaiming these terms, however, requires looking beyond the obvious connection between photography and policing, or at least asking questions about it from different angles. When the Communards mounted their barricades and faced the camera, what sparked this convergence between the repertory of revolutionary performances that was already well-established in Paris and the collective aspirations that Parisians projected on the emerging technology of photography?[6] How did the Communards' choice to "live revolution as an image" embody a bid to put photographic reality itself up for grabs? In sum, how did this choice set their claims to a place of visibility in the iconography of urban Paris and their desire for an intimate and engaged relation to its history on a collision course with the equal impetus of "the powers that be" to use photography in ways both ostensibly "disinterested" and "objective" to fix identity, define place, and write history from above?[7]

Answering such questions, I suspect, must begin by taking seriously those aspects of contemporary accounts of photography and the barricades that have been overlooked because they seem to us more frivolous or dated—a matter of petty aesthetic judgments and the same old class-based disdain. "In fact, the *fédérés* weren't bad at striking a pose," Huart allowed—before concluding his spoof on the Communards' photographic bid for "posterity" with the story of a non-combatant who couldn't resist the temptation the barricades offered to have a portrait

5. On the "simple refusal to move" as one measure of "the degree of recalcitrance, on the part of Parisians, at having Paris provided in doses by the powers that be," see T. J. Clark, *The Painting of Modern Life: Paris in the Art of Manet and His Followers* (Princeton: Princeton University Press, 1984), 68–69.

6. On barricades and the repertory of images of collective action, see Mark Traugott, "Barricades as Repertoire: Continuities and Discontinuities in the History of French Contention," in Mark Traugott, ed., *Repertoires and Cycles of Collective Action* (Durham and London: Duke University Press, 1995), 43–56. On the desire for photography as a "conceptual . . . production" and as a "social imperative," see Geoffrey Batchen, *Burning with Desire: The Conception of Photography* (Cambridge: MIT Press, 1997), 36.

7. On "living an event as an image," see Maurice Blanchot, "The Two Versions of the Imaginary," in *The Space of Literature*, trans. Ann Smock (Lincoln: University of Nebraska Press, 1982), 261–62.

made on the cheap. Protestations of innocence aside, the evidence of the photograph was irrefutable: he ended up in the crowded cellars of L'Orangerie, the makeshift prison at Versailles. Du Camp describes a typical March scene on the rue de Belleville, where a barricade was built expressly for picture-making. Once the Communards had crowded close and arranged themselves in suitably menacing postures, they held still while an obliging passerby ran for the local photographer. After the exposure was made, the paving stones were put back and traffic resumed as usual.

A caricature of the "*Barricades artistiques*" appearing in *La Parisienne* hits just as close to its mark. By heightening the appearance of Communard preening and posing, it holds up a kind of funhouse mirror to photographs like the one of the barricade spanning the rue Basfroi, thickly layered with national guardsmen and *cantinières*, and bristling with guns and swords (Figs. 2 and 3). By including the camera in the sketch, the caricature affirms the crucial role that photography played in the visual economy of the Commune's barricades, while calling attention to one of the most forceful effects of this photograph in particular, in which aperture is matched to aperture, and the monocular stare of the camera lens is perfectly aligned with the circular barrel of the cannon ready to fire. The effect was not lost on contemporary observers. "Don't move!" Du Camp gleefully repeated the familiar exhortation shared by photographer and police officer alike as he lined up the Communards in his hostile literary sights. "The photographer *shoots* the barricade and its defenders," Huart sneered, "the print/proof [*l'épreuve*] is excellent." No less than the mortar shells with which the caricaturist framed his sketch, Huart's choice of words brings to mind the grim events that so decisively put an end to the Commune. Between twenty and forty thousand were killed during the eight May days of street fighting, fires, and summary executions that became known as the *semaine sanglante.* Many thousands more were arrested, twenty-three were formally put to death by order of military tribunal (another thousand died under miserable conditions while awaiting trial). Nearly three thousand were deported to New Caledonia. Those lucky enough to survive did not return to France until the general amnesty of 1880.[8] This is where the work of writing history draws closest to redemption. It is in the full knowledge of the enormous human cost of the Com-

8. Jacques Rougerie, *Procès des communards* (Paris: Gallimard, 1978), 17–24.

I. — BARRICADES ARTISTIQUES. — Construites sur les dessins du « Maître ». Le soleil, réquisitionné pour la circonstance, reproduira les traits du bataillon disposé avec art : au premier plan, le colonel et ses bottes; derrière lui, lascars et pétroleuses variées, dans une attitude imposante; au fond, tous les bons b... tels qu'ils étaient au combat qui aurait pu avoir lieu.

Figure 2. Anonymous, "Barricades artistiques," *La vie parisienne* (30 September 1871): 932. Lithograph. University of California, Berkeley.

Figure 3. Anonymous, Barricades, rue Basfroi, intersection of rue de Charonne, 11th arrondissement, March 1871. Photograph, Bibliothèque national, Paris.

mune's suppression that it seems so necessary to look again at the relation between the Commune, the material history of photography,
and the representational politics of the barricades.

*   *   *   *   *

The first thing that should be said is that Du Camp's acid contempt for
the barricade photographs and Huart's gloating parody were nothing
new. They join in a larger body of nineteenth-century criticism ex-
pressing dismay at the public's fascination with the automated ease of
photographic "reality"—its vulgar mimeticism, cheap theatrics, and
aesthetics of the lowest common demonimator. Among others, Charles
Baudelaire took elegant aim at photography in his essay on the Salon of
1859. Photography confused exactitude and truth, he complained, offering mere artifice in place of art. Just as bad, it seemed to attract a
crowd, an "idolatrous mob [demanding] an ideal worthy of itself and
appropriate to its nature" who found in the photographer a suitable
agent of its newly industrialized aesthetic. "By bringing together a
group of male and female clowns," Baudelaire continued,

> got up like butchers and laundry-maids at a carnival, and by begging
> these *heroes* to be so kind as to hold their chance grimaces for the time
> necessary for the performance, the operator flattered himself that he
> was reproducing tragic or elegant scenes from ancient history.[9]

Baudelaire's now classic *cri de coeur* against the tastelessness of
photography's imitative capacities prefigures with startling accuracy
the mainstream response to the barricade photographs. It indulges in a
similar pattern of fault-finding, annoyed with the confusion of history
and play-acting that photography seemed to encourage, and deeply suspicious of its complicity with society's baser predilections for facile legibility and sensationalistic pleasures. Most importantly, it pits Baudelaire's aesthetic elitism against what he saw as a broader culture of
narcissism linking the fortunes of the photographic entrepreneur as
one of the "industrial nomads" spawned by the rapid transformation of
Paris under Haussmannization to the desire of an increasingly unset-
tled population for an image of itself.[10] Of course in Baudelaire's day, it

9. Translated in Vicki Goldberg, ed., *Photography in Print: Writings from 1816 to the
Present* (New York: Simon and Schuster, 1981), 124.
10. Victor Fournel, *Paris nouveau et Paris futur* (Paris: Lecoffre, 1868), 129–30. On
the photography industry during the Second Empire, see Elizabeth Anne McCauley, *Industrial Madness: Commercial Photography in Paris, 1848–1871* (New Haven: Yale University Press, 1994).

JEANNENE M. PRZYBLYSKI   63

was hardly a "mob" of laundresses and butchers who had comman-
deered the camera; it would be quite a while before the average worker
could afford the luxury of a session in the photographer's studio. During the Second Empire, photography functioned as an art of self-representation largely for the bourgeoisie, who embrraced it as a means to
approximate the more privileged realm of painted portraiture. Their
early and enthusiastic patronage of the new technology ensured that
what Roland Barthes characterized as photography's alignment with
"the body's formality," its considerable power as "an art of the Person,"
would be inextricably mingled with the signifiers of public identity,
civil status, and social affiliations worn on the surface of the bourgeois
body in particular.[11]

The barricades, however, made things look different—transforming the photographic genre scenes Baudelaire detested into a kind of
portraiture by voluntary association that was to be equally decried by
the Commune's critics. Not for nothing were all those March stories of
the Commune as street party, in which passersby were gaily invited to
join the impromptu construction crews or suffer the consequences:
Contribute a *pavé* and become one of us![12] The spontaneous and celebratory quality of these actions led Henri Lefebvre to characterize the
Commune as the "last popular festival," a turn of phrase that had as
much to do with registering the barricades' ceremonial power as with
lamenting their military ineffectiveness (in 1871, they could amount
to little more than ritual—even before Haussmann's new boulevards
allowed the military to make an end run around the barricades, the cannon, introduced in 1830, had effectively spelled their doom).[13] The
group photo opportunity functioned as a similar intervention in the
practices of everyday life, bringing together the Commune's true believers and mixing it up with those more like Huart's hapless Com-
munard-impersonator, whose barricade antics were little more than a
moment's whim. But this heterogeneity also went to the heart of the
Commune's act of photographic provocation. When the Communard

11. Roland Barthes, *Camera Lucida: Reflections on Photography*, trans. Richard
Howard (New York: Hill and Wang, 1981), 79.

12. See, for example, "La Journée," *La patrie* (20 March 1871): 2; "À l'Hôtel de Ville.
Dimanche matin, neuf heures," *Le petit journal* (20 March 1871): 2; "La journée d'hier.
Les barricades et l'Hôtel de Ville," *La patrie* (21 March 1871): 1.

13. Henri Lefebvre, "La Commune. Dernière fête populaire," in James A. Leith, ed.,
Images of the Commune—Images de la Commune (Montreal: McGill University Press,
1978), 33–45. See also Kirstin Ross, *The Emergence of Social Space: Rimbaud and the
Paris Commune* (Minneapolis: University of Minnesota Press, 1988), 33.

crowd faced the camera, they added another layer to the already sub-
stantial iconography of the barricade. Even more importantly, they also
widened the realm of possibility for claiming a relation of confident entitlement to and playful familiarity with photography itself.

This was at least part of the problem: when the Second Empire's "industrial nomads" took their cameras to the streets, they also, if only
hypothetically, opened the doors of the photographic studio to the
Communards, and made of studio portraiture a comparable battlefield,
where the signifiers of likeness were too readily counterfeited, and
difference threatened to collapse into the same photographic performances. Photography's instantiation of the real, its eye for detail, its
authority as evidence, and its paper-thin promise of immortality
seemed to turn the barricades into a stage populated not by actors, but
by ordinary people who, awakened to the expressive potential of their
own bodies, acted as if they might define themselves by playing willingly and casually, almost thoughtlessly, to the camera. In other words,
the Communards posing on the barricades explicitly laid claim to the
theatricality that is intrinsic to photographic reality, to the performativity that is the counterpart to its opticality, especially in the commercialized realm of the photographic portrait. In doing so they put to
the test what Pierre Bourdieu has called the "mediate relationship" of
photography to social identity, contesting the ways in which an individual's stance before the camera not only inscribes him or her within
a group, but intersects the whole structure of group identity as negoti-
ated through photography.[14]

This photographic dispute did not end with the Commune's demise,
but continued in the prison yards of Versailles, where the autumn
months of 1871 would have found yet another "nomad" setting up his
camera to document the Communard detainees. Ernest Eugène Appert
had struck an especially good deal. In return for providing images of the
accused to the government, he also retained exclusive rights over their
reproduction. And to better facilitate the orderly procession of Communards before his camera, he promised each sitter a number of portraits for their own use.[15] In their memoirs of the Commune, both
Marc-Amédée Gromier, secretary to the Communard leader Félix Pyat,
and the Communard activist Louise Michel reported having their portraits made by Appert. Gromier remembers waiting in the photogra-

14. Pierre Bourdieu, *Photography: A Middle-Brow Art*, trans. Shaun Whiteside (Stanford: Stanford University Press, 1990), 9.
15. *Gazette des tribunaux* (29 October 1872): 1049–50.

pher's line with the journalist Abel Peyroutin and the Commune's Delegate of War, Louis Rossel, both of whom greeted him with some surprise, since notices of Gromier's death had been widely published in the papers.[16] Small wonder that the Communards so willingly submitted to Appert's camera. Amid all the confusion and counterinformation, his photographs offered some means of assuring the subjects' loved ones that they were still alive.

Appert's prison portraits are poignant images. More often than not tired and gaunt faces confront the camera; the Communards' abjection is obvious. But so is their stake in the photographic confrontation. Look closely and notice that if clothes are torn and dirty, they have also been hastily tidied. Arms were neatly folded, hair smoothed in make-do style; one woman struck a self-conscious air, hand to chin; two sisters posed together, as did fathers and sons, mothers and daughters. While a few Communards continued to affect the attitudes of defiance more typical of the barricade photographs (a barrel-chested man in *képi* stood arms akimbo; one *cantinière* straddled her chair and jauntily smoked a cigar), most opted for respectability. When his turn in line came, Rossel leaned almost confidingly toward the camera, his dark, full hair and bushy mustache framing deep-set eyes that look squarely into the lens (Fig. 4). Thumb hooked into waistcoat over a dangling pocket watch, he looks more like a lawyer or a journalist than a military traitor and dangerous insurgent who would stand a few months later before a firing squad on the plain of Satory.

On the one hand, their very respectability reveals these images to be no less theatrical inventions than the barricade photographs. Respectability could also be a kind of playing for the camera, a set of postures and a way of holding the body that had been seen often enough in the photographer's window to be copied and performed almost by rote. For most of the Communard prisoners, the choice to mime the practices of bourgeois decorum before the camera must have seemed not much of a choice at all; it was one of the few options available at a moment when self-preservation seemed inextricable from self-representation. But on the other hand, the prison portraits also implicate the poses of bourgeois respectability as themselves signifiers of disciplinary subjection. By envisioning the honorific become interchangeable with the repressive, the consensual become indistinguishable from the imposed, they suggest just how deeply plotted together these two mod-

16. Marc-Amédée Gromier, *Journal d'un vaincu* (Paris: Havard, 1892), 217. Louise Michel, *La Commune* (Paris: Stock, 1898), 305.

Figure 4. Ernest Eugène Appert, *Louis Rossel,* 1871. Carte de visite photograph. Bibliothèque nationale, Paris. Bibliothèque Nationale de France.

alities have been historically—not only as products of photographic technology but as embodied relations to it. Like some of the sketches that appeared in the popular press during the first decades of photography (Daumier's observational joke about the uncomfortable lengths to which the bourgeois would go to facilitate the camera's exact transcription of his features, for example, or *L'illustration*'s sober illustration of the difficulty in getting a good-enough likeness from a resistant detainee), Appert's prison photographs threaten to collapse functional distinctions between the portrait and the police photograph (Figs. 5 and 6). They also dramatize the degree to which the mugshot could not completely come into its own as an authoritative means of constructing the criminal subject until the external supports enforcing compliance had become superfluous, the mugshot's ability to typify deviance as fully internalized (its truths so seemingly inevitable) as those photographic genres and their generic conventions celebrating individuality.

So the challenge of the prison portraits to the usual order of things cut both ways. They offered the Communards a second chance in the face of disaster while continuing, like the barricade photographs, to taint the prerogatives of bourgeois self-representation by association. Stabilizing this challenge could not be a police matter alone, all the more so since the images circulated widely; Appert busily sold them off to curiosity-seekers, and licensed them to the press. To the extent that an equally commercial counter-initiative was called for, something like Appert's *Crimes de la Commune* would seem to better fit the bill. These panoramic scenes of the most notorious of Communard atrocities, punctuated by a retributory re-staging of the executions of Rossel, Sergeant Bourgeois, and Théophile Ferré, are the ersatz history paintings worthy of a Baudelaire's disdain—cut and paste extravaganzas combining the faces of the imprisoned Communards with the bodies of actors hired to pose on the rue des Rosiers, rue Haxo, in Mazas and La Roquette prisons where, in the last desperate days of the Commune, its enemies (both real and imagined) had been put to death. Appert's transposition of Rossel's living image (made in September) to the moment of his death (in November) is disturbing enough; how callous a hand it must have taken to glue a tiny white blindfold over his eyes. But even stranger is another Appert production, a composite collectible of the Communard "celebrity" Rossel, restored to the full military regalia he had earned in the fight against Bismarck and photographically relocated from the detention yards at Versailles to the drapery-swagged and pedestal-cluttered interior of the portrait studio (Fig. 7).

Figure 5. Honoré Daumier, "Les bons bourgeois. Position réputée la plus commode pour avoir un joli portrait au daguerréotype," in *Le charivari* (24 July 1847). Lithograph. University of California, Berkeley.

Figure 6. H. Meyer, *La photographie dans les prisons,* c. 1875. Lithograph. Bibliothèque nationale, Paris.

Figure 7. Ernest Eugène Appert, *Louis Rossel*, c. 1871. Carte de visite composite photograph. Bibliothèque nationale, Paris.

It has been pointed out often enough that Appert's *Crimes* are a nasty business, part of a long history of trumped up attempts to trick a gullible public with photographically manipulated propaganda.[17] But Appert's composite portraits strike me as even more insidious, not merely because they are falsified images masquerading as real, but because they potentially expose all photographic portraits as fictions, unmasking even the fragile decorum of the Communard prisoners as little more than disguise. By ironically reimposing the most reified photographic accouterments of bourgeois entitlement on the mimetic gambits of the prison portraits, and stifling the expressiveness of the body's "formality" in a mocking straitjacket of military rank, the composite Rossel provides the pendant image to his death at Satory that his prison portrait alone could not be—laminating Rossel's identity as a Communard with the artifacts of his dishonorable betrayal of his class and his commission as an army colonel. But it is more than that: look at the composite long enough and feel Rossel's body solidifying beyond the body's solidity, the photomontaged dress uniform framing his head like a sarcophagus. By willfully flattening the self-sustained stillness of the body as it gathers itself for presentation to the world into the immobilization of the body displayed, Appert's composite has the uncanny effect of aligning the portrait studio with the executioner's wall. The photograph's "likeness," powerfully convincing and unsettlingly inert, becomes like nothing so much as a corpse (Blanchot, 258).

This is the haunting power of Appert's parodic embalming of Rossel in the portrait studio: by externalizing the mortifying effects of the photographic pose, it raises the specter of the dead. Of course, in the weeks following the Commune, one would not have had to look far afield to find more concrete manifestations of their presence. Communard casualties began to accrue in earnest in April and the Communard government, hard pressed to see to the orderly return of remains to family and friends, commissioned photographers to help in the process of identification. When faced with an exponentially greater body count in May, the Versailles government appears to have authorized the continuation of photographic operations. These "morgue" photo-

17. On this series, see Jeannene M. Przyblyski, "Moving Pictures: Photography, Narrative and the Paris Commune of 1871," in Leo Charney and Vanessa Schwartz, eds., *Cinema and the Invention of Modern Life* (Berkeley: University of California Press, 1995), 253–78; and "Between Seeing and Believing: Representing Women in Appert's *Crimes de la Commune*," in Dean de la Motte and Przyblyski, eds., *Making the News: Modernity and the Mass Press in Nineteenth-Century France* (Amherst: University of Massachusetts Press, 1999), 233–78.

graphs would seem to provide a vision of grim finality to the Commune's embrace of a spurious, photographic aestheticism (Fig. 8). Heads are crumpled at unnatural angles, teeth are bared, clothing is torn and muddy, faces are swollen with bloat and eroding in decay. As examples of the extreme violence with which the corpse unmakes the body's "cultural content," this stripping away of the social signifiers animating the body in life provides the context for the rumors abounding in post-Commune Paris that photographs of Confederate casualities of the U.S. Civil War were being hawked to souvenir hunters as images of dead *fédérés;* in the continuing climate of vicarious blood lust that followed the repression of the Commune, one picture of a dead rebel was as good as another.[18] But such grisly opportunism also demonstrates the degree to which these images, so anaesthetic in their instrumental bleakness, remained deeply complicit in the Baudelairean vision of Parisian photographic practices as thoroughly commercialized and fashionably of the moment. In ways both banal and chilling, the morgue photographs function as the literal image of photographic fashionability's allegorical pairing with death.[19]

*   *   *   *   *

For the Commune's detractors, the difference between mere fashion and this latest revolutionary incarnation amounted to very little, especially with respect to photography. Huart saved his most damning sally against the Communards on the barricades for last. "In '93," he chided, "even if photography had existed, the revolutionaries of the time would have never thought to pose before the cameras of Disderi, Nadar, and their colleagues." As an accusation of the "crime" of a hankering for the trendy photographic emporiums of the *grands boulevards,* Huart's insult, like Appert's commodified souvenirs, was part of a host of gambits by which the Commune was to be retrospectively trivialized in the popular press as a kind of insurrectionary dandyism— the latest *article de Paris,* as *La vie parisienne* was fond of declaring.[20] Just as significantly, however, it yokes the discredited representational

18. Viator, "From Across the Water," *Anthony's Photographic Bulletin* (December 1871), 397. My thanks to Alisa Luxenberg for this citation. On the "emptying of the body of cultural content" in death, see Elaine Scarry, *The Body in Pain: The Making and Unmaking of the World* (New York: Oxford University Press, 1985), 118–19.

19. Walter Benjamin, "Paris: Capital of the Nineteenth Century," in *The Arcades Project,* trans. Howard Eiland and Kevin McLaughlin (Cambridge: Harvard/Belknap, 1999), 18–19.

20. "Petite chronique," *La vie parisienne* (16 September 1871): 905.

Figure 8. Anon., *Insurgés non réclamés*, 1871. Photograph. Gernsheim Collection. Harry Ransom Humanities Research Center, University of Texas at Austin.

politics of revolution *à la mode* to the Commune's self-conscious relation to the revolutionary heritage of 1793, most particularly as it was
claimed by the followers of Auguste Blanqui, the legendary insurrec-
tionist whose incarceration for the duration of the Commune did not
prevent him from being a significant force in its ideological formation.[21] The Blanquists might well have joined with Huart in admitting
that the barricade photographs—cheap and brash, "the historical event
iself become a mass article," swept up into a circuit of mass, promis-
cious desire—were not quite what they had in mind when they dreamed
of recreating the elaborate popular festivals of Thermidor (the hastily
organized toppling of the Vendôme Column, also much photographed,
would not be much of an improvement). But insofar as the barricade
photographs *as* mass articles conjure up the image of revolution as
"eternal return" (revolution come back yet again but as it never was in
'93 or '30 or '48, its photographic difference the very figure of the ac-
celerated pace of revolutionary crisis), then this effect was also, in Walter Benjamin's words, inextricable from the "traces of economic circumstances to which [they] owed [their] sudden currency."[22]

Here, according to Benjamin, is the relevant passage from Blanqui's
L'éternité par les astres, the book on cosmology he wrote in prison in
1871:

> The entire universe is composed of astral systems. To create them, na-
> ture has only a hundred *simple bodies* at its disposal. . . . [T]he result is
> necessarily a *finite* number, like that of the elements themselves; and
> in order to fill its expanse, nature must repeat to infinity each of its *orig-
> inal* combinations or *types*. So each heavenly body, whatever it might
> be, exists in infinite number in time and space, not only in *one* of its as-
> pects but as it is at each second of its existence, from birth to death. . . .
> Every human being is thus eternal at every second of his or her exis-
> tence. What I write at this moment in a cell of the Fort du Taureau I have
> written and shall write throughout all eternity—at a table, with a pen,
> clothed as I am now, in circumstances like these. And thus it is for
> everyone. . . . The number of our doubles is infinite in time and space.
> One cannot in good conscience demand anything more. These doubles
> exist in flesh and bone—indeed in trousers and jacket, in crinoline and

21. On Blanqui and the Commune, see Patrick H. Hutton, *The Cult of the Revolutionary Tradition: The Blanquists in French Politics, 1864–1893* (Berkeley: University
of California Press, 1981), 49–54.

22. Quoted in Eduardo Cadava, *Words of Light: Theses on the Photography of History* (Princeton: Princeton University Press, 1997), 31. On Benjamin, photography, and
Blanqui, see Cadava, 31–42.

chignon. They are by no means phantoms; they are the present eternal-
ized. Here, nonetheless, lies a great drawback: there is no progress. . . .
What we call "progress" is confined to each particular world, and van-
ishes with it. Always and everywhere in the terrestrial arena, the same
drama, the same setting, on the same narrow stage—a noisy humanity
infatuated with its own grandeur. . . . The same monotony, the same immobility. . . . The universe repeats itself endlessly and paws the ground
in place. In infinity, eternity performs—imperturbably—the same rou-
tines. ["Paris," 25–26]

For the Communards who struck one repertory of poses on the barricades of the boulevard de Puebla, the rues de Charonne, des Pyrénées,
de Belleville, de Basfroi, and elsewhere, only to strike another pose in
the prison yards of Versailles, or to end up staring sightlessly at the camera in a numbing parade of anonymous corpses, *l'actualité éternisée* is
the image of cosmological repetition as catastrophe—the doomed repetition of a limited set of possibilities whose finitude can only be dimly
grasped from the prison house of the present. It is also the image of cosmological repetition as a photographic image, proliferated through
copies, infinitely reproducible, each image little more than typical; Blanqui's "noisy humanity infatuated with its own grandeur" is deeply resonant with the ragtag figures of Baudelaire's "tragic or elegant scenes
from ancient history." Equally significantly, in Blanqui's cosmology
this photographic repetition works not with but against the authority
of progress as an animating force of the disciplinary narrative, not with
but against the tendency to wed the trajectory from revolution to repression to the promise of the perfectibility of photographic technolo-
gies of ordering and overseeing the world. Instead it sets the sameness,
the monotony, and the static immobility of the photographic copy
against photography's equal affinity for lifelikeness, illusory mobility,
and fashionable novelty ("crinolines and chignons")—in a word, the effects of instantaneity and ephemerality that inform photography's
dominant aesthetic myths.

I said at the outset that the barricade photographs did not seem adequately described as modern. This is what I mean: for the Communards facing the camera, the catastrophic is instantiated by *holding
still*. Du Camp was right: "*Ne bougeons plus!*" The Communards' voluntary assumption of the pose might be contrasted on the one hand to
"arrest" (the imposition of stillness through police restraint) and, on
the other, to the endless stillness of the morgue. The immobility of the
Communards on the barricades is not yet the funereal stillness of

death, but rather the stillness of historical contingency. As the embodiment of the photographic "currency" that linked the fortunes of the barricades and the camera in 1871, this stillness defines the photographic relation to actuality and mortality, everyday life and history, commercial camera practice, its technological limitations and its attendant tactics of self-representation that allowed the uncertain play of identity to open up—all too briefly—in the space between the street, the portrait studio, and the prison. In this respect, the vision provided by the barricade images of photography as a habitable state of mind for those on the economic and social margins was not only a matter of too-little-too-late (it is not merely a question of faulting the foolhardy Communards for posing on the barricades when they should have been organizing for battle). It was also too-much-too-soon, an apparently unregulated vision of photographic immortality that would not be safely permissible until it had been transformed into the ephemeral instantaneity of a standardized and thoroughly commodified "Kodak moment."

This then is the power (and the threat) of the barricade photographs as revolutionary images. In their banal repetition, their purloined aesthetics, and their tragic inability to imagine any other relation to the camera than the ones that had already been, they remind us that the risk of an engaged relation to history as performative, self-conscious, deeply (and yet casually, almost thoughtlessly) invested in the "battlefield of representations," is the surrender of voluntary will (even as it appears as voluntary, a matter of the brave or imprudent choice to stand on the barricades, to be photographed, and to fight) (Clark, 6). The risk is to give one's self up to the symbolic order, to mourn that there is no hopeful way to see oneself outside it. But this risk also resists the dominant fiction of the disciplinary regime of the photographic archive, the fiction that anyone can stand apart from the archive—using it, ordering it, and bending it to social imperative while remaining oneself above the fray, safely segregated by the line drawn between the celebratory and repressive practices of photography, a boundary line imposed not only by cultural conceit but by the institutionalized history of photography and its uses. This is the fiction that must be fought at all costs—because it is the fiction that allows the distinction between "them" and "us," the false distinction upon which theories of domination and repression rest. The photographs of the barricades in 1871 allow us to glimpse this fiction for what it is; they demand that we recognize that we are all joined together as "doubles," in the body's "for-

Figure 9. Anon., *Barricades, rue des Amandiers, near Père Lachaise cemetery, 20th arrondissement,* March 1871, Photograph. Bibliothèque nationale de France, Paris.

mality," its mortality and in its persistence (its infinitude) as a universe of photographic copies.

*   *   *   *   *

Look at them. Grouped around the fortifications of earthworks and paving stones built on the rue des Amandiers near Père Lachaise cemetery, where the last of the Communards would make a desperate stand only a few weeks later (Fig. 9). Crouched in a pit fronting the barricades, the National Guardsmen posed arms to the ready while the neighborhood looked on. We know only too well that the men will prove better at menacing the camera than the Versailles troops, and the pit is the same place where many of those who had fallen during the "bloody week" would later be buried. Why *were* these photographs made? Perhaps it *was* for the fun of it—out of the sheer giddiness of playing at revolution, or out of the boredom that arose when the Versaillais failed to attack in March and the jubilant Communards were left, if only for a short while, with nothing else to do. The men on the barricades shake their fist at history, they seem prepared to will the Commune into being. Look at them. If the Communards seem to us now to already have one foot in the grave, it is worth recalling, in the words of Benjamin, that "only that historian will have the gift of fanning the spark of hope in the past who is firmly convinced that even the dead will not be safe from the enemy if he wins. And this enemy has not ceased to be victorious" ("Theses," 255).

HOWARD G. LAY

Beau geste!
(On the Readability of Terrorism)*

For Bernadine

la fonction référentielle est
un piège, mais inévitable
—Paul de Man, 1983[1]

Vive le son,
D'l'explosion!
—Anon., *La Ravachole*, 1892[2]

On a Wednesday evening in April 1894, the fashionable neighborhood
just north of the Luxembourg Garden was shaken by a deafening explosion, the echoes of which resonated as far away as the Opéra and the
Hôtel de Ville. Rafters shuddered, windows shattered, and jagged shards
of glass and metal sliced through the air in search of random targets.[3]
By the time the dust had settled, the restaurant Foyot (rue de Vaugirard)
was a shambles. Two dinner guests, a waiter, and a cashier had been injured. Doctors were summoned. The police arrived in short order.

*This essay has greatly benefited from the suggestions of Erika Naginski, Caroline
Weber, Alyson Waters, Patricia Simons, Jean-François Cardoso, Nina Bernstein, and
Christopher Leichtnam. Joan Halperin kindly shared invaluable information where
Fénéon is concerned, and Amy Freund provided timely assistance from Paris. T. J. Clark
and Ross Chambers have contributed significantly to the formulation of my arguments,
although neither of them should be held accountable for my conclusions. All translations
in this essay are my own.
    1. Cited in Paul de Man, *Aesthetic Ideology*, ed. Andrzej Warminski (Minneapolis
and London: University of Minnesota Press, 1996), 1.
    2. Anon., *La Ravachole*, published in *Almanach du père Peinard pour 1894—an 102*
(Paris: Le père Peinard, 1893), 43.
    3. For a description of the explosion and the resulting damage to both the restaurant
Foyot and surrounding buildings, see "Nouvel attentat. L'explosion du restaurant
Foyot," *Le matin*, 5 April 1894. See also "Une bombe. Un attentat anarchiste au restau-
rant Foyot," *L'éclair*, 6 April 1894.

YFS 101, *Fragments of Revolution*, ed. Weber and Lay, © 2002 by Yale University.

The following morning, 5 April, the renowned criminologist Alphonse Bertillon recorded the damage in a photograph (Fig. 1): four windows have been blown out; a gaping hole (about a meter and a half in
diameter) disfigures the façade like a wound; "ESTAU" is all that's left
of a sign that had read, just a few hours earlier, "RESTAURANT."[4] But,
provisionally at least, order has been restored. To the far left, a waiter—
apron secured, napkin in hand—reassures us that commerce (and fine
dining) will prevail; the policeman, standing confidently to the right,
attests to the strength of the law's long arm. These figures appear in the
picture as makeshift allegories of containment, of damage control, and
of sheer wishful thinking. For as everyone knew in the spring of 1894,
the restaurant Foyot had just fallen victim to an anarchist *attentat* [at-
tack]—the significative repercussions of which were launched, like flying debris, when the detonation of a home-made bomb brought dinner
to an abrupt conclusion.

There was no ignoring anarchist terrorism in fin-de-siècle Paris. It
had made its presence felt repeatedly between 1892 and 1894 with a
succession of bombings and an estimable quotient of violence, destruction, and bloodshed. It had also established itself as a rudimentary
mode of communication, an inchoate language through which a stal-
wart revolutionary subculture sought simultaneously to speak and to
act, or more precisely, to speak by acting. The Foyot *attentat*, in other
words, was like a primal utterance, a solitary "!" reduced to its bare
bones without a word, a phrase, or a sentence to precede it.[5] Yet once
voiced, it began inexorably to take on meaning as an object of interpretation—as a text, that is, destined from the outset to perform as a
function of entirely divergent orders of reading. So it was that a detonation in 1894 could inspire impassioned cries of *Vive l'anarchie!* and
Assassins! with equal facility; despite their differences, the inferences
thus expressed were bound, both of them, to the same (radically "free-
playing") signifier. This explosive signifier, however, was also a mate-

4. "La bombe Foyot," *Le matin,* 6 April 1894. Bertillon was called upon to make
crime-scene photographs at the sites of each of the terrorist bombings in the early
nineties. The images, some of them quite gruesome, are in the collection of the Archives
de la préfecture de police, Paris.

5. This is not to suggest that "speaking" and "acting" are somehow antithetical (since
speech itself *is* an act), nor that terrorism manages to signify "extra-linguistically." On
relations between cognitive and performative orders of language, see Paul de Man, "Kant
and Schiller," in *Aesthetic Ideology,* 132–34. On the convergence of "saying" and "doing," see J. L. Austin, "Performative Utterances," in *Philosophical Papers* (Oxford: Clarendon Press, 1961), 220–39.

Figure 1. Alphonse Bertillon, *Le restaurant Foyot*, 5 April 1894. Photograph. Archives de la préfecture de police, Paris.

rial event so brutish that it seemed somehow to signify the insignifi-
cance, where revolutionary action was concerned, of discourse itself.
Hence its communicative muscle, the refractory dumbness of which
served the dual purpose of generating the illimitable indexicality of the
Foyot "!" and of refusing readability altogether.

LE FAIT

I doubt that the police thought much about language, signification, and
interpretation. Theirs were more pressing concerns. By the spring of
1894, the outbreak of terrorism—or *la propagande par le fait* [propa-
ganda by deed], as militants preferred to call it—that had gripped Paris
for more than two years had reached epidemic proportions. The notorious *dynamiteur* Ravachol had already authored three explosions, and
Emile Henry, a brilliant student-turned-revolutionary, another two; a
journeyman worker named August Vaillant had flung a bomb into a
crowded session at the Chambre des Députés. These were only the most
sensational of a rash of terrorist acts that had yielded ten deaths and
property damage in the tens-of-thousands of francs.[6] So by the time the
restaurant Foyot added its numbers to the statistics in April, the Chief
of Police was already under enormous pressure to muzzle what had become an extremely disruptive form of revolutionary (anti-)discourse.[7]

As "informed" readers of anarchist terrorism, the police knew all
about its propagandistic agenda. As agents of the law, they also knew
that the most effective means of delimiting its communicative power
was to conflate its revolutionary message with criminality, to neutralize *la propagande* by investigating *le fait*—and by collaring a perpetrator around whom a terrorist act might be reconfigured as a *symptom*
(of a sociopathic personality) rather than a *statement* (of revolutionarly
intransigence). Within minutes of the Foyot explosion, the restaurant

6. On the so-called "*ère des attentats*" in Paris (1892–94), see Jean Maitron, *Le mouvement anarchiste en France*, 2 vols. (Paris: François Maspero, 1983), vol. 1, 206–50. See
also, Henri Varennes, *De Ravachol à Caserio* (Paris: Garnier frères, 1895). As this issue
of *Yale French Studies* goes to press, an important new book on fin-de-siècle anarchist
terrorism has appeared in France; see Uri Eisenzweig, *Fictions de l'anarchisme* (Paris:
Christian Bourgois éditeur, 2001).
7. The day after the Foyot *attentat*, a police informant reported considerable agita-
tion among *habitués* of the "cafés du boulevard," as well as frustration with the Republic's inability (despite additional taxes levied to aid police investigations) to effectuate
"la découverte et l'éxtermination des anarchistes" [the apprehension and extermina-
tion of the anarchists]. See Archives de la préfecture de police (hereafter APP), B A/142
(125), unsigned report of a secret agent. For a brief summary of newspaper commentary,
see "Les journaux de ce matin," *Le matin*, 5 April 1894.

had become a "crime scene" in which telltale clues were systematically plucked from scattered rubble and eyewitnesses grilled for information. Several fragments of the bomb were recovered, and it was quickly determined that the device had consisted of a mixture of dinitrobenzene and ammonium nitrate, a handful of bullets, and a detonator, all of which had been concealed in an ordinary flower pot; the municipal laboratory dutifully fabricated a replica (Fig. 2).[8] Three witnesses agreed that a man in dark clothing had been seen in the vicinity of the restaurant the afternoon before the *attentat*, and two more remembered a similar figure walking quickly away immediately after. But additional testimony revealed that still other suspicious characters, both male and female, had apparently lingered for no good reason near the intersection of the rue de Vaugirard and the rue de Condé.[9] With remarkable efficiency, the police had gathered a wealth of evidence—none of which pointed to a plausible suspect or, for that matter, to any other means of containing the significative potential of the Foyot "!". Standard procedure dictated that they turn their attention to a long list (compiled through the combined efforts of informants, spies, and intelligence officers) of suspected anarchist militants.

A day or two after the explosion, they interrogated the art critic and editor, Félix Fénéon, whose involvement with *L'endehors*, an avantgarde weekly of anarchist persuasion, had made him the object of police surveillance for several months. The interview was unproductive, and a thorough search of his apartment yielded nothing more incriminating than the *carte de visite* of Laurent Tailhade—a poet who had been the most severely injured of the Foyot's dinner guests on the evening of 4 April.[10] Tailhade's was an uncomfortable situation. The side of his face had been mutilated by slivers of glass, and he had lost his right eye. And to make matters worse, his sympathy for anarchist terrorism was already a matter of public record. Only a few weeks earlier, his blithe remark to a newspaper reporter about the Vaillant bombing—"Qu'importe que les vagues humanités disparaissent, si le geste est beau?" [What does it matter if insignificant lives are lost, as long as the gesture is beautiful?]—had raised more than a few eyebrows. The

8. "Nouvel attentat. L'explosion du restaurant Foyot," *op. cit.*
9. For depositions of "eye witnesses," see APP, B A/142 (97–115).
10. On Fénéon's difficulties with the police, see "Les anarchistes. Arrestation de M. Félix Fénon [sic]; interview de Mme Fénon [sic]; l'anarchiste Meunier," *Le jour*, 28 April 1894, and "L'arrestation de M. Félix Fénéon," *Le temps*, 28 April 1894. The police also discovered *cartes de visite* from Camille Pissarro and Octave Mirbeau, both of whom were well-known anarchist partisans.

Figure 2. La bombe du restaurant Foyot, 1894. Police facsimile. Musée de la préfecture de police, Paris.

same remark now provided journalists with a victim of comeuppance and the police with a possible suspect.[11] Tailhade was interrogated in his hospital bed at La Charité, but like Fénéon he proved to be an in-

11. *Le journal*, 6 February 1894, 1. According to a police informant, socialist activists from the *18e arrondissement* suspected that Tailhade, "un homme ambitieux qui ne

vestigative dead end. Neither man was detained. Days passed, and speculation about the Foyot explosion proceeded unchecked, even as scores
of suspected anarchists were rounded up in an ongoing police dragnet.

VIVE LA RÉ . . .

There was nothing new in the early nineties about *la propagande par
le fait*. Its virtues as a means to inspire insurrection, to give material
form to revolutionary consciousness, had been rehearsed in anarchist
journals for years, and a considerable number of militants thought it a
far more persuasive communicative model than *la propagande théo-
rique*. There was, of course, a theory behind their dissatisfaction with
theory. This is Paul Brousse, the future leader of the Possibilist socialist party, writing from exile in the *Bulletin de la fédération jurassienne* in 1877:

> L'idée sera jetée, non sur le papier, non sur un journal, non sur un tab-
> leau, elle ne sera pas sculptée en marbre, ni taillée en pierre, ni coulée
> en bronze: elle marchera, en chair et en os, vivante, devant le peuple. Le
> people la saluera au passage.[12]

> The idea will not appear on paper, nor in a journal, nor in a painting; it
> will not be sculpted in marble, nor carved in stone, nor cast in bronze:
> it will walk, in flesh and bone, alive, before the people. The people will
> salute it as it passes by.

What better way to account (in theory) for the eruption of figuration
generated by a terrorist act than through figurative language itself.
"Elle marchera, en chair et en os, vivante": the words allegorize the revolutionary *"idée"* even as they presume to dispense with the allegorical disguises it had traditionally assumed in painting, sculpture, and
literature (the feminine *elle* further facilitates the slippage here); but
they say precious little about what (in practice) the *"idée,"* stripped
bare, might amount to—other, that is, than a would-be revolutionary
wake-up call to the masses. Hence, I think, the unconscious hankering
for allegory, for personification, for figuration in general, even among
the same anarchist propagandists who would distinguish detonations
from more conventional forms of communication.

cherche qu'à faire parler de lui" [an ambitious man who wants only to attract attention],
was himself the author of the Foyot explosion. See APP, B A/142 (127), 6 April 1894, report signed "Argus."

   12. Anon. [Paul Brousse], *Bulletin de la fédération jurassienne*, 5 August 1877. Cited
in Maitron, *Le mouvement anarchiste*, vol. 1, 77.

Hence, also, the irresistible urge they felt to produce verbal translations of a nonverbal language and, in effect, to bind the significative impact of exploding dynamite to words. By 1883 Jean Grave, the indefatigable editor of *La révolte,* had already insisted on the crucial role of propaganda (both oral and written) to promote action and to explicate revolutionary deeds.[13] By the time the restaurant Foyot was bombed a decade later, a hermeneutics of terrorism had been well established. With each *attentat* came a period of intense after-the-fact deliberation during which any number of interpretive readings were proposed, assessed, and debated. Ravachol's targets—a magistrate's home on the boulevard St. Germain, a deputy prosecutor's in Clichy, an army barracks—were clearly connected to the brutal beatings and severe sentences doled out in 1891 to a trio of anarchist protesters in the aftermath of an unruly May Day demonstration. *Compagnons* tended accordingly to read the explosions as acts of individual reprisal against the various agencies of authority responsible for the injustice, each of them a proven enemy. Vaillant's attack on the Chambre des Députés in December 1893 made sense too, precisely because it took direct aim at the symbolic and administrative heart of bourgeois society. When just two months later, Henry threw a bomb amid the after-work clientele at the café Terminus (gare Saint-Lazare), interpretation became a more difficult business—until, during his trial, he explained his intent to retaliate against the complacency of *"les bons bourgeois"* and of the low-level employees who always end up taking sides with their masters.[14]

Of course the readability of these *attentats* was further complicated by the deployment of the Republic's own variation of *la propagande par le fait*—one that involved arrests, trials, and the spectacularly material, punitive, and figurative power of the guillotine. Heads rolled, and terrorists like Ravachol, Vaillant, and Henry were transformed instantaneously into anarchist martyrs. In the interim between a terrorist act

13. See Jehan Le Vagre [Jean Grave], *Organisation de la propagande révolutionnaire* (Paris: Publications du groupe des 5e et 13e arrondissements, 1883), 10.

14. "Déclaration d'Emile Henry," *L'écho de Paris,* 30 April 1894. For Octave Mirbeau (who had voiced his support of Ravachol in 1892), Henry's assault on the café Terminus was incomprehensible (*Le journal,* 19 February 1893): "Un ennemi mortel de l'anarchie n'eût pas mieux agi que ce Emile Henry, lorsqu'il lança son inexplicable bombe, au milieu de tranquilles et anonymes personnes, venus dans un café, pour y boire un bock, avant de s'aller coucher . . . [A mortal enemy of anarchism could not have acted more effectively than did this Emile Henry, when he threw his inexplicable bomb amid a crowd of tranquil and anonymous people gathered in a café to drink a beer before going home to bed . . .].

and its macabre official rejoinder, the effects of a succession of public disclosures—the comportment of an author at trial, say, or the relative merits of his testimony, or the measure of his personal sacrifice for the anarchist cause—could make of interpretation a matter of incessant arbitration. It was reported in the newspapers that Ravachol's last words, "Vive la ré . . . ," were cut short by the blade of the guillotine; the ensuing speculation about the severed syllables (". . . volution!" or ". . . publique!") typified the instability of an ongoing discharge of signification that had commenced a few months earlier with an explosion on the boulevard St. Germain.

Yet speculation about a last-second change of heart hardly mattered, for if nothing else the guillotine had served to draw attention away from the terrorist act itself and toward its author. A great deal of anarchist eulogia was produced on Ravachol's behalf. The colloquial verb, *ravacholizer* (to exact revenge; to vanquish one's enemies), was coined in his honor. The novelist Paul Adam would name him the modern world's "Rénovateur du Sacrifice Essentiel" [Reformer of the Essential Sacrifice].[15] The artist Charles Maurin would make a commemorative woodcut of similar conviction (Fig. 3) in which Ravachol stands steadfast before the guillotine, a field of grain, and the rising sun—each of them a fitting attribute for anarchism's most venerated martyr. The stylistic conceits at work in the image—the *japoniste* perspective, the robust linearity, the schematization of form—coalesce to produce a studied naiveté that had already become one of the characteristic affectations of both modernist painting (van Gogh and Gauguin in the late eighties) and printmaking (Henri Rivière and Félix Vallotton in the early nineties). But more to the point, it contributes to the picture's iconic bearing, to the saintly stature of its protagonist, and to a graphic limpidity reminiscent of the popular woodcuts that had issued from provincial workshops for more than two enturies. In January 1893, Maurin exhibited his *Ravachol* at the Boussod and Valadon gallery in a two-artist show he shared with his friend Toulouse-Lautrec; by the end of the year it had found a more appropriate home in the propagandist Emile Pouget's *Almanach du père Peinard*, where its stylistic overtures to artless sincerity—to the presumed forthrightness of Ravachol and the people alike—provided a compelling visual equivalent for the rough-and-tumble *Hébertiste* rhetoric that had made Pouget's the most

15. Paul Adam, "Éloge de Ravachol," *Entretiens politiques et littéraires* 5/28 (July 1892), 28.

Figure 3. Charles Maurin, *Ravachol*, 1893. Woodcut. L'institut français d'histoire sociale (14 AS 41 1), Paris.

staunchly proletarian and widely disseminated anarchist publications in France.[16]

Maurin's woodcut drew cleverly from both popular and Christian sources, and to anarchist eyes it presumably represented a powerful hagiographic challenge to the authority of a familiar cast of saints and martyrs. But the visual vocabulary it deployed could in turn be reconfigured to serve the interests of commerce, and its revolutionary zeal metamorphosed into rote sensationalism. Lautrec himself would make a promotional poster of similarly feigned artlessness (Fig. 4) in which *japoniste* illusionism and an ungainly ensemble of grim caricature, ominous silhouettes, and (elegantly) mishandled outlines serve to articulate the brute instrumentality of the guillotine rather than the "*Sacrifice essentiel*" of its victim. The ghoulish executioner; the beneficent man of God (good book in hand); the grimacing prisoner who struggles with shackles and self-control: these are the stock-in-trade characters of the hack, of the daily papers, of a commercially driven narrative consecrated in equal measure to mawkishness and cheap thrills. Lautrec's poster, in other words, was the perfect visual complement to a promotional campaign launched by the newspaper *Le matin* in 1893 for a series of articles by l'Abbé Faure, a priest from the Roquette prison, whose recollections of last rites and executions were sure to captivate even the most complacent of readers.[17] That the image shares a pictorial lexicon with Maurin's *Ravachol* attests to the significative mutability of modernism's appropriations of "popular" (and otherwise "exotic") orders of representation. That both address themselves to the guillotine is testimony to good police work and to the efficacy of the Republic's program of punitive terrorism. For regardless of anarchist vows to avenge fallen martyrs (and thus to extend the series of propagandistic deeds), a timely execution could upstage the disruptive effects of an explosion with a gripping melodrama, the

16. Fénéon, who reviewed the exhibition for *L'endehors*, praised Maurin's *Ravachol* for its "sentiment apothéotique [*sic*] et populaire" [apotheosizing and popular sentiment]. See Anon. [Félix Fénéon], "Peintures: Henri de Toulouse-Lautrec et Charles Maurin, chez Boussod et Valadon, 19, boulevard Montmartre," *L'endehors*, 12 February 1893. The image was published in *Almanach du père Peinard pour 1894—An 102*, 45. Pouget made clever use of the insolently off-color revolutionary argot first deployed a century earlier in the pages of Jacques Hébert's notorious *Le père Duchêne* (1790–93). The police estimated in 1891 that each issue of Pouget's anarchist weekly, *Le père Peinard* (1889–1900), reached as many as one hundred thousand working-class readers. See APP, B A/77 (22), "Les anarchistes. Bulletin de quinzaine," 5 November 1891, report signed "4."

17. The collected articles appear in Jean-Baptiste Faure, *Au pied de l'échafaud. Souvenirs de la Roquette* (Paris: M. Dreyfous, 1893).

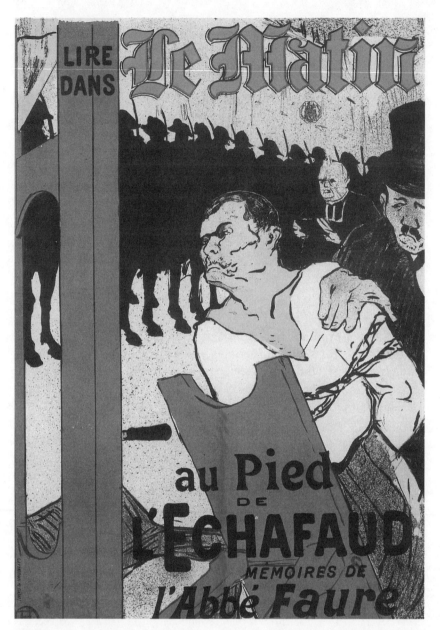

Figure 4. Henri de Toulouse-Lautrec, *Au pied de l'échafaud*, 1893. Color lithograph. Private collection.

gory details of which were jointly orchestrated by the State and the commercial press.

UNE LUEUR SOMMAIRE

This is not to suggest that anarchism's retorts to the arrests and executions of its heroes failed to encourage collective action; Ravachol, after all, would be avenged on more than one occasion.[18] My point is rather that the communicative potential of a terrorist act, once refocused on perpetrators and their intentions, was immediately delimited by the discourses to which it was accordingly conjoined—discourses attuned less to the obdurate materiality of a detonation than to the more familiar orders of (verbal or visual) rhetoric habitually deployed to assess the relative virtues of a particular individual. In the process, the power of a refractory "!" to operate at the edges of discourse, to make language itself shake in the wake of a deafening explosion, was effectively defused—not only by the police, the judiciary, and the press, but also by the same anarchist partisans who most adamantly subscribed to *la propagande par le fait*.[19] Yet in the absence of authorial identity and interpretive legibility, the same explosive "!" was liable to stretch language to its limits, to reveal both its ideological constitution and its deficiencies as a system of representation, to contest both its powers of containment and its capacity to establish the parameters of cognition. Such was the case, I want to argue, when in the spring of 1894 an exploding flower pot laid waste to one of the Latin Quarter's finest restaurants.

From the very beginning, the logic behind the *attentat* seemed to defy logic. Why strike the Foyot, when (with the exception of Henry's assault on the café Terminus) attacks against judges, prosecutors, legislators, policemen, banks, and churches had so clearly functioned as retaliatory gestures against abuses of justice, of force, of capitalism, and of institutional authority? Had the bomb been intended for the nearby Sénat, or perhaps the Odéon? How could such a senseless gesture pos-

18. The first of these acts of retribution was directed at the restaurant Véry (boulevard Magenta) where Ravachol, with three bombs already to his credit, had finally been identified and captured on 15 March 1892. An explosion there on 25 April took the lives of the proprietor and a customer; the perpetrator was never apprehended. See Maitron, *Le mouvement anarchiste* I, 215–16.

19. For related reflections on an "outside" to language, see Gilles Deleuze, "He Stuttered," in *Essays Critical and Clinical*, trans. Daniel W. Smith and Michael A. Greco (Minneapolis: University of Minnesota Press, 1997), 107–14.

sibly serve as revolutionary propaganda? The newspapers were filled with questions like these, as well as with obligatory hypotheses of the "whodunit" variety and more than a few jabs at police incompetence.[20] The police apparently deserved the abuse, since their best efforts had yielded little more than the embarrassing arrest of a young working man from St. Denis who, it was soon discovered, had been hospitalized at the time of the Foyot *attentat.*[21] More embarrassing still was the fact that a week after the explosion, they were no closer to apprehending a suspect than they had been when their investigations began on the evening of 4 April. The press would have a field day. *Le matin* noisily launched its own investigations, starting with the publication on 13 April of a lengthy interview with Jacques Prolo, an anarchist militant who was sure of two things about the Foyot affair: first, that the bombing was *not* the work of an anarchist, since the restaurant was hardly a fitting target for a right-thinking *compagnon;* and second, that the explosion was engineered by a woman, since "l'idée ne peut venir qu'à une femme de cacher la dynamite dans des fleurs" [only a woman could come up with the idea of hiding dynamite in flowers].[22] The Foyot *attentat,* according to Prolo, was a personal act of revenge directed specifically at Tailhade, who had presumably managed to make enemies among a group of *femmes de lettres* and feminists.

Meanwhile, Tailhade was busy holding forth from his bed at the Charité. In response to *Le matin*'s inquiries, he acknowledged a history of violent disagreements with a woman of literary ambition (who, he made sure to add, possessed negligible talent and was given to wearing men's clothing in public). Yet Prolo's intuitions about matters of gender somehow escaped him, and he penned an official pardon—brimming with elocutionary bravado—on behalf of the anonymous *"frère"* he assumed to have authored the explosion.[23] These were appetizing

20. See "Les journaux de ce matin," *op. cit.*

21. "L'arrestation de l'auteur de l'attentat du restaurant Foyot," *L'intransigeant,* 15 April 1894.

22. "Bombe passionnelle?," *Le matin,* 13 April 1894.

23. *Ibid.* "Le pardon du poête" was published in facsimile on 13 April: "Puissent les vertus magiques et propitiatoires du sang épanché accoiter [*sic*] l'âme douloureuse du rêveur qui m'a féru! Puissent les Esprits que délivra la rouge libation de mes veines conduire ce triste frère pardonné vers les calmes et hautes pensées qui aident à supporter le mal de vivre ainsi que l'infamie perpétuelle de nos iniques jours" [Would that the magical and propitiatory powers of spilt blood calm the disconsolate soul of the dreamer who smote me. Would that the Spirits liberated by the red libation of my veins guide this sad brother, hereby forgiven, toward the peaceful and lofty thoughts that help us to tolerate the disquietude and perpetual infamy of these iniquitous times].

contributions to an ongoing journalistic feeding-frenzy. But even more savory were Tailhade's responses to the inevitable questions inspired by the declaration he had made, back in February, concerning *vagues humanités* and *beaux gestes*. On the subject of his alleged anarchist sympathies, he had this to say: ". . . ma phrase ne voulait point dire que j'étais anarchiste, mais seulement ami de toutes les manifestations esthétiques quelles qu'elles fussent" [. . . my statement was in no way meant to suggest that I was an anarchist, but rather that I support all aesthetic acts, no matter what they might be]. And on revolution, this: "Toute révolution . . . commence et finit par le pochard! . . . C'est la marche vers le Néant!" [Revolution . . . always begins and ends with some wino! . . . It leads straight to the Void!]. For Tailhade, anarchism's revolutionary objectives were irrelevant, if not downright pathetic. What mattered were the aesthetic merits of its means and methods: "Il n'y a d'intéressant," he concluded, "que les gestes" [There's nothing of interest, except for gestures].[24]

An aesthetic gesture; feminine guile; cross-dressing; the futility of revolution; the Void: needless to say, the interpretive possibilities afforded by the Foyot *attentat* had multiplied exponentially in a matter of days. So I think it makes sense to propose a direct correspondence between the radical textual instability the explosion generated and its intractable illegibility; the greater its resistance to verbal recuperation, it seems, the more inventive were the attempts to translate its obstinate mutness into words. Tailhade was probably right to applaud the anarchist *beau geste* on aesthetic grounds, since terrorists tended to ply their trade in consonant reciprocity to the inequities of a society he described as even more monstrous than terrorism itself.[25] But he was probably wrong to assume that the Foyot "!" (and *la propagande par le fait* in general) had nothing else of interest to say, especially since it possessed the paradoxical capacity both *to signify* and *to refuse signification*, to point everywhere and nowhere at the same time, and in the process to frustrate the desire, among approbatory and antagonistic interpreters alike, for significative closure, for dialogic congruity, for an order of understanding to which the *attentats* engineered by Ravachol, Vaillant, and Henry—once yoked to their authors (and to readably didactic intent)—had ultimately been made to conform. As an anonymous act of indeterminate import, the Foyot explosion succeeded in-

24. André Picard, "M. Laurent Tailhade et l'anarchie. Interview de M. Laurent Tailhade," *Le gaulois*, 6 April 1984.
25. *Ibid.*

stead in emitting a summary glow of (in)comprehension, the radiance of which fleetingly illuminated the undercarriage of representation, its structural mechanisms, and the ideological smoke and mirrors it routinely deploys.

A summary glow; *une lueur sommaire*. I borrow the turn of phrase from Mallarmé, whose brief aside on terrorism in "La musique et les lettres" is sandwiched between a blistering dismissal of Max Nordau's *Entartung* [*Degeneration*] and an ardent defense of free verse. The essay first appeared in *La revue blanche* (with impeccable timing) in April 1894. Here is the passage in question:

> Les engins, dont le bris illumine les parlements d'une lueur sommaire, mais estropient, aussi à faire grand'pitié, des badauds, je m'y intéresserais, en raison de la lueur—sans la brièveté de son enseignement qui permet au législateur d'alléguer une définitive incompréhension; mais j'y récuse l'adjonction de balles à tir et de clous.[26]

> Explosive devices—the detonation of which illuminates parliaments with a summary glow, but that maims, just as regrettably, the curious onlooker—would interest me for the glow they produce, were it not for the brevity of its lesson, which permits the legislator to claim a definitive lack of understanding; but I question the addition of bullets and nails to these devices.

Although Vaillant's assault on the Chambre des Députés instantly comes to mind here, the plural forms of "*engins*" and "*parlements*" suggest that the passage addresses anarchist terrorism in more general terms. So too does the redolently figurative "*lueur sommaire*," a metaphor that simultaneously conjures up the luminous discharges of home-made bombs and the faint glimmering, not quite discernible, of indeterminate orders of intuition to which language can only allude. The noumenal illuminations thus evoked operate in direct opposition to the phenomenally delimited "*incompréhension*" of the Republic's official position on terrorism, while steering the reader toward the same liminal boundaries that the "*législateur*"—for obvious reasons— would prefer not to cross. Mallarmé voices two reservations: the first, about terrorism's tangential victims; and the second, about the brevity of its potentially revelatory "*enseignement.*"

This second reservation, muted to a certain extent by the first, treads on dangerous ground. For what would a sustained "*lueur*" and a more enlightening "*enseignement*" amount to in this context, if not an explosive challenge to the authority of parliaments and of rhetoric alike? To elude the tentacles of government, to navigate around the referential trap of language, to pass beyond the cognitive borders that governments and language both patrol: all this, I suspect, is what constitutes the dialectical flip side of the *Mallarméan* coin—if not the very essence of signification to be distilled from unprocessed aggregates of words and letters. I also suspect that this same convergence of "*lueur*" and "*enseignement*" is related to what Brousse—despite his weakness for allegorization—had imagined in 1877 to be a specifically revolutionary *idée*, the effusion of which was the primary objective of *la propagande par le fait*. Readers of Schopenhauer will recognize vague correspondences here with the Idea, and readers of Kant's third *Critique*, with the Sublime. But the more important point is that an explosion in the spring of 1894 could stage critical encounters between imagination and reason, between the noumenal and the phenomenal, between mind and matter, that had the effect both of testing the perimeters of consciousness and of alluding to alternative modalities of thought.

FÉNÉON

To stage these critical encounters was not to resolve them. And to stage them "explosively" was to insist—violently, concretely, unequivocally—on the innate contrariety of their terms. Now resolution, as I have already argued, was the shared desire of the Republic, the police, and the press, as well as of the large majority of anarchist sympathizers. It involved the redirection of the significative impetus of a revolutionary act toward a perpetrator who, once apprehended and convicted, became the sign of interpretive closure—at the expense of the disruptive effects of the act itself. What was lost along the way was the potential actualization, almost entirely contingent upon material, intellectual, and emotional destabilization, of the intolerable conditions under which revolution typically occurs. What was gained was readerly gratification, punctuated by the congenial placidity of false consciousness.

Which brings me to the remarkable afterlife of the Foyot *attentat*. The police failed to get their man (or woman) in 1894; and anarchism failed, in the wake of massive repressions, to sustain its program of material reprisal.[27] The assassination of President Sadi-Carnot in June marked the end of more than two years of terrorist assaults, and many among the anarchist rank-and-file would seek greener pastures in the nascent revolutionary-syndicalist movement; the defiant sensationalism of *la propagande par le fait* accordingly gave way to the work-a-day pragmatics of *l'action directe* (including strikes, sabotage, and labeling). But the Foyot explosion would continue to inspire conjecture, even as the memory of its historical moment grew faint. In April 1948, Alexandre Zévaès, the socialist historian, journalist, and politician, revealed in the pages of *L'ordre* that Paul Delasalle, the recently deceased syndicalist revolutionary, had placed the bomb on the window sill of the restaurant some fifty years earlier. Delasalle's widow publicly disputed the claim; Zévaès insisted in turn that his information had come directly from her husband the morning after the incident.[28] The anarchist historian Jean Maitron, having conferred with both parties, would devote a chapter of his 1952 biography of Delasalle to the controversy.[29] Then in 1959, the poet-critic André Salmon complicated things further by attributing the explosion to an unnamed *homme de lettres* who had apparently boasted of his deed to a close anarchist friend.[30] Five years later, the American scholar Joan Halperin acquired information from an acquaintance of Salmon's indicating that the literary man in question had been none other than Fénéon—whose anarchist predilections had aroused the suspicions of the police in the immediate aftermath of the *attentat*. Halperin would go on to write the definitive biography of Fénéon, two extended passages of which propose wonderfully provocative accounts of her protagonist's activities on the evening of 4 April 1894. When the book was published in 1988, the Foyot controversy flared up once again, this time in the pages of journals like the *New York Review of Books* and *La quinzaine littéraire*.[31]

The vagaries of hearsay notwithstanding, Fénéon makes for a very good suspect. His deep involvement with fin-de-siècle anarchism's most militant factions—with the terrorist Henry and the propagandists

27. Police informants reported (on 25 June 1894, and again on 26 March 1895) rumors among anarchist partisans that the propagandist Armand Matha had engineered the explosion. See APP, B A/142 (168–69).

28. See *L'ordre*, 13 and 28 April, and 13 May, 1948.

29. Jean Maitron, *Le syndicalisme révolutionnaire. Paul Delasalle* (Paris: Les éditions ouvrières, 1952), 42–48.

30. André Salmon, *Le terreur noir* (Paris: J.-J. Pauvert, 1959), 356–67.

31. Joan Ungersma Halperin, *Félix Fénéon: Aesthete and Anarchist in Fin-de-Siècle Paris* (New Haven and London: Yale University Press, 1988), 3–4, 276.

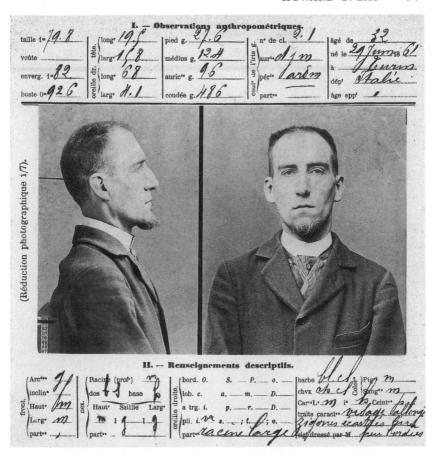

Figure 5. Alphonse Bertillon, *Félix Fénéon*, 1894. Photograph. Archives de la préfecture de police, Paris.

Pouget and Armand Matha—was a matter of record. And when, on 25 April, he was finally arrested in connection with the Foyot affair, a box of detonators and a flask of mercury were discovered in his office at the Ministry of War (where, in keeping with avant-garde tradition, he held a day job as a clerk). Once in police custody, Fénéon was measured, weighed, inspected for distinguishing features, and then photographed (Fig. 5) in Bertillon's studio at the préfecture de police. On 3 May he was transferred from a holding cell to Mazas prison, where he would remain for over three months awaiting prosecution on charges of having participated—with twenty-nine other suspects (nineteen of them leading anarchist writers and activists)—in a criminal association of malefactors. During the so-called Trial of the Thirty in August, his sophistication and wit ran circles around the prosecuting attorney. Both Mallarmé and the prominent psychologist Charles Henry testified warmly on his behalf. That he was acquitted by the skin of his teeth (the jury was evenly divided on the Fénéon verdict) did not deter him from remarking to the painter Paul Signac, less than a year and a half after the trial, that terrorism had done much more for anarchist propaganda than twenty years' worth of pamphlets by Elisée Reclus or Peter Kropotkin.[32] In short, there is every reason to believe that his interest in explosives was more than a simple question of intellectual curiosity.

But all this evidence has less to do with the Foyot bombing than it does with Fénéon, or rather with the fabrication in Fénéon's absence of a likeness informed by a level of conjecture entirely foreign to the descriptive information and anthropometric observations that adorn the margins of Bertillon's mug shots. That the *attentat* can still help both to substantiate and to falsify that likeness is all in keeping with the warning it had sent a century earlier to interpreters who would exchange the factious effects of insistent illegibility for the illusion of comprehension. I imagine that Fénéon, the archetypal fin-de-siècle ironist, would have understood the interests at stake when the allure of easy answers contrives to neutralize the destabilizing effects of a terrorist act. I imagine, too, that he would have recognized the power of a terrorist act to resist recuperation altogether, even by anarchist luminaries like Reclus and Kropotkin—the authority of whose writings was, after all, subjected to implicit critique by the violent materiality of *la propagande par le fait.*

ENSEIGNEMENT

Let me conclude, then, with two final points concerning the Foyot *attentat.* The first has to do with the strained relationship it articulates between materiality and signification, and therefore with the peculiar nature of its textuality. There has been no shortage over the years of interpretative readings of the explosion: retribution for the executions of Ravachol and Vaillant; retaliation against the complacency of the well-to-do (who enjoy fine cuisine while others starve); the vengeance of a literary woman run amuck; a *beau geste;* the chicanery (why not?) of

32. Cited in John Rewald, "Extraits du journal inédit de Paul Signac," *Gazette des beaux-arts* 6/36 (December 1949): 113.

an *agent provocateur.* The incongruities among them are entirely predictable, since each of these explications rests on a different set of hypotheses—all of which (including the assumption that the *attentat* was in fact "anarchist") cling precariously to an event so grossly material that it inflects the act of reading with the haunting specter of an *hors-texte* to which language has no access. Hence the uneasiness that informs *any* account of the explosion (including my own), whether it purports to solve a mystery or to rehearse an assemblage of possible meanings. What took place at the restaurant Foyot, in other words, was a violent collision between the materiality of the world and the phenomenality of the sign; what made the incident revolutionary was the resulting evocation of an alienated state of being, of a radical alterity, for which the sign (and interpretive reading) no longer mattered.[33]

So it would seem—and this is my second point—that the communicative authority of the Foyot *attentat* was largely contingent upon its apparent refusal to communicate. The paradox is a function of textuality or, more precisely, of the readability of unreadability. But it nonetheless points to an unsettling distinction between a monadic subject's phenomenal experience of the world (wholly circumscribed by the boundaries of individual consciousness) and the incontrovertible actuality (individual consciousness notwithstanding) of flying projectiles and mangled bodies. The concreteness of the latter, I want to suggest, pressures the conceptual primacy of the former to the breaking point, since to invoke distinctions between phenomenality and materiality where terrorism is concerned is to suggest, finally, that signs are somewhat less material than explosions (even when explosions function as signs). Small wonder that by the spring of 1894, *la propagande par le fait* would have lost much of the tentative approbation it had enjoyed among anarchism's most prominent theoreticians—great believers, all of them, in both the sanctity of the integral self and the power of words. As the last in a two-year sequence of eleven bombings, the Foyot *attentat*—and the performative (il)legibility of its indexical "!"—was perhaps destined to serve as a nagging corrective for the interpretive domestication of the previous ten. For it is well to remember that the "*enseignement*" that made terrorism interesting to the likes of Mallarmé had less to do with musings about reprisal and sacrifice than with the "*lueur sommaire*" emitted in turn by each of the explosions, regardless

33. On phenomenality and signification, see de Man, "Hegel on the Sublime," in *Aesthetic Ideology*, 111.

of the rhetoric subsequently formulated to dim its ephemeral illumi-nations. The lessons thus taught were hard to swallow, if only because of the violence involved when revolutionaries turn their attention away from words and toward more material orders of persuasion. But equally unpalatable, I suspect, was the anxiety inevitably generated when recurrent acts of terror force interpretive consciousness to go toe-to-toe with its own cognitive limitations.

II. Narrative Tactics

DARRIN M. McMAHON

Narratives of Dystopia in the French Revolution: Enlightenment, Counter-Enlightenment, and the *Isle des philosophes* of the Abbé Balthazard

One of the oldest and most obdurate fictions of the Revolution is that of its gestation and birth. For like all young upstarts to the city, the men and women who gathered in Paris in 1789 were eager to fashion for themselves a tale of respectable origins. Aristocratic lineage, to be sure, would no longer do. And timeless Catholic tradition, ancient roots, and ancestral heritage—all this gave off the musty smell of the former régime. At a time when the point was to be new, the past seemed, well, *passé*. Yet even those intent on starting afresh had to have a history. Only God, after all, could create *ex nihilo*, and he too would no longer do. Where did one begin?

There were many answers to this question—many narratives to give the revolutionary's break with the past paternity and legitimation.[1] But as Hans Ulrich Gumbrecht and Rolf Reichardt observe, the "spontaneous and almost conventional conviction" of the men and women of 1789 was that their rupture had been prepared by *philosophie*, by the thought of the great *philosophes* of the eighteenth century who had tirelessly battled for light in what was otherwise a dark age.[2] Thus, when "Voltaire's disciple," the venerable *homme de lettres*, Jean François La Harpe, led a delegation of playwrights before the National

---

1. For an overview of the Revolution's encounter with history, see Joseph John Zizek, "The Politics and Poetics of History in the French Revolution, 1787–1794," PhD dissertation, University of California, Berkeley (1995).

2. Hans Ulrich Gumbrecth and Rolf Reichardt, "*Philosophe, Philosophie,*" *Handbuch politisch-sozialer Grundbegriffe in Frankreich 1680–1820,* 10 vols., ed. Rolf Reichardt and Eberhard Schmitt (Munich: Olddenbourg Verlag, 1985–), vol. 3, 61. Translations throughout this essay are my own unless otherwise noted.

YFS 101, *Fragments of Revolution,* ed. Weber and Lay, © 2002 by Yale University.

Assembly in 1790, his claim that "men of letters had been the first mo-
tors of this grand and happy revolution" was already a deeply held certainty. "They and they alone," La Harpe continued grandiloquently,
"liberated the human spirit," breaking the chains of ignorance placed
on man by religious, political, and moral oppressors.[3] He was preaching to the converted. Just months later, the National Assembly would
vote to inter Voltaire in the Pantheon, honoring him as a great revolutionary forefather. And when, in 1794, the remains of Jean-Jacques
Rousseau were placed by his side, no one, surely, could scoff at the revolutionaries' lineage. They had, it seemed, noble parentage indeed.

This, at any rate, was the Revolution's story of itself, a "catechism"
of origins and birth recounted to schoolchildren in the 1790s, and re-
stated and reformulated down to the present day.[4] For despite the fact
that scores of historians have complicated any simple and ineluctable
causal relationship between the enlightenment and the Revolution,
many continue to see 1789, and what followed, as the "strange offspring of *philosophie.*"[5] To what degree this represents an unreflexive
acceptance of the Revolution's own beliefs about itself is a question
worthy of serious consideration.[6] Here, however, I would like to draw

3. *Archives parlementaires de 1787 à 1860, recueil complet des débats législatifs &*
politiques des chambres françaises, Série 1 (1787–1799), ed. M. J. Mavidal and M. E. Laurent, et al., 82 vols. (Paris, 1867–1913), vol. 8, 250. La Harpe delivered his discourse, accompanied by André Chénier, Louis-Sébastien Mercier, Nicolas Sébastien Roche Cham-
fort, and others on 24 August 1790.
4. See the *Alphabet des sans culottes, ou Premiers éléments d'éducation républi-*
caine (Paris, 1793), cited in Gumbrecht and Reichardt, "*Philosophe, Philosophie,*" 64.
The primer queries students in the following manner:

Q: Who are the men who by their writings prepared the Revolution?
A: Helvétius, Mably, J. J. Rousseau, Voltaire, and Franklin.
Q: What do you call these great men?
A: *Philosophes.*

5. This is the formulation of François Furet, in his highly influential *Interpreting the*
French Revolution, trans. Elborg Forster (Cambridge: Cambridge University Press, 1989),
28–29. Furet qualifies this statement in a parenthetical immediately following the
quoted sentence "(its offspring at least, in a chronological sense)," but the thrust of his
work, I would argue, favors the original proposition.
6. This is the line of inquiry pursued by Roger Chartier, in his *The Cultural Origins*
of the French Revolution, trans. Lydia G. Cochrane (Durham and London: Duke University Press, 1991). Chartier argues here that rather than affirming that "it was the Enlightenment that produced the Revolution," we should consider "that it was the Revolution that invented the Enlightenment by attempting to root its legitimacy in a corpus
of texts and founding authors, reconciled and united, beyond their extreme differences"
(5). Keith Baker also reflects with insight on the complex relationships between Enlightenment and Revolution in his classic essay, "On the problem of the ideological ori-

attention to another narrative of the Revolution's origins and subsequent trajectory—that provided by the counter-revolutionary priest, the abbé Balthazard, in his 1790 dystopian fiction, the *Isle des philosophes* [Island of the Philosophers].[7] As we shall see, Balthazard's narrative shared a number of similarities with the more positive tale told by his revolutionary adversaries, as well as with later critics of the *siècle des lumières*. This odd coincidence, I will suggest, has important things to tell us about subsequent interpretations of the Enlightenment and of the Revolution to which it allegedly gave birth.

The reader may be excused if he or she has never heard of the abbé Balthazard or of the *Isle des philosophes*, a minor text by a minor author, whose only other work, published in Paris in 1789, was a devotional breviary, the *Année chrétienne, ou Précis de la vie du Saint* [Christian Year, or Précis of the Saint's Life], a book of exercises, psalms, and readings joined to the Christian calendar. Himself an obscure priest in the diocese of Metz, Balthazard has left us little more than his surname and these two books. Little wonder, then, that he is hardly a household name. Yet it is also true that Balthazard's work, and particularly the *Isle des philosophes*, formed part of a much larger current of "anti-philosophic" literature that flourished in the second half of the eighteenth century. In turn part of what I have called the "French Counter-Enlightenment," this wider literature, too, has been almost completely ignored, testimony to the one-sidedness with which scholars have addressed the intellectual world of the *siècle des lumières*.[8] As Robert Palmer observed many years ago, "it must be confessed that the thought of the age of Enlightenment, more than that of any equally important period in modern history, has been studied from writings which express only one side of the question."[9] Over fifty years later, his assertion still holds largely true.

What, then, was anti-philosophic literature, and what was the French

---

gins of the French Revolution," in *Inventing the French Revolution: Essays on French Political Culture in the Eighteenth Century* (Cambridge: Cambridge University Press, 1990).

7. [Abbé Balthazard], *L'isle des philosophes et plusieurs autres, nouvellement découvertes, & remarquables par leurs rapports avec la France actuelle* (n.p., [1790]).

8. See Darrin M. McMahon, *Enemies of the Enlightenment: The French Counter-Enlightenment and the Making of Modernity* (New York: Oxford University Press, 2001), especially Chapter 1.

9. Robert R. Palmer, *Catholics and Unbelievers in Eighteenth-Century France* (Princeton: Princeton University Press, 1939), 4.

Counter-Enlightenment? These are questions that necessarily lie beyond the scope of this essay, but some insight can be gained by a close reading of the *Isle des philosophes* itself. For published at an early stage in the Revolution, this work is emblematic not only of a militant strain in early counter-revolutionary thought, but also of a host of well-developed anti-philosophic arguments, to which the Counter-Revolution itself was direct heir.

Organized in epistolary format, the text unfolds through a series of eight extended letters from the so-called "Chevalier du Haut-Mont," an enthusiastic partisan of modern philosophy, now living in Italy, to his young nephew in Paris, the silent but ostensible editor of the volume. Chronicling his recent voyages to a series of fantastic islands in the Atlantic (discovered when his ship to New France is shipwrecked in a storm), the Chevalier's letters comprise a sort of anti-*philosophe Candide* in which the misguided protagonist confronts the world not through the distorting lens of Voltaire's Dr. Pangloss, but through Enlightenment philosophy itself. Penned during the crucial first year of the Revolution (from May 1789 to the Spring of 1790), the letters comment intermittently as well upon news of events in France, providing an appropriately "philosophic" reading of this allegedly philosophic event. The two, we are meant to see—*philosophie* and Revolution— are inextricably linked: the follies and horrors of the one beget the follies and horrors of the other.

This is, however, more than merely transparent satire. For the reader is also privy to the suitably "antiphilosophic" views of the Chevalier's faithful traveling companion, the Vicomte de Bisval. A devout Catholic and ardent opponent of the Revolution, Bisval had succumbed in his youth to the dangerous maxims of *philosophie*, but has since been cured of his "idiotic vanity" and "criminal complaisance," and so offers here an orthodox assessment of all that the two travelers see and hear on their exotic travels. On good terms despite their opposing views, the two friends debate with passion, but no ill will, united by "a secret penchant of the heart," whose ultimate source is revealed when the myopic Chevalier acknowledges the distortions of his gaze, likewise converting to Catholicism at the story's end (8). Repulsed by the ruins wrought by *philosophie*, and saddened by the untimely death of his bosom friend, the Chevalier repents his former creed, withdrawing not, however, to cultivate his garden, but his soul, through a rejuvenating faith in the Catholic religion.

It is within this conventional narrative of philosophic temptation and Christian redemption, then, that Balthazard launches his two "diametrically opposed" voyagers on their spiritual journey from France (7). Whereas the Chevalier is an embodiment of the spirit of philosophic innovation and nascent revolutionary change, the Viscount represents the viewpoint of the author himself, that of a Catholic traditionalist—a man, we are told, "who still thinks in 1790, as all France thought in 1788" (vi). Their experience of the world could not be more different. Thus, when the two are shipwrecked at the first of the story's fantastic islands, the *Isle de la fortunée* [Island of Fortune], the Chevalier's predicament is severely aggravated by his philosophic beliefs, whereas the Viscount's fate is rendered infinitely more tolerable. Taken captive by the island's primitive inhabitants, the two spend a night in prison facing death. The Viscount, "sustained and consoled" by his religious convictions, awaits his fate with patient courage and fortitude, whereas the Chevalier, taught by his "philosophical principles" that there is no life after death, gives himself over to "an impotent despair that only multiplies his afflictions" (29). When, the next day, the travelers are not killed, but rather sold into slavery, the Viscount adapts to his new situation with forbearance, eventually earning the trust of his masters, who free him, promising passage to the New World. The Chevalier, by contrast, though treated kindly by his new masters, proceeds to corrupt their children, attempting to seduce the daughter with philosophic maxims ("virtue," he tells her, "is a chimera," and the respect for chastity, a "prejudice" invented by tyrants), while pumping the son full of similar beliefs (38–39). Soon, this once sensible and respectful child has become a *petit philosophe*, scornful of duty and disobedient to his parents, a libertine and a liar. Learning of the source of his corruption, the father threatens to kill the Chevalier, who only manages to escape through the help of the more forgiving children. Forced to spend the next six days hiding in a forest before fortuitously rejoining the Viscount, the Chevalier nearly perishes from the hunger and cold of the wild. Bisval cannot help remarking on the irony. *Eh bien*, he jests, "according to your Jean-Jacques and other *philosophes*, this is the way men once lived, free, content, and happy. To listen to you, this was the golden age of nature, and we were fools to have left it" (45). The Chevalier is forced to concede that there is a "great difference between practicing a doctrine and preaching it." After his brief novitiate, he is ready to take a "well seasoned chicken" over "all the acorns of the forest" (46).

It is through such farcical escapades, then, that the shallowness, hypocrisy, and naiveté of the Chevalier's *philosophie* is revealed. In their encounters on other islands (the rough seas of the Atlantic ensure a steady supply of nautical deviations), the two men are able to observe the absurdities of Enlightenment *philosophie* first-hand. Thus, on the *Isle des ours* [Islands of Bears], suggestions by the French *philosophes* Guillaume-Thomas Raynal and Julien Offray de La Mettrie minimizing the differences between human beings and animals are taken to their "logical" conclusion. Here, bears are the highest race, having developed, in a world without providence or divine order, the faculties of speech and reason. Walking upright and living with all the benefits of society, they are nonetheless contemptuous of their present lot, philosophizing a former "golden age of nature," a time of "perfect equality without distinctions of rank, honor, or power" to which they long to return (72–73).

Similarly, on the *Isle du hasard* [Island of Chance], the travelers find the "systems" of eighteenth-century savants "realized in fact" (61). Here, nature rules through "blind chance," and "random combinations" in keeping with the speculations of such radical materialist philosophers as Holbach and Boulanger. In accordance with a suggestion by Helvétius, who in *De l'esprit* related the development of human intelligence to the development of the human hand, men and women have horses' hooves, and hence are stupid brutes. Horses, by contrast, possess hands, and so think and reason like human beings. Likewise, the travelers encounter a monkey who paints portraits with perfect skill, and come across a school of talking animals who reason as sophisticated philosophers, apparently lending credence to d'Alembert's conjectures in the *Alambic moral* that the sole barrier to the cultivation of animal intelligence is the inability to use language. Finally, the two men discover a three-thousand-year-old race which seems to confirm La Mettrie's belief that human beings have naturally evolved from less perfect forms in the absence of a directing intelligence. With perpendicular mouths, eyes behind the head, ears in the middle of the face, and a host of other irregularities, these "masses of flesh still have thousands of years to go before they become perfect men" (106).

This lampoon of Enlightenment science and materialist metaphysics may seem as far from the urgencies of contemporary France as Balthazard himself believed *philosophie* to be far from the truths of the natural world. Yet when the travelers journey to the *Isle des philosophes* itself, the parody takes a decidedly more pointed turn. The maxims of modern *philosophie*, we learn, are not only absurd in their denial of a providential order and divine purpose to man and the universe, they are extremely dangerous as well. In stripping away all that makes us decent—the respect for religion and tradition, the gentle yoke of hierarchy and authority, and the fear of an afterlife—modern philosophy turns us over to our selfish passions and pleasures, to our most depraved lusts and longings. So exposed, we are prey to the anarchy of dissolution and desire. The account of the island of the *philosophes*, then, is meant as a cautionary tale, of the thinnest possible transparency.

Thus, upon their arrival, the two travelers learn that the wise rulers of the country have only recently liberated themselves from a despotic government. As the rector of the island's philosophic academy explains:

> Our ancestors were dupes enough to have submitted themselves to those tyrants and despots called kings, princes, monarchs, and sovereigns. But we cried "despotism" and "tyranny" so loud and with such force that we were able to inspire in the people the love of liberty—to make them appreciate their rights, and to understand that millions of men were stronger than a single one. When we had so electrified their spirits with our countless brochures and writings, a happy revolution was carried out on this island that has rendered us free. It is to *philosophie* that we owe this great service. [117]

Long mediated, and secretly prepared, the Revolution has triumphed on the back of modern *philosophie*, whose acolytes wisely determined that the nation's woes stemmed entirely from religion, the hand-maiden of despotism. But given that many of the country's inhabitants retained atavistic beliefs in the "chimeras" of God and an afterlife, the island's *philosophes* unveiled their attack slowly. They began with ridicule, spreading jokes and sarcasm against the church and clergy in a variety of forms: brochures, *bons mots*, stories, novels, and songs. Gaining in audacity, they sponsored essay prizes at the island's academy for the best treatises arguing that morality was based solely on reason, not on God. At the same time, they adopted the standard of "universal tolerance" in order to disseminate the belief that all revealed religions were equally good, so as to be able better to prove that they were all equally false. From deism, they progressed to atheism, finally openly preaching the complete destruction of the Church—a task that had only recently been effected through the sale of its lands (119–30).

Now liberated from oppressive superstition, the inhabitants of the *Isle des philosophes* were free to live totally in accordance with the maxims of modern philosophy. These held, among other things, that in a world without God or soul, morality was a function entirely of utility, pleasure, and pain. "Virtue is all that is useful to us, and vice is all that is harmful," a professor tells the travelers, quoting directly from Helvétius's *De l'esprit,* Holbach's *Système de la nature,* and the abbé Raynal's *Histoire des deux Indes* to the great delight of the Chevalier. Our only "duty" is to "make ourselves happy" (218–19). And happiness, for soulless animals, is but the maximization of pleasure, "the sensual satisfaction of the body" (219). When the Viscount protests that surely such an ethics would encourage selfish egotism, breaking all ties of duty and authority, the islands' inhabitants demur. They have taken, it seems, a maxim of Voltaire to heart: *Voulez vous être heureux, vivez toujours sans maître* (116–17) [If you wish to be happy, live always without a master]. And now, having unburdened themselves of all oppressive masters—political, religious, and moral—they plan to usher in a reign of perfect freedom and happiness.

With all these ecstatic pronouncements, the Chevalier is in perfect agreement. The Viscount, by contrast, though polite to his hosts, warns that things in Europe would be very different were its inhabitants to fully embrace this dangerous creed. For "we," he observes,

> are not like you. Your sublime maxims would be extremely dangerous. This liberty would quickly degenerate into license, into murder, violence, conflagration, and civil war. Disorder of all kinds would overthrow the most beautiful kingdoms, and in the place of the despotism of kings would succeed an infinitely more deadly despotism of the people. [118]

And this, of course, is the heart of the matter, the central message of the text. *Philosophie* leads, in the end, to meaningless death and destruction on the social scale, just as it leads to meaningless death for *individuals* who adopt it to the detriment of their religious convictions. When, having wearied of the progressive *isle philosophique,* the two voyagers manage to board a return ship to Europe, Balthazard insists on this theme relentlessly. Fellow passengers exchange lurid stories of the crimes committed by ordinary men and women ("*des domestiques & des gens simples*" [servants and simple folk]) who have lost their faith in *philosophie.* As one French victim allegedly repents on the scaffold, before receiving his just reward:

> I have had accomplices whom it is well that you know—dangerous corrupters who placed the dagger in my hand. They are the works of your celebrated unbelievers—your Voltaires, your Raynals, your Boulangers,

and this entire crowd of skeptics, deists, atheists, and materialists who open the door to all heinous crimes with their abominable maxims and pernicious principles. Alas, these are the perverse masters who led me down the path of crime . . . by assuring me that there is no avenging God, that all dies with us. They crushed in me the remorse of conscience, treating it as yet another prejudice, and so took away the only restraint (*frein*) able to contain the fire of my passions. [285–86]

And lest there be any doubt as to the metonymic relationship between individual and nation, Balthazard has the guilty party warn his countrymen directly.

Enfin, French nation . . . heed my words. If you lend an ear to the seductive oracles of a false *philosophie,* and to the impetuous declamations of these new preachers of license who cloak their words behind the beautiful name of liberty, soon they will carry trouble, anarchy, and desolation into your breast. [287]

This is a dead certainty. And though the crowd of onlookers is allegedly moved to exonerate the repentant *philosophe,* allowing him to end his days in a monastery, Balthazard leaves little hope that philosophic France will be so lucky.[10] The book ends on a dark note, with the Chevalier recounting to his nephew the news of the Viscount's death from illness in Italy, where the two travelers have remained since returning from the island of the *philosophes.* The Chevalier himself, it is true, is moved by this traumatic event to embrace Bisval's cherished faith. But this is only a small glimmer of light before a gathering dark storm. The text's final pages are bleak, chronicling the triumph of *philosophie* over the Church in France with the passage of the Civil Constitution of the Clergy, and the defeat in the National Assembly of dom Gerle's motion to declare Catholicism the national religion (13 April 1790). In such a philosophic state—the logic of the entire text is designed to show—the future can only be one of anarchy, death, and destruction.

---

10. After uttering his warning, the condemned continues, "But where does my zealousness get me and what good is it to uselessly tire myself? It is in vain that that you are urged to feel the snakes that you caress, that you warm with complacence in your breast, and from which you swallow in gulps the mortal poison. Far from prohibiting these public poisonings, you extol them as genius' wonders, you shower praise on them as if they were divinities, you give them prizes in your academies, you coronate them in your theaters, you erect statues of them in your museums, you spread their lampoons with all of your effort" (238).

The patient reader will have discerned by now that the *Isle des philosophes* is hardly a masterpiece of intellectual satire in the tradition of
the lofty models to which it makes allusion (*Candide, Gulliver's Travels, Don Quixote*). Nor is it an archetype of philosophical nuance and
subtlety. But for these very reasons, it is important to resist the temptation to simply reject the work out of hand, to write it off as a silly,
reactionary response to two of the major intellectual and political phenomena of the modern age, the Enlightenment and the French Revolution. For it is precisely this impulse that has long deafened scholars
to the distressed cries of horror uttered in the dark eighteenth century,
to the plaintive, uncomprehending outrage of men and women like
Balthazard. In one camp, those sympathetic to the Enlightenment and
the Revolution have historically been all too ready to accept the *philosophes'* own polemical characterizations of their enemies as the collective *infâme*, dismissing them without further thought as so many idiots
and reactionaries standing in the way of the sun. Scholars more sympathetic to the study of religion, by contrast, have frequently appeared em-
barrassed by the vehemence of voices such as those of Balthazard, making efforts, as a consequence, to emphasize that not all religious souls
in the eighteenth century were so adamantly opposed to reason and
light.[11] Finally, as I will have occasion to remark further at the end of
this essay, many modern (or postmodern) critics of the Enlightenment
seem blissfully unaware that the *philosophes* ever had enemies at all.
In their view, the Enlightenment itself is the force to be condemned.

In light of this concurrence, Balthazard and his kind have gone
largely unheard in academic circles. Yet however poorly attuned the
ears of modern scholars, Balthazard's eighteenth-century contempo-
raries had no choice but to hear him, if not to listen. For since the middle of the century, men and women sharing exactly his views had
voiced their outrage at the apparent triumph of *philosophie* in great volume—not just in France, but throughout Catholic Europe, and even the
New World.[12] Looking on in baffled disbelief, they watched as the *phi-*

11. This was the tack adopted by Robert Palmer who purposefully set aside "the more
absurd productions of the orthodox," excluding "writings that were only cries of horror,
wild assertions and promiscuous calling of names." He acknowledged, however, that this
process "may well give a false view of the real ideas of the time" (*Catholics and Unbelievers*, 21). Similarly, Albert Monod, in his classic study *De Pascal à Chateaubriand.
Les défenseurs français du Christianisme de 1670 à 1802* (1916), dismissed the more extreme writers of this ilk, commenting simply, "they deserve to be forgotten" (472).
12. On the international dimension of the Catholic Counter-Enlightenment, see my
"Seeing the Century of Lights as a Time of Darkness: The Catholic Counter-Enlighten-

losophes and *philosophie* made huge inroads into polite society, dominating patronage networks, conquering the salons and academies, and insinuating their views into the mainstream of educated European life in a massive publishing campaign that is now well documented. What from the vantage point of the early twenty-first century might seem the inevitable progress of light, struck many eighteenth-century Catholics as the most concerted campaign against the Christian faith in human history. As the assembled clergy of France noted in a pastoral letter circulated in every parish in the country in 1775, "In previous centuries there were impious persons here and there—but without party and results. There were books that taught impiety, but [they were] obscure and little read. Today the unbelievers form a sect, divided as it should be over the objects of its belief; united in the revolt against the authority of divine revelation."[13]

This was a frightening prospect, and of course neither the Church nor its supporters took it lying down. On the contrary, they sought continually to respond to the *philosophes*, blow for blow, in a Counter-Enlightenment literature comprising not just printed sermons and formal religious apologies, but a wide range of anti-*philosophe* novels, poems, plays, and other *genres*, of which the *Isle des philosophes* is a fitting example.[14] As I have tried to show elsewhere, though much of this production was not terribly sophisticated, it was adept—in part for this very reason—at putting forth a simple, reified portrait of what *philosophie* was. Reducing the varied and variegated opinions of the age of Enlightenment to a number of worst-case propositions (atheism, materialism, sensual hedonism, individualism), anti-*philosophes* argued that *philosophie*, collectively, was working toward common, pernicious ends. It destroyed respect for religion and superordinate authority, subverted the patriarchal family, and urged sexual license. It taught disrespect for law and tradition, ridiculing as "prejudice" the wisdom of the ages. By preaching "universal tolerance," it sapped the legiti-

ment in Europe and the Americas," in Florence Lotterie and Darrin M. McMahon, ed., *Les Lumières européennes dans leur relation avec les autres grandes cultures et religions du XVIIIᵉ siècle* (Paris: Champion, 2001).

13. [Jean-George Le Franc de Pompignan], *Avertissement de l'assemblée-générale du Clergé de France aux Fidèles de ce royaume sur les avantages de la religion chrétienne et les effets pernicieux de l'incrédulité* (1775), 5.

14. In addition to *Enemies of the Enlightenment*, Chapter 1, see McMahon, "The Counter-Enlightenment and the Low-Life of Literature in Pre-Revolutionary France," *Past & Present* 159 (May 1998), which deals specifically with the secular, anti-*philosophe* world of letters.

macy of the one true faith, and by enjoining men and women to indulge their passions, maximizing pleasure in the pursuit of happiness, *philosophie* corrupted the social whole, creating egotistic individuals who scorned duty and social obligation. To be sure, this was hardly a fair portrait (though it must be said in justice that the *philosophes*, for their part, seldom spoke of religion with the intent to be fair). Deeply biased, incendiary, ideological, the view of the *siècle des lumières* put forth in this collective anti-*philosophe* discourse—a discourse reproduced in full in Balthazard's *Isle des philosophes*—nonetheless possessed the great virtue of coherence. It is an irony worth contemplating, in fact, that the Enlightenment was defined—was constructed—as much by its enemies as by its partisans.

Be this as it may—and the vehemence of this anti-*philosophe* onslaught notwithstanding—by the last decade of the Old Regime, many enemies of the Enlightenment were beginning to admit defeat. "I no longer recognize my nation," grumbled an altogether typical commentator in the *Journal ecclésiastique*, the leading professional publication of the clergy. "The *philosophes* are the men of the day. . . . What changes in our morals, in our writings, in our religion, in all our being!"[15] Just what such changes might entail was an object of intense speculation, and enemies of the Enlightenment left little to the imagination. Drawing on two fecund sources—the apocalyptic rhetoric of the Old Testament, and the cultural memory of the European religious wars—Catholic partisans warned that like the Biblical and Protestant apostates of old, the *philosophes* were precipitating a new reign of violence and destruction. In a sermon celebrating the birth of the new dauphin, for example, delivered at the church of the Mazarin college in Paris in 1781, the orator painted a frank picture of the dangers posed by the triumph of "false philosophy." "From this anarchy of the physical and moral universe results necessarily," he stressed, "the overthrow of thrones, the extinction of sovereigns, and the dissolution of all societies. Oh Kings! Oh Sovereigns! Will you be strong enough to stay on your thrones if this principle ever prevails?"[16] Clearly, the speaker implied, they would not.

15. "L'inoculation du bon sens," *Journal ecclésiastique, ou Bibliothèque raisonnée des sciences ecclésiastiques*, lxxxiii, Part 2 (May 1781): 156–57.

16. *Discours sur la naissance de Monseigneur le Dauphin, le 22 d'Octobre 1781, prononcé en présence de l'Université de Paris, pendant l'Office divin, le 12 du mois de décembre suivant, dans l'Église du College Mazarin*. Printed in *Supplément au Journal ecclésiastique*, x, Part 3 (December 1786): 231–55.

Such graphic descriptions of the destruction to be wrought by *philosophie* were commonplace in the last decades of the Old Regime, and it is in just such a context that Balthazard's *Isle des philosophes* is most interesting. For the work provides a running account of the way in which many devout Catholics responded to the Revolution in its early stages, interpreting it as the logical outcome of a battle they had waged, and lost, during the Old Regime. To see the Revolution in this way was perforce to give it narrative coherence—not just a present, but a past and a future. Looking backward, it seemed abundantly clear that the upheaval of 1789 had been consciously foreseen, and in fact will- fully prepared. Just as the rulers of the *Isle des philosophes* carefully or- chestrated their eventual triumph—ridiculing religion, conquering the academies and *beau monde*, spreading tolerance and *philosophie* to the farthest reaches of society—the French *philosophes*, too, had master- minded the present upheaval. And if the present was thus the direct outcome of the premeditated conspiracy of the past, it seemed equally clear that the future portended even greater upheaval still.[17] For *philosophie* was always worse than it seemed. It hid horrors behind be- guiling phrases—liberty, humanity, tolerance—while plotting further conquests beneath its specious allure. When viewed from this per- spective, the events of the first year of the Revolution—culminating, as Balthazard emphasizes, in the national expropriation of the Church —seemed to provide convincing evidence that the revolutionaries shared the maximalist intentions of their philosophic forefathers. The next step, surely, would be the total annihilation of the faith, of the monarchy that it upheld, and of the nation that, for hundreds of years, had been nurtured in the protective arms of altar and throne. To see be- hind the veil was to understand that France had been seduced—with terrible consequences, the worst effects of which were yet to be re- vealed.

This reading of the Revolution rested, needless to say, on a number of untenable assumptions—the coherence of the *philosophes* and *phi- losophie* as a unified force, the ineluctable causal relationship between Enlightenment thought and revolutionary rupture, and the conscious, conspiratorial agency of men of letters and their revolutionary min- ions. But then again, it is worth remembering that these same as- sumptions were shared entirely by supporters of the Revolution it-

17. On *Philosophe* conspiracy theories in the eighteenth century, see Amos Hofman, "The Origins of the Theory of the *Philosophe* Conspiracy," *French History* 2 (June 1988), and McMahon, *Enemies of the Enlightenment*, Chapter 2.

self—both with regard to the *philosophes*, and with respect to their sinister enemies—fanatical priests, despots, and lords, who had long conspired to keep humanity in darkness and who were, the revolutionaries continually affirmed, forever plotting still. When the Revolution placed Voltaire in the Pantheon in July of 1791, could it have chosen a more perfect means to confirm the worst suspicions of a Balthazard? Viewed through the lens of the Catholic Counter-Enlightenment literature of the second half of the eighteenth century, this text, and others like it, took on a "logic" that could claim considerable explanatory power.

And how much more was this the case, when those same events long predicted by Counter-Enlightenment partisans *actually* occurred? In the wake of the destruction of the Church, the persecution of priests, civil war, regicide, and a terror involving the massacre of tens of thousands of individuals, yesterday's "paranoid" fanatics could not be so easily dismissed. On the contrary, they were able to claim with some plausibility that they had been right all along, having predicted, with extraordinary foresight, the "inevitable" consequences of Europe's flirtation with hideous *philosophie*. Such retrospective logic made sense to many, including none other than "Voltaire's disciple," Jean-François La Harpe, mentioned above. After time spent in a Jacobin prison, La Harpe converted to Catholicism, and embraced, in its totality, the anti-*philosophe* discourse examined in this paper. For him, *philosophie* was a God that had failed. Many young Europeans at the beginning of the nineteenth century shared his disillusion.[18]

The story of the post-revolution fate of this Catholic Counter-Enlightenment discourse is fascinating. For in literally thousands of pulpit sermons, political tracts, published histories, and philosophical interpretations, observers in the nineteenth and twentieth centuries recycled the convictions of men like Balthazard, passing on a construction of the Enlightenment that, largely discounted in the academy, has had tremendous endurance in the wider (especially Catholic) world. But this, in the end, is another story. Here we would do well simply to ask what might be learned from a close reading—and careful consideration—of works such as Balthazard's *Isle des philosophes*.

18. On the case of La Harpe, and others like him, see McMahon, *Enemies of the Enlightenment*, Chapter 3. La Harpe's most incendiary anti-*philosophe* publication was the infamous, *Du fanatisme dans la langue révolutionnaire, ou De la persécution suscitée par les barbares du dix-huitième siècle, contre la religion et ses ministres* (1797).

In the first place, the text—and the larger discourse of which it forms a part—makes clear that there were men and women inclined from the very outset to oppose the French Revolution in its entirety. Indeed, well before Balthazard, in the very first days of 1789, Catholic anti-*philosophes* began to transfer the categories and assumptions formed in response to the Enlightenment to the Revolution itself. From this perspective, as we have seen, the Revolution was simply the logical evolution of the corruption of *philosophie,* and hence would continue to run its terrible course until it was stopped. In the minds of these anti-*philosophes,* then, there was every reason to oppose the Revolution from the start as destined for cyclical destruction and ever-increasing radicalization. Contrary to the claims made by a number of important revisionist historians—chief of whom is the late François Furet—the Revolution did not need to "invent" its enemies in its early stages as part of a "frenzied preoccupation with power" that demanded the creation of imaginary scapegoats.[19] These enemies were real. Only by considering them in the context of the heated political dynamics of 1789–90 can one properly understand the contingent nature of the early Revolution, and the fears of its supporters. If there was, to be sure, something delusional about the Jacobins' early obsession with conspiracy, it was matched by the anti-*philosophes'* obsession with conspiracies of their own. The two visions re-enforced one another, and in fact gave them each some measure of truth.[20]

Reading a text like the *Isle des philosophes,* then, helps to remind us that neither the early Revolution nor the Enlightenment occurred in a vacuum. This fact is of crucial importance, not least of all for an understanding of the Enlightenment itself. For just like the event that succeeded it in time (if not in effect), the Enlightenment evolved in the context of bitter opposition and was challenged at every juncture by men and women who saw in its collective principles a deeply destructive force. Inevitably, this process of dialectical struggle—of Enlightenment and Counter-Enlightenment—had the effect of shaping both sides in the conflict, of binding them together, while at the same time pushing them apart. Indeed, I would argue, there were doubtless greater similarities between *philosophes* and anti-*philosophes* than either camp would have cared to admit. Perhaps La Harpe's conversion was not such a radical defection after all? Perhaps, we might say, something

19. Furet, *Interpreting the French Revolution,* 54.
20. This is an argument I make in detail in *Enemies of the Enlightenment,* Chapter 2, "From Anti-philosophe to Counter-Revolutionary, 1789–92."

deeper than a "secret penchant of the heart" bound together the Chevalier and Viscount, the Enlightenment and the Counter-Enlightenment?

These are genuine questions—questions of language, form, content, and style. They will only be answered, however, when critics begin to take seriously the shadow side of the age of Enlightenment, the *context* from which its light shone. For to ignore this context is to run the risk of fundamentally distorting the nature of what is too often termed the "Enlightenment project" (as if there were only one)—an error, it seems clear, that has characterized a good deal of what has passed as postmodern scholarship on the century of lights. Fortunately, scholars armed with rather more than a tattered copy of Foucault's *Discipline and Punish* and Bentham's *Panopticon* have, of late, begun to expose the gross generalizations and unhistorical over-simplifications of those who would charge that the Enlightenment was nothing more than a germinating source of totalizing discourse, political oppression, misogyny, racism, and holocaust.[21] In the meantime, these latter critics can at least take comfort in that fact that the abbé Balthazard would doubtless have agreed with them. Philosophy, like politics, it seems, makes strange bedfellows. And strange bedfellows breed even stranger children.

---

21. See, for example, Robert Darnton's spirited article, "George Washington's False Teeth," *New York Review of Books* xliv, No. 5 (27 March 1997): 34–38, and the many trenchant articles in Daniel Gordon, ed., *Postmodernism and the French Enlightenment*, a special edition of *Historical Reflections-Réflexions Historiques* 25/2 (Summer 1999).

PETER BROOKS

Balzac: Epistemophilia and the Collapse of the Restoration

Near the end of Balzac's *Splendeurs et misères des courtisanes*, when Jacques Collin, alias Vautrin, alias Carlos Herrera, passes from chief of the underworld to chief-designate of the police and aids the leaders of society in their effort to suppress evidence and pervert justice in order to prevent a scandal that would throw discredit on some of the Faubourg Saint-Germain's greatest ladies—deeply compromised by their passion for Lucien de Rubempré—the Garde des Sceaux, Comte des Lupeaulx, explains to the Procureur-Général, Comte de Granville:

> Le Roi ne veut pas, à la veille de tenter une grande chose, voir la pairie et les grandes familles tympanisées, salies . . . Ce n'est plus un vil procès criminel, c'est une affaire d'état. . . .[1]

> The King, on the eve of an important move, doesn't want to see the peerage and the great families vilified, dragged in the mud . . . This is no longer a sordid criminal trial, it's a matter of state. . . .

The "*grande chose*" King Charles X is about to attempt is the promulgation of the "Ordonnances de Juillet," the reactionary decrees of July 1830 that would precipitate the revolution that dethroned Charles X within three days, and sent this last of the Bourbon monarchs into permanent exile.

Splendeurs et misères des courtisanes—which makes at least two other references to the coming events of 1830—may demonstrate the inevitability and even the necessity of the July Revolution, in its flam-

---

1. Balzac, *Splendeurs et misères des courtisanes* (Paris: Gallimard/Folio, 1999), 604. Most other references to Balzac will be to Folio editions, and will be given in parentheses in my text. Translations are my own. Parts of this essay were originally presented at the conference, "L'érotique balzacienne," at the University of Pennsylvania, in November 1999, at the kind invitation of Lucienne Frappier-Mazur and Jean-Marie Roulin.

YFS 101, *Fragments of Revolution,* ed. Weber and Lay, © 2002 by Yale University.

boyant depiction of a world where those responsible for justice and politics cooperate with the arch-criminal to suborn justice and create fictive versions of reality. The *"grande chose"* of Charles X comes to appear, in context, as merely another attempt to rewrite reality, to deny the corruption and arbitrariness of the exercise of power exposed in the novel, to claim a legitimacy for a ruling class that has forfeited the right to rule, and to impose an autocratic, hierarchical meaning on a world where even sign-systems—including language—seem to have lost their authority, to be subject to a constant play of disguise, reversal, subversion, to a vertiginous and sinister play. Balzac, as a self-proclaimed monarchist and Catholic who by the time he wrote *Splendeurs et misères* had declared publicly his reactionary politics, had little use for the July Revolution and the bourgeois monarchy that issued from it. But he nevertheless judged that the Restoration brought revolution upon itself through its corruption and incapacity. In this novel—as in most of the *Comédie humaine*—he writes about the Restoration from the perspective of the period that followed it. This critical distance in time allows him to see the Restoration as a completed epoch, brought to its end by revolution—and enables him to pass judgment on the Restoration as a whole.

His judgment on the Restoration is severe, and expressed perhaps most fully and dramatically in the novella *La Duchesse de Langeais*, notably in a long passage introducing chapter 2 of that text which is often considered something of an excursus but which I think is in fact crucial. His principal indictment of the Restoration concerns its egotism, its fixation on class privilege rather than on national good, and most of all its failure of intelligence. In order to understand fully why the Restoration collapsed through lack of intelligence—through an insufficiency of intellect—it may be useful to say something about the place of intelligence and the drive for knowledge in Balzac's understanding of the human and social worlds, and specifically about his version of "epistemophilia."

EPISTEMOPHILIA

There is in Balzac's fiction a form of the lust to know that begs for the Freudian label of "epistemophilia." I believe that we owe that lovely word to James Strachey, who in the *Standard Edition* of Freud's work translates Freud's term *Wisstrieb* as "epistemophilic instinct." Like many of Strachey's translations, this takes a compound of two simple Germanic words and passes it through Greek to arrive at English. "Drive for knowledge" would have been a simpler solution. But "epistemophilia" strikes me as a felicitous complication, since it preserves the erotic sense in which Freud conceives *Wisstrieb*, and because it points us not just to knowledge, but to the roots of knowing.[2]

The core Freudian scenario of epistemophilia is probably that of his essay on Leonardo da Vinci, where he describes the infant's desire to look as "an instinctual erotic activity," focused on the genitals, and particularly on the mother's penis (Freud's infantile scenarios, alas, almost always concern boys). The search for this imaginary object "leaves indelible traces on the mental life of the child, who has pursued that portion of his infantile sexual researches with particular thoroughness."[3] Leonardo's subsequent restless investigative energy and creativity are at root an eroticized search for an imaginary object.

More directly relevant to our purposes is Freud's discussion of "the epistemophilic instinct" in the case-history of "The Rat Man" ("Notes Upon a Case of Obsessional Neurosis"), where he notes that "the histories of obsessional patients almost invariably reveal an early development and premature repression of the sexual instinct of looking and knowing [the scopophilic and epistemophilic instinct] . . . ," to add in a footnote: "The very high average intellectual capacity among obsessional patients is probably also connected with this fact."[4] Obsessional neurosis is the intellectual's problem. In Freud's description:

> Where the epistemophilic instinct is a preponderant feature in the constitution of an obsessional patient, brooding becomes the principal symptom of the neurosis. The thought-process itself becomes sexualized, for the sexual pleasure which is normally attached to the content of thought becomes shifted on to the act of thinking itself, and the satisfaction derived from reaching the conclusion of a line of thought is experienced as a *sexual* satisfaction. . .procrastination in *action* is soon

2. The term "epistemophilia" was brought to my attention by a fine essay by Toril Moi, "Patriarchal Thought and the Drive for Knowledge" (1988), reprinted in Moi, *What is a Woman?* (New York: Oxford University Press, 1999); I then used it in my book, *Body Work* (Cambridge: Harvard University Press, 1993).

3. Sigmund Freud, "Leonardo da Vinci and a Memory of his Childhood" (1910) [Eine Kindheitserinnerung des Leonardo da Vinci], *Standard Edition of the Complete Psychological Works* (London: Hogarth Press, 1957), vol. 11, 96.

4. Freud, "Notes Upon a Case of Obsessional Neurosis" (1909) [Bermerkungen über einen Fall von Zwangneurose], *Standard Edition*, vol. 10, 245.

replaced by lingering over *thoughts*, and eventually the whole process, together with all its peculiarities, is transferred into the new sphere, just as in America an entire house will sometimes be shifted from one site to another. [245]

Now, Balzac's world contains a number of brooding intellectuals, perhaps most strikingly Louis Lambert, but others as well, such as Gobseck, who vicariously participates in the dramas of others from his usurer's vantage, or the narrator of *Facino Cane*, who enters into visionary possession of others' inner lives, or the antiques dealer of *La peau de chagrin*, who formulates the famous antinomy of *vouloir/pouvoir* on the one hand, and *savior* on the other. The choice of *savior* is explicitly the repression of sexual practice—Gobseck is of "the neuter gender," Lambert attempts self-castration—and the choice of self-pleasuring in intellectual activity. These thinkers conserve their sexual substance where the orgiasts, the *viveurs*, the gamblers spend. They may live beyond the normal span. Yet theirs is a dangerous form of activity: often they go mad, are struck dumb like the musician Gambara, or destroy their creations in the manner of Frenhofer in *Le chef d'oeuvre inconnu*, or are punished, like the antiques dealer, who is made to fall in love with a courtesan. *Savoir* is not, it turns out, wholly to be insulated from *vouloir/pouvoir*; it is in fact predicated on their repression, and takes into itself their dynamic, since knowledge, thinking, is itself sexualized, an auto-erotic activity.

Nor should one evoke only the self-declared thinkers, since, as Baudelaire first noted, all Balzac's characters, even the porters, are stuffed with genius. His ambitious young men may not be brooding intellectuals, but they are theorists of their destinies, and quickly come to understand that the realization of *vouloir/pouvoir* depends on a certain social *savoir*. Thus Rastignac during his first visit to Madame de Restaud: "Il voulait pénétrer ce mystère, espérant ainsi pouvoir régner en souverain sur cette femme si éminemment Parisienne" (Folio, 93) [He wanted to penetrate this mystery, hoping in this manner to be able to reign as sovereign over this so eminently Parisian woman]. Or when Lucien de Rubempré, after his spectacular rejection by Madame de Bargeton and the Marquise d'Espard, vows to learn the codes of Parisian success: "je triompherai! Je passerai dans cette avenue en calèche à chasseur! j'aurai des marquises d'Espard!" (Folio, 202) [I'll triumph! I'll drive down this avenue in a carriage with a footman! I'll have a Marquise d'Espard!] The language of knowledge is closely linked to the language of desire and power because knowing is essentially, at its root, a sexualized activity. When sexuality wholly breeches the bar of repression, it makes you lose your wits, as when Lucien, "heureux tous les jours" with Coralie—sexually satisfied—"n'eut plus alors cette lucidité d'esprit, cette froideur de tête nécessaires pour observer autour de lui" (Folio 391, 412) [no longer had that mental lucidity, that cool head necessary to observe what was going on].

Balzac in fact gives us the basic, infantile scenario of epistemophilia in *La peau de chagrin*, in that very strange scene where Raphaël de Valentin hides behind the curtains in the bedroom of Foedora, the "woman without a heart," "pour examiner cette femme corporellement comme je l'avais étudiée intellectuellement, pour la connaître enfin tout entière" (Folio, 202) [to examine this woman corporally as I had studied her intellectually, in order at last to know her entirely]. Examining her corporally means seeing her naked, peeping at her from his hiding place in the embrasure of the window. And what is he looking for? An "imperfection" that would make her fear "les yeux furtifs de l'amour." These furtive eyes find no imperfection, indeed they find nothing, since he is blinded by her beauty: "son corps blanc et rose étincela comme une statue d'argent qui brille sous son enveloppe de gaze" (Folio, 209) [her pink and white body sparkled like a silver statue that shines under its gauze envelope]. As in the infantile scenario, there is both an affirmation and a denial, the classic: "Je sais bien mais quand même." The woman's penis both is and isn't there. The lack of imperfection is possibly too much perfection. The woman without a heart may also be a woman without a sex. But you can't tell, since even though we are promised Foedora naked, she remains veiled by the "gauze" of her shift. The woman's sex remains an imaginary object to the little boy looking for it, and Raphaël is condemned to his fixation, and then to the potent but shrinking skin that lets him live with excess—and die young.

Many texts would serve to focus these general evocations of epistemophilia. I turn to *La Duchesse de Langeais* because it shows with particular clarity the importance of the epistemophilic paradigm, how it reaches beyond the more obvious instances of sexual curiosity to include the theory of society and history, and because it brings this paradigm to bear on a sociopolitical analysis of the failure of the Restoration. *La Duchesse de Langeais* turns on the paradigm, and then, in that "excursus" that heads chapter 2, uses it to generalize on a moment of history the tale is supposed to illustrate.

LA DUCHESSE DE LANGEAIS

General Montriveau is a grown man, but curiously infantile when it comes to love. He has returned to Paris from his exploration of Africa. "Il était, à son âge, aussi neuf en amour que l'est un jeune homme qui vient de lire Faublas en chachette" [He was, despite his age, as novice in love as a young man who has just read Faublas in secret].[5] He is *"vierge de cœur"* [a virgin in his heart], and his desire for Antoinette de Langeais is correspondingly absolute, whereas she takes seduction and resistance as a game, refusing to give herself to him but indulging in a long strip-tease where parts of her body are sequentially offered to his adoration. Her foot, her hand, the ringlets of her hair, and accessories such as her scarf, become invested with erotic passion, in scenarios that correspond fully with Freud's description of the fetishist's approach to and avoidance of the problem of the woman's phallus. Montriveau lifts one by one the "veils" that envelope the *"adorable personne"* of the Duchess. Everything with her is "la plus douce préface . . . pour ce que le monde appelle *une faute"* (281) [the sweetest preface . . . to what society calls *a lapse*]. In particular, there is an evening when Montriveau is on his knees in the Duchess's boudoir: "Il baisa le bas de la robe de la duchesse, les pieds, les genoux; mais, pour l'honneur du faubourg Saint-Germain, il est nécessaire de ne pas révéler les mystères des ses boudoirs, où l'on voulait tout de l'amour, moins ce qui pouvait attester de l'amour" (280) [He kissed the hem of the Duchess's dress, her feet, her knees; but, for the honor of the Faubourg Saint-Germain, we cannot reveal the mysteries of its boudoirs, where one desired everything from love, except that which could prove love]. The unrevealed mysteries would seem to have to do with how far Montriveau advances, upwards, in these kisses that start with the hem of the dress, then move to feet, then to knees, to fade out thereafter.

We have a situation, then, in which the desire for sexual possession is maintained at the level of a prolonged foreplay which, for Montriveau, is marked by an intense curiosity about the Duchess's body, revealed only in its parts, metonymically, gradually. Sexual curiosity is all the more intense because of the body's veiling, the need to penetrate mysteries in order to conquer, to recall Rastignac's phrase. And this need to penetrate surface veils and façades is evidently crucial in the

5. Balzac, *La Duchesse de Langeais,* in *Histoire des Treize* (Paris: Garnier, 1966), 248. Subsequent references are to this edition, and will be given in parentheses in my text. *Faublas* is of course the mildly erotic novel by Louvet de Couvray.

project of knowing that engages most of Balzac's protagonists. They all encounter troubling surfaces that both conceal and suggest that there is something to be revealed, a behind that the observing glance alone cannot penetrate—that requires a movement through the surface, a visionary moment of revelation. This can be a peep through—Raphaël in Foedora's bedroom, Rastignac peeping through a keyhole in the Pension Vauquer to see Goriot twisting a silver plate into an ingot. Or it can be another form of intense vision—Nucingen perceiving Esther by night in the Bois de Vincennes; or a listening through walls—how we learn of Rastignac's way to fortune in *La Maison Nucingen;* or the pedagogical moment provided by Vautrin, especially, in explanation of the world as it really is. It is the also the visionary moment of the novelist, as his descriptive prose warms up, takes off, pierces the appearance of Parisian streets and façades of houses to see what is hidden from view—the kind of penetrative creative vision celebrated, and punished, in *Facino Cane* and a number of other stories. The desire subtending the observing gaze in Balzac, whether in characters or narrators, is always intensely epistemophilic, a desire to penetrate and to possess.

La Duchesse de Langeais opens with an exemplary instance of such desire, on the Mediterranean island where the Duchess has become Soeur Thérèse in a convent of barefoot Carmelites, following the misunderstanding that ends her romance with Montriveau, and prevents "la femme vraie" from becoming visible to him. In this narrative prolepsis—it precedes the chapters that will tell of the earlier development of their romance—Montriveau must seek the lost object of his desire in a sanctuary where desire and even the male gaze is strictly prohibited, and where the Duchess is considered to have lost the attributes of woman, and of temporality, and thus to be immune to the dynamics of desire. Her presence in the convent is revealed, or rather suggested, by the slightest indication, through music: first, as I understand the text, her voice in the *Te Deum,* then her style of playing the organ in the *Magnificat.* The narrator, at this moment, launches into what promises to be a somewhat embarrassing Balzacian meditation on the arts: "L'orgue est certes le plus grand, le plus audacieux, le plus magnifique de tous les instruments créés par le génie humain. Il est un orchestre entier, auquel une main habile peut tout demander, il peut tout exprimer" (202) [The organ is truly the greatest, the boldest, the most magnificent of all the instruments created by human genius. It is an entire orchestra, from which a practiced hand can demand anything, it can express everything]. But this excursus on the organ is in fact crucial. For the "poet" listening to the organ understands that "entre les hommes age-nouillés et le Dieu caché par les éblouissants rayons du Sanctuaire les cent voix de ce chœur terrestre peuvent seules combler les distances, et sont le seul truchement assez fort pour transmettre au ciel les prières humaines . . . " [between men on their knees and God hidden in the dazzling rays of the Sanctuary the hundred voices of this terrestrial choir alone can abolish the distances, and are the only interpreter powerful enough to transmit to heaven human prayers . . .].

The music of the organ is thus doubly a *truchement*, a translation and a translator, between the Duchess hidden in the nun and Montriveau, and between God hidden in the sanctuary and men on their knees. Or triply so, since it also offers the only means to transmit human prayers to heaven. A *truchement*, as a go-between, an interpreter, offers the possibility of penetrating the unknown, of gaining knowledge ordinarily closed to one dealing with a foreign language. Since the interpreter, the organ, is here bringing knowledge of both the woman hidden in the nun, and of God in his sanctuary, it is the vehicle, or metaphor—figure of a *translatio*—of knowledge both sacred and profane, and in both cases eroticized by the desire to know. (I note that the Littré gives as a citation for *truchement* this phrase from Chateaubriand's *Le génie du Christianisme:* "Le ministre chrétien, dit encore Saint-Jérôme, est le truchement entre Dieu et l'homme." [The Christian minister, Saint Jerome also says, is the only interpreter between God and man.] The authorities evoked are interesting in suggesting the profane nature of Balzac's *truchement*.) And of course the organ as interpreter is itself being interpreted, played by the *"main habile"* of the Duchess in a manner that contains clues to her French nationality, and to her identity as the other figure in his romance when she weaves into her playing echoes of the *romance, Fleuve du Tage,* which earlier she played for Montriveau in her boudoir. The organ is indeed the complete instrument in providing a multivalent translation machine for knowledge passionately desired, sublimely figured, and partially withheld. That *"main habile,"* which earlier Montriveau spent much time kissing, has here found the perfect vehicle of its knowledge game.

When Montriveau finally obtains an interview with Sœur Thérèse through the grille of the *parloir*, it is by way of her lie to the Superior, that he is her brother; when his demands that she leave the convent become too insistent, she denounces her own lie, crying out to the Superior, "je vous ai menti, cet homme est mon amant!" (214) [I lied to you, this man is my lover!]. With the translation from the general "he is one of my brothers"—an "admirable jesuitism," according to the narrator —to the specific "he is my lover," the sacred is denounced as profane, specifically erotic, and indeed based on a desire to "la disputer à Dieu, de la lui ravir" (204) [to quarrel with God for her, to abduct her from him], and the possibility of translation collapses. The curtain of the *parloir* falls. Montriveau is now pushed to the expedient of literally ravishing her, abducting her from the convent. And, of course, when he finally carries her out of the convent, it is as a dead body, no longer available to desire.

The scene of desiring to know very often in Balzac needs the *truchement* here represented by the organ. Readers of the *Comédie humaine* will recognize the role of *truchement* frequently played by various older and wiser figures who explain the true meaning of social codes and human behavior to young protagonists: Madame de Beauséant and the Duchesse de Langeais herself with Rastignac, Lousteau and Blondet with Lucien, Vautrin with both of them and so many others. The pedagogy of the *truchement* works because the pupil is eager for knowledge. That is of course an understatement. The pupil is avid for knowledge, burning with a passion to know. "Que faut-il que je fasse?" dit avidement Rastignac" (Folio, 155) [What do I need to do? said Rastignac avidly]. To gain knowledge, which is the precondition of having power, nearly always implies an erotic pedagogy, one that unfolds in fullest flower at the end of *Illusions perdues,* where Vautrin, alias Carlos Herrera, takes Lucien's arm, on the road from Angoulême, and proposes a lesson never taught in the schools.

THE FAILURE OF THE RESTORATION

The indictment of the Faubourg Saint-Germain, of the aristocracy, and of the Restoration that heads the second chapter of *La Duchesse de Langeais* shows the Balzacian narrator assuming his not uncommon role of pedagogue, presenting a historical lesson leading to the conclusion: "Ce fut une époque froide, mesquine et sans poésie. Peut-être faut-il beaucoup de temps à une restauration pour devenir une monarchie" (234) [It was a cold, petty, unpoetic age. Perhaps a restoration needs a long time to become a monarchy]. The real problem of the Restoration, in the narrator's analysis—and it is Balzac's also—was the egotism of its ruling caste. The monarchy and the Faubourg Saint-Germain thought only in terms of consolidating their own power, riches, and privileges, and did not establish roots in the hearts and minds of the whole nation. Like one of Balzac's old misers of desire—the antiques dealer of *La peau de chagrin*, Gobseck—the ruling gerontocracy of the Restoration conserved desire within its narrow circle, and never created the libidinal national economy it needed to become a well-established monarchy, on the model of English Toryism.

At the heart of the Restoration's failure, in this analysis, lay its unwillingness to reach out to include the young intellectuals who could have given it dynamic life: "les mesquins meneurs de cette grande époque intelligentielle haïssaient tous l'art et la science" (224) [the petty leaders of this time of great intelligence all hated art and science]. Since the governing elite didn't have within itself the intellectual talent it needed, it should have sought it in the aspiring youth of the middle class: "si ce génie n'était pas en elle, aller le chercher jusque dans le froid grenier où il pouvait être en train de mourir, et se l'assimiler, comme la chambre des lords anglais s'assimile constamment les aristocrates de hasard" [if genius wasn't within it, to go and look for it even in the cold attic where it might be dying, and to assimilate it to itself, as the English House of Lords constantly assimilates aristocrats created by circumstance]. Instead, the governing elite chose to combat young talent if it didn't have aristocratic credentials: "il pouvait priver la bourgeoisie de ses hommes d'action et de talent dont l'ambition minait le pouvoir, en leur ouvrant ses rangs; il a préféré les combattre, et sans armes . . . " (225) [It might have deprived the bourgeoisie of its men of action and talent whose ambition was undermining authority, by opening its ranks; it preferred to fight them, and without arms . . .]. Youth was excluded from the real affairs of the state, ruled by an aged monarch whose ministers shared his allegiance to the Old Regime into which they were born (Charles X, brother of Louis XVI, was born in 1757). The result of this exclusion is of course chronicled throughout the *Comédie humaine,* perhaps most forcefully in *Illusions perdues,* in the chapter on "Les viveurs," the young men of talent who spend their lives in a kind of "moral slavery," disempowered, with nothing to do but play destructive and self-destructive games—leading, in Balzac's view, straight to the collapse of the legitimist monarchy in 1830.

The heart of Balzac's argument may appear in the lines that urge the importance of the intellect as one of the pillars of the modern state. "Un beau théorème vaut un grand nom" [A great theorem is worth as much as a great name]. He continues:

Ainsi, le talent de la parole, les machines à haute pression de l'écrivain, le génie du poète, la constance du commerçant, la volonté de l'homme d'état qui concentre en lui mille qualités éblouissantes, le glaive du général, ces conquêtes personnelles faites par un seul sur toute la société pour lui imposer, la classe aristocratique doit s'efforcer d'en avoir aujourd'hui le monopole, comme jadis elle avait celui de la force matérielle. [221]

Thus: the talent of the word, the high-pressure machinery of the writer, the genius of the poet, the constancy of the tradesman, the will of the statesman who concentrates a thousand dazzling qualities in himself, the sword of the general, these personal conquests by which an individual dominates society—the aristocratic class should work to have a monopoly of them today, as in the past it had a monopoly of physical force.

All the Balzacian vocabulary of desire, knowledge, and power (as well as the themes of so many of his novels) can be found here. The writer is comparable to a high-compression steam engine; talent results in a personal conquest of the individual over society, imposing one's power through the energy of the intellect. The mention of the general's sword evokes not only Napoleon, but Balzac himself as the writer who would finish the work of that sword with his pen. A ruling class that does not include within itself the dynamic principles of the desiring machine is doomed . . . to run out of steam. It has no source of energy to propel it forward: "enfin, loin de se rajeunir, le faubourg Saint-Germain s'est avieilli" (224) [finally, far from rejuvenating itself, the Faubourg Saint-German made itself aged]. It lacks sexual force, and the intellectual curiosity and dynamism that are driven by that force.

Balzac's case against the Restoration stresses its epistemophilic failure, the lack of a sexualized, energized kind of knowing and taking possession. One could indeed analyze the Revolution of 1830 as the direct product of such a failure: as an attempted absolutist *coup d'état* by a ruling elite that did not know the country it was governing, that was out of touch with the forces transforming France, and, further, was stupid enough to issue the *Ordonnances* that provoked revolution at a moment when the crack army regiments that might have defended the regime were off conquering Algeria. And in the vanguard of revolution in July 1830 were journalists and students: the intelligentsia of a younger generation.

The plot of *La Duchesse de Langeais* could be said to illustrate Balzac's sociopolitical analysis throughout. If the Duchess herself appears to lack true sexuality—"Pour l'honneur de cette femme, il est nécessaire de la croire vierge, même de cœur" (274) [For the honor of this woman, we must believe her to be a virgin, even in her heart] comments the narrator—Montriveau's passion for her will nonetheless provoke her conversion to "la femme vraie," when he proposes to mark her with a branding iron. But this sadistic act of possession never takes place, and Montriveau shows himself incapable of understanding the passion he has created. He misses the rendezvous set in the Duchess' ultimatum, and loses her to the convent. And when he concentrates on her abduction from the convent all the occult power represented by the shadowy brotherhood of *les Treize*, all he can possess is her dead body.

Montriveau's problem is not a lack of desire, but a lack of intellectualism linked to that desire. Early in the text, we are told that he is "un homme de passion, un homme dont la vie n'avait été, pour ainsi dire, qu'une suite de poésies en action, et qui avait toujours fait des romans au lieu d'en écrire" (196) [a man of passion, a man whose life had been only, so to speak, a series of poems in action, and who had always lived novels instead of writing them]. And his failure to perceive the Duchess' conversion to passion arises from his blindness to the libidinal economy of others. As Ronquerolles says to him, "tu as commis la faute dont sont plus ou moins coupables les hommes de ton énergie. Ils jugent les autres âmes d'après la leur, et ne savent pas où casse l'humanité quand ils en tendent les cordes (340–41) [you committed the mistake that men of your energy tend to be guilty of. They judge other souls according to their own, and don't know at what point humans break when you stretch their ligaments]. The brute force of passion is not enough, it must be matched by theory, by the curiosity to understand how the cords of humanity work. By the end of the novella, Ronquerolles seems to suggest to Montriveau that he give up intellectualism in love, in favor of a prudent bourgeois investment: "Désormais, aie des passions; mais de l'amour, il faut savoir le bien placer . . . (349–50) [Henceforth, have your passions; but as for love, you have to know how to invest it].

I see in *La Duchesse de Langeais* a kind of counter-demonstration to those provided in many of the novels about desiring young men—*La peau de chagrin*, *Le Père Goriot*, *Illusions perdues* come most obviously to mind—where an initial bafflement and frustration at how to know and possess the world leads to a thought-process that can validly be considered the construction of a theory. Recall that line from Balzac's critique of the Faubourg Saint-Germain: "Un beau théorème vaut un grand nom." Constructing a theory—as the infant baffled about sexual difference does in Freud's scenarios—is the prerequisite to conquest, precisely because theory is the result of epistemophilia, the constraining of desire into knowledge. Too much theory leads to the intellectual's "brooding," to recall Freud's analysis of the "Rat Man"—as in the extreme case of Louis Lambert's brooding on his Theory of the Will—and to a self-enclosed erotic economy in which thought-processes are sexualized for their own sake, rather than for their leverage on the world. But the lack of theory can result in Montriveau's kind of failure, desire as force without idea or perception.

It may seem strange to conclude with a kind of apologia for the place of theory in Balzac's work, since we so often tend to discount Balzac's theories—which, as Taine remarked, he has on everything—as most often outmoded and indigestible, part of the "*rabâchage*" of the text that is often unreadable. But all his heroes are theoreticians—think not only of those I have already mentioned, but also of Rabourdin in *Les employés* or Benassis in *Le médecin de campagne,* and his fictional writers, from Daniel d'Arthez to Félicité des Touches—and the capstone of the *Comédie humaine* was to have been in those analytic works such as the "Théorie de la démarche" that reveal the ultimate principles of the will at work on the world. Louis Lambert's prediction of a reverse Scripture, in which the flesh will be made Word, remains the unreachable goal. The ultimate principles of theory in Balzac are all rooted in the epistemophilic paradigm, in the sexualization of knowing as desiring, including the desire to know. And if the Revolution of 1830 is just around the corner in *Splendeurs et misères des courtisanes* and a number of other novels, it is because of the Restoration's epistemophilic failure.

DEBARATI SANYAL

The Tie That Binds: Violent Commerce in Baudelaire's "La corde"

Les illusions—me disait mon ami,—sont aussi innombrables peut-être que les rapports des hommes entre eux, ou des hommes avec les choses. Et quand l'illusion disparaît, c'est-à-dire quand nous voyons l'être ou le fait tel qu'il existe hors de nous, nous éprouvons un bizarre sentiment, compliqué moitié de regret pour le fantôme disparu, moitié de surprise agréable devant la nouveauté, devant le fait réel.

—Baudelaire, "La corde" (1864)[1]

Baudelaire's prose poem "La corde," inspired by the suicide of one of Edouard Manet's models, recounts how a painter took in a little boy to pose and to do minor chores around his studio. The child's initially sunny disposition gives way to mysterious fits of melancholy and an excessive taste for sugar and liqueurs. After threatening to send the child back to his parents, the painter goes off to take care of some business. Upon his return, he discovers that the boy has hanged himself. The painter informs the mother of the tragic news, and she begs him to give her the remains of her son's noose. Only when the painter receives letters of solicitation from his neighbors does it dawn on him that the mother, exploiting the superstition that to own a hanged person's rope brings luck, intends to sell its pieces as profitable consolation.

"La corde" does not only demystify the "givenness" of maternal love by suggesting that it, too, has its price. It also examines the nature of art's attachment to its model, leading to a broader meditation on the threads that tie together the postrevolutionary community, or the *corde* of *concorde*. The poem may be read as a testament to Baudelaire's

1. "Illusions—my friend used to say—are perhaps as innumerable as the relationships between people, or between people and things. And when the illusion disappears, that is to say, when we see the creature or the thing as it exists outside of us, we experience a strange feeling, complicated half by regret for the vanished phantom, half by pleasant surprise before the novelty, before the real fact." Charles Baudelaire, *Oeuvres complètes.* 2 vols. (Paris: Gallimard, 1976), I: 328. All references to Baudelaire's work are to this edition, and all translations, unless otherwise indicated, are mine.

YFS 101, *Fragments of Revolution,* ed. Weber and Lay, © 2002 by Yale University.

profound political disillusionment in the aftermath of 1848, and to a general crisis in representing the contemporary political body through the symbolic legacy of the revolution. The "unnatural" mother of the poem points to the emergence of an entirely different conception of the social family, one whose latent violence, I will suggest, harbors unexpected affinities with revolutionary terror.

The alleged purpose of "La corde" is to show that even an emotion as immutable, sacred, and *natural* as maternal love cannot be taken for granted. Indeed, the painter defends his initial blindness to the nature of the mother's request for the rope by invoking the unquestionable naturalness of the maternal instinct, an instinct that provides the foundation for the nuclear and social family alike: "S'il existe un phénomène évident, trivial, toujours semblable, et d'une nature à laquelle il soit impossible de se tromper, c'est l'amour maternel" [If there exists a phenomenon that is obvious, trite, immutable, and of a nature that would be impossible to mistake, it is maternal love]. Yet this self-identical and immutable given, "l'illusion la plus *naturelle*" [the most natural illusion; my italics], as the painter calls it, turns out to be the deceptive product of established cultural assumptions about the "nature" of the maternal instinct. Natural instincts and empirical phenomena, as the poem gradually discloses, are culturally produced illusions that have acquired the status of nature over time.

Initially a trial of the maternal instinct, the poem swiftly engages in a broader consideration of the natural grounds for filiation, of the *nature* of man's relationship to men, and to things. From the outset, the bonds that tie the boy to the painter and to his parents are not natural or affective, but economic and contractual. The painter, seduced by the boy's appearance, asks his parents to surrender their son to his care. His proprietary attitude toward the child suggests a repressed and denatured paternity not unlike the mother's own travestied maternity: "je priais un jour à ses parents de vouloir bien me le *céder*" [one day I asked his parents to hand him over]. The violence of the maternal contract, it turns out, will be fully matched by that of the artistic contract.

At stake in the demystification of the "naturalness" of maternal love, then, is a parallel demystification of the life-enhancing powers of the artistic imagination. The aesthetic production of *l'illusion la plus naturelle* will have deadly repercussions on *le fait réel,* the empirical fact of another's body. The painter evokes his attraction to the boy in singularly acquisitive terms: "Ma profession de peintre me pousse à regarder attentivement les visages, les physionomies, *qui s'offrent dans ma route,* et vous savez *quelle jouissance nous tirons* de cette faculté qui rend à nos yeux la vie plus vivante et plus significative que pour les autres hommes (my italics)" [My profession as a painter impels me to examine the faces, the physiognomies, that offer themselves up/that I encounter on my way, and you know what delight we draw from that faculty that makes life more alive and more meaningful for us than for others]. The aristocratic and appropriative thrust of the artist's perception is typical of the Baudelairean poet-*flâneur* of "Les foules," who assumes the vacancy of all beings before his expropriating imagination: "Pour lui seul, tout est vacant" (I:291) [For him alone, everything is vacant]. A similar evacuation of the model's intrinsic properties occurs in his successive metamorphoses under the painter's brush: "Je l'ai transformé tantôt en petit bohémien, tantôt en ange, tantôt en Amour mythologique. Je lui ai fait porter le violon du vagabond, la Couronne d'Epines et les Clous de la Passion. . . . Cet enfant, débarbouillé, devint charmant . . . " [I sometimes turned him into a little gypsy, sometimes into an angel, sometimes into a mythological Cupid. I made him bear the vagabond's violin and the Crown of Thorns. . . . Once washed clean, this boy was delightful]. At once painted and unpainted, transformed into so many conventional cultural and religious icons (several of which invoke martyrdom), the boy is docile and supple material in the painter's hands. No instance of reported speech breaks his conspicuous silence throughout the tale. The only details that rupture the proprietary, aesthetic economy established by the painter are the child's "crises singulières de tristesse précoce" [strange fits of precocious sadness]. These fits, significantly, remain uninterpreted by the painter, who merely notes their literal manifestations in the boy's excessive taste for sweets and liqueurs; "un goût immodéré pour le sucre et les liqueurs" [an immoderate taste for sugar and liqueurs]. Melancholy, as that which exceeds cultural assumptions about childhood ("précoce"), and which challenges the painter's representational authority ("crises singulières"), erupts as an "immoderate" taste for the superfluous ("le sucre et les liqueurs"). This fissure in the painter's economy, however, is immediately suppressed by the re-establishment of the implicit contract between artist and model, one resting upon the painter's right to dispose of the child as he deems fit: "je le menaçai de le renvoyer à ses parents" [I threatened to return him to his parents].

The socially sanctioned commodification and aesthetic manipulation of the boy culminate in the portrait of his hanging body, significantly described by the painter as "le premier *objet* qui frappa mon regard" [the first *object* to strike my gaze; my italics]. The dangling corpse bears mute testimony to the underlying violence of a social and artistic process that puts real, living bodies into circulation for profit. The nature of the relationship between model and painter is eloquently conveyed in the pun, "Le dépendre n'était pas une besogne aussi facile que vous pouvez le croire" [to take him down was not as easy as you might think]. *Dépendre* is but a letter away from *dépeindre*, which is precisely what the painter does in his clinical account of the cadaver's "unhanging," suggesting thus the link between *painting* and *hanging*, representation and execution.

Yet, the boy's *mise-en-scène* of his own death also endows his previously imprinted body with an undecipherable opacity, a weight that challenges the painter's previous representational mastery. Baudelaire conveys the fleshly opacity of the child's body in vivid, tactile detail, and foregrounds its resistance to manipulation. Indeed, rigor mortis is so advanced by the time the painter discovers the gruesome scene that the clothes have to be torn from the child's body: "la rigidité cadavérique était telle que, désespérant de fléchir les membres, nous dûmes lacérer et couper les vêtements pour les lui enlever" [the cadaverous rigidity was such that we gave up on bending his limbs, and were forced to slash and cut his clothes in order to take them off]. The puffiness of the boy's face, the folds of his neck, the stiff resistance of his limbs, and the dense weight of his body are ironic counterpoints to the fluidity of his previous incarnations. While the *illusion la plus naturelle* ostensibly demystified in the poem is maternal love, whose *fait réel* appears to be the more fundamental and natural instinct of greed, it is a demystification that, unbeknownst to the painter, fully implicates the artistic process itself. For the *fait réel* that the painter fails to acknowledge throughout the poem ultimately designates the facticity of the child's dead body, its obdurate materiality and resistance to the "naturalizing" illusions that have been painted upon it.

The trial of maternal love thus fully implicates the process of artistic figuration.[2] The underlying price of both the maternal and the artistic contracts is unveiled in all its violence when the boy stages himself as his own *nature morte*: "le petit monstre s'était servi d'une ficelle fort mince qui était entré profondément dans les chairs, et il fallait main-

2. See Steve Murphy, "Inquest and Inquisition in 'La corde,'" *Dalhousie French Studies* 30 (1995): 65–91, for an in-depth reading of the relationship between painting and poetry in "La corde" and the significance of the dedication to Manet in the context of Baudelaire's personal relationship with him and of their divergent aesthetic programs.

tenant, avec de minces ciseaux, chercher la corde entre les deux bour-
relets de l'enflure, pour lui dégager le cou" [the little monster had used
a very thin string that had dug deep into his flesh, and I had to pry, with
narrow scissors, into the swollen folds of his neck in order to release
him]. The image of the painter digging deep into the child's flesh to extract the noose captures the violence of this rapport, a violence matched
by the mother's own extraction of the rope from the painter's home:
"soudain, je compris pourquoi le mère tenait tant à *m'arracher* la ficelle" [I suddenly realized why the mother was so intent on snatching
the rope from me]. The artist, however, disavows any responsibility for
the boy's suicide, blithely dismissing a police officer's suspicious queries
as motivated by "une habitude d'état de faire peur, à tout hasard, aux
innocents comme aux coupables" [the professional habit of randomly
frightening the innocent along with the guilty]. Yet even after accom-
plishing the necessary rites in order to dispose of the cadaver and exor-
cise its bothersome ghost by returning to his artistic labors, the painter
is nevertheless unable to "extract" the boy from his conscience. The
allusion to the boy's corpse embedded in the folds of the artist's brain
("ce petit cadavre qui *hantait les replis* de mon cerveau") [the little
corpse haunting the recesses of my brain] recalls that of the rope embedded in the folds of the child's flesh, in an analogy that reiterates the
association of *peindre* [to paint] with *pendre* [to hang]. But the capture
of matter by aesthetic form is never entirely complete, as the model's
unyielding body and its continued life suggest. It leaves behind a stub-
born residue, a remnant lingering in the recesses of the artist's imagination.

The poem does not only scrutinize the act of painting but meditates
more generally on the underlying price of transfiguring living bodies
and things through "cette faculté qui rend à nos yeux la vie plus vivante
et plus significative que pour les autres hommes" [that faculty that
makes life more alive and more meaningful for us than for others]. What
animates life into signification, it would seem, is the ability to extract
from the *fait réel* the intensity and coherence of illusion. Poetry is also
implicated in this meditation on representational violence, as the
painter's allusion to a *"nous"* contaminating the silent interlocutor
and author of the poem suggests. This typically Baudeairean ripple of
complicity becomes all the more significant when we recall that the
poem was inspired by the real suicide of Manet's model, Alexandre.
Baudelaire is said to have read the text aloud before the painter, at a
gathering shortly after the boy's tragic death. The image of Baudelaire

uttering the words attributed to the painter-figure in the poem, in front of a silent Manet (thereby reversing the relationship between the speaking painter and the silent poet in the text) conveys the ways in which poetry and painting can be seen to converge in their potential violence toward a represented object. Indeed, "La corde" could be read as a parodic literalization of Baudelaire's claim that his prose poems stand as worthy *pendants* to the lyric corpus of *Les fleurs du mal*.[3] If we picture the painter as a poet, the rope as the lyre's string, then what the boy's *nature morte* suggests is nothing less than the price of lyric production. Far from the felicitous concordance of sights, sounds, and smells celebrated in *correspondances*, the vital chain of analogies in this poem is frozen into a set of conventional, dead representational equivalences imposed on a vulnerable—though ultimately recalcitrant—human body.

"La corde" thus reveals the discrepancy between *le fait réel* and *l'illusion la plus naturelle*, between the body and its artistic representation, and between the ambiguous nature of the maternal instinct and its cultural construction. As the title's near homonym—*concorde*—suggests, also at stake in this demystification of art and maternity is the social contract itself. The mother's betrayal of the umbilical cord radiates outward and implicates the *concorde* that binds together the larger social family. The thread weaving together the social family, "*la corde*" of "*concorde*," has quite literally fallen into pieces.

Significantly, when the artist discovers the hanging body, his neighbors turn a deaf ear to his cries for help: "J'ai négligé de vous dire que j'avais vivement appelé au secours; mais tous mes voisins avaient refusé de me venir en aide, fidèles en cela aux habitudes de l'homme civilisé qui ne veut jamais, je ne sais pourquoi, se mêler aux affaires d'un pendu" [I forgot to mention that I had called loudly for help; but none of my neighbors came to my assistance. In that, they were faithful to the habits of civilized man, who, I know not why, never wants to get tangled up in the business of the hanged]. Civilized man, Baudelaire

3. "Le spleen de Paris, pour faire pendant aux *Fleurs du mal* (en prose)," Baudelaire, Note pour M. Hippolyte Garnier, 6 fév. 1866, in *Correspondance* II (Paris: Gallimard, 1973), 591. See also the preface to the collection attributed to Gustave Bourdin in *Le Figaro*: "'Le Spleen de Paris' est le titre adopté par M. C. Baudelaire pour un livre qu'il prépare et dont il veut faire un digne pendant aux *Fleurs du Mal*," *Le Figaro*, 7 February 1864. Although he cannot establish for a fact that Baudelaire wrote this preface himself, Raymond Poggenburg nevertheless believes that Baudelaire, and not Bourdin, wrote, or at least dictated its contents to the editor. See *Baudelaire: Une micro-histoire* (Paris: Corti, 1987), 390–91. Certainly the reappearance of the term *pendant* in Baudelaire's letter marks it as his own.

suggests with grim humor, will only entangle himself in the affairs of the hanged in the most literal sense of the expression. For it is the rope (*l'affaire*) of the hanged, and the business (*affaires*) it enables, that define a new community, one bound (*mêlé*)—albeit anonymously—by the ritual purchase of the noose. "La Corde," then, does not only put on trial the metaphorical process through which the artist transforms his material—the bodies and things that nourish his art. It simultaneously questions the symbolic threads that bind together the postrevolutionary social fabric, and the illusions they weave around the nature of man's bond with men and things.

Baudelaire's *oeuvre* is suffused with allusions to the legacy of the Revolution. His profound ambivalence toward his republican fervor in 1848 manifests itself in vengeful outbursts that confront the utopianism of revolutionary rhetoric with the bankruptcy and concealed violence of actual social and political practice. The prose poems in particular ironically recollect the linguistic vestiges of the revolution—its vocabulary of equality, fraternity, concord, *patrie*—in order to expose their travestied afterlife in the bourgeois order of the Second Empire.[4] These *défigurations du langage politique* [disfigurements of political language] disclose the ways in which the revolution's utopian rhetoric has been coopted, homogenized, and short-circuited.[5] They also reveal a profound shift in the conceptualization of violence. No longer displayed in the spectacular and bloody purges of the Terror, violence is an invisible force woven into the very fabric of postrevolutionary social life. Baudelaire's enigmatic celebrations of the revolution as radi-

4. Linda Orr views the saturation of Baudelaire's writings with revolutionary rhetoric as symptomatic of a failed attempt to use and transcend the omnipresent and omnivorous political vocabulary of his time. She shows how his ostentatious repugnance toward the Revolution (shared by Marx and Flaubert) deflects from his actual engagement in—if not cooptation by—its shameful discursive legacy: "Baudelaire protests that he is an aristocrat of art, but he knows, as Vigny knew before him, that the only language possible is the one steeped in Rousseau and the Jacobins, twisted by contemporary 'democratic' literature . . . Baudelaire succeeded in making us forget the degree to which his words were saturated with the ubiquitous discourse of his century." Orr, "Repulsive Recollections: After the Revolution, French Romantic Thought," *Stanford Literary Review* 6/1 (Spring 1989): 36. While I agree with Orr's assessment, I want to suggest that, far from making us forget this saturation, Baudelaire takes great pains to remind us of it. By displaying how even poetry is bogged down in the clichéd and defunct vocabulary of republican idealism, he provides an ironic critique of the Revolution's failure to make good on its promises.

5. I am of course alluding to Barbara Johnson's seminal work on the prose poems, *Défigurations du langage poétique*, an essay that throughout suggests the homologous functioning of poetry and politics.

cal destruction—"Je dis *Vive la Révolution!* comme je dirais: *Vive la Destruction! Vive l'Expiation! Vive le Châtiment! Vive la Mort!*" (II: 961) [I say *Long live the Revolution!* as I would say *Long live Destruction! Long live Expiation! Long live Punishment! Long live Death!*]— are attempts to resuscitate the violence so visibly displayed and acknowledged during the Terror, and so insidiously disarticulated under the reign of Napoleon III. His poetry's distorted allusions to the revolution's discursive legacy, I will suggest, press into visibility the latent violence of the Second Empire.[6]

Given Baudelaire's fascination with the fate of the revolution's discursive legacy, it is not surprising that he found Robespierre's rhetoric, his "style de glace ardente, recuite et congelé comme l'abstraction" (I:592) [his style of fiery ice, glazed and frozen like abstraction] more worthy of interest than his actions.[7] Echoes of what the poet called his "style sentencieux dont ma jeunesse s'est enivrée" [the sententious style on which my youth got drunk] may be discerned in the most startling places. Consider, for instance, Robespierre's famous *rapport du 18 Floréal* and its celebration of fraternal bonds tying together the universal human family: "Le véritable prêtre de l'Être suprême, c'est la nature, son temple l'univers, son culte, la vertu, ses fêtes la joie d'un grand peuple rassemblé sous ses yeux pour resserrer les doux noeuds de la fraternité universelle et pour lui présenter l'hommage des coeurs sensibles et purs."[8] It is tempting to hear reverberations of this imagery in

6. See Richard Terdiman's *Present Past: Modernity and the Memory Crisis* (Ithaca: Cornell University Press, 1993) for a powerful study of the relationship between commodity-production, the formalist literary project, and the Second Empire's masking of sociopolitical instability through a forgetting of history (an amnesia staged, for example, by Napoleon III's declaration of amnesty). For Terdiman, intertexuality and other forms of interpretive undecidability in an author such as Baudelaire reveal the "semiological disquiet" latent in the attempt to make the present—and the work of art—immobile and absolute entities cut off from the history of their production.

7. "Robespierre n'est estimable que parce qu'il a fait quelques belles phrases" (I:680) [Robespierre only deserves to be esteemed for coining a few beautiful sentences], Baudelaire declares, repudiating any substantive affiliation to revolutionary politics. Yet during the active phase of his republicanism, Baudelaire actually joined the *Société républicaine centrale* founded by Blanqui in 1848. As Claude Pichois notes, Baudelaire saw in Blanqui a Robespierre of the nineteenth-century: "By the integrity and intransigence of his republicanism, and by his revolutionary spirit, Blanqui was for Baudelaire a sort of nineteenth-century Robespierre." Claude Pichois and Jean Ziegler *Baudelaire*, trans. Graham Robb (London: 1989), 162.

8. "Nature is the true priest of the Supreme Being, his temple is the universe, his worship is the joy of a vast people gathered before his eyes to tighten the sweet knots of fraternity and to present the hommage of pure and sensitive hearts." Cited in Marcel David, *Fraternité et Révolution française 1789–1799* (Paris: Aubier, 1987), 127.

the opening lines of Baudelaire's "Correspondances" and its hymn to an anthropomorphic nature: "La nature est un temple où de vivant piliers / Laissent parfois s'echapper de confuses paroles" [Nature is a temple in which living pillars / Sometimes release confused utterances], a connection that may not be entirely fanciful if we recall that the principle of universal analogy professed in this sonnet is proposed by Robespierre as the foundation for fraternity. More relevant to "La corde" and its implicit scrutiny of the body politic, however, is the image of fraternity as a knot tying together the human family. Robespierre's *doux noeuds de la fraternité* mutate into a strangulating noose whose severed fragments, once put into circulation, will foster a chilling parody of universal brotherhood. The transparency of hearts, or Robespierre's "coeurs sensibles et purs" constituting both the etymological root and principle of *concorde*, is travestied into a cluster of anonymous transactions feeding greed and superstition.[9] As the portrait of the parental figures and their neighbors suggest, "La corde" attests to a crisis in representing a community through metaphors of natural filiation.

The poet's later works insistently implicate the utopian vocabulary of communion, fraternity, equality, and concord with the reality of collective violence, of terror. Nowhere is the perversion of fraternity into fratricide more compellingly staged than in "Le gâteau" (1862), published two years before "La corde." The prose poem details the poet's journey through an idealized, romantic landscape. In a beatific moment of lyric elevation, the voyager, soaring on the wings of *l'universelle analogie*, succumbs to Rousseauist reflections on the essential goodness of man: "dans mon total oubli du mal terrestre, j'en étais venu à ne plus trouver si ridicules les journaux qui prétendent que l'homme est né bon" [in my complete oblivion to earthly evil, I no longer found so ridiculous those newspapers proclaiming that man is born good]. His epiphany, however, is brutally interrupted by a typically Baudelairean fall. Having offered some bread to an urchin on the streets, another little fellow, "si parfaitement semblable au premier qu'on aurait pu le

9. See Baudelaire's "La solitude" for another instance in which fraternity is associated with commerce and violence. The poet-figure derisively describes "les belles agapes fraternelles" as the collectivity's attempt to co-opt individual thought as if it were an economic category, a common good to be homogeneously distributed and consumed. In the 1855 version, the poet-figure responds to the chattering and appropriating throng by ironically reifying his vision of the sublime as an inalienable private property ("ce coup d'oeil lui a conquis une propriété individuelle inaliénable") [this glance has conquered for him an inalianable private property], thus mimicking the discourse he derides.

prendre pour son frère jumeau" [so perfectly like the first that he could have been his twin brother], surges out of nowhere and wrestles his "brother" to the ground. The unsuspecting narrator has engendered a vicious struggle in which the twins quite literally "break bread" until only crumbs remain, as they tear each other to pieces.[10] The poet concludes wryly, "Il y a donc un pays superbe où le pain s'appelle du *gâteau*, friandise si rare qu'elle suffit pour engendrer une guerre parfaitement fratricide!" [there is a superb country where bread is called *cake*, a treat so rare that it suffices to engender a perfectly fratricidal war]. The individual poet's fall from an edenic correspondence between men and things finds its historical correlative in the fall from the illusion of fraternity to the reality of fratricide, from the the idealism of revolution to the reality of terror.

A similar allegory is subtly embedded in "La corde" and its ironic commentary on the bankruptcy of a unified body politic, one whose underlying corruption is figured through the mother's unnatural body, her loyalty to the economic chain rather than the umbilical cord.[11] Robespierre's *doux liens de la fraternité* have mutated into a strangulating noose that points to the emergence of an anonymous community around the dead body of a child. Could we then read the child's suicide as an allegory for the slain republic? Certainly the child-martyr who dies in suicidal loyalty for the *patrie* is a familiar figure in the iconography of the revolution. The thirteen-year old Joseph Bara, for example, died opposing the Vendée rebels and became a cult republican figure extolled by Robespierre, along with the young Agricola Viala, shot by the federates in 1793. Both children, in their intransigent and literal espousal of the Jacobin motto *liberté, égalité, fraternité ou la mort*, incarnated the ideal of Terror. Their suicidal opposition, made in the name of the republic, and memorialized in paintings such as David's *Death of Bara*, was part of a symbolic legacy that may

10. The allusion to the boys as twin brothers locked in vicious combat seems to parody familiar representations of "fraternité" as two cherubic boys locked in an embrace. See for instance the illustrations in Marcel David, *op. cit.*: plates 17–18.

11. Baudelaire tirelessly contested utopian theories of progress, arguing that "Il faut toujours en revenir à de Sade, c'est à dire à l'*Homme Naturel*, pour expliquer le mal" (I: 595) [To explain evil, one must always return to Sade, that is to say, to Natural Man]. The fallenness of nature is often represented through the abjection of the female body, as Baudelaire's well-known misogynist declaration attests: "La femme est *naturelle*, c'est-à-dire abominable" (I:677) [Woman is natural, that is to say, abominable]. It is not surprising, then, that Baudelaire should figure the corruption of the body politic through a woman's betrayal of the maternal instinct.

well have informed Baudelaire's portrait of Manet's boy-model in "La corde."[12]

Still another sacrifical figure and scene are invoked in the poem's final, ironic gesture toward the collective consumption of the noose: Louis XVI, his decapitation and the alleged distribution of his clothing and body.[13] As Lynn Hunt has shown, the parsing out of the king's body and possessions—his blood, hair, and clothing—was a rite intended to disseminate his sacredness onto the people. Louis-Sebastien Mercier gives a gruesome account of the festivity surrounding the King's decapitation and the alleged circulation of his body and belongings:

> Son sang coule; c'est à qui y trempera le bout de son doigt, une plume, un morceau de papier; l'un le goûte, et dit: *Il est bougrement salé!* Un bourreau sur le bord de l'échafaud, *vend et distribue* des petits paquets de ses cheveux; *on achète le cordon qui les retenait;* chacun remporte un petit fragment de ses vêtements ou un vestige sanglant de cette scène tragique. J'ai vu défiler tout le peuple se tenant sous le bras, riant, causant familièrement, come lorsqu'on revient d'une fête.[14]

12. See Baudelaire's *Le musée du Bazar Bonne-Nouvelle* for his appraisal of David's work, including "Marat" and "La mort de Socrate." No mention is made of "La mort de Bara," but the description of "Marat" is full of admiration and suggestively called a "gift to the grieving nation" (II:410). For a discussion of the cult of Bara, see Thomas Crow, *Emulation: Making Artists for Revolutionary France* (New Haven: Yale University Press, 1995) and *La mort de Bara* (Avignon: Fondation du Museum Calvet, 1989). It is interesting to note—in the context of "La corde" and its perversion of the relationship between mother and son—that Joseph Bara joined the army to support his widowed mother and was commemorated as an exemplary son.

13. Could we read an allusion to the guillotine's blade in the chilling detail of the painter's scissors cutting into the boy's neck? It is interesting to note that Baudelaire had initially written *"col"* (which directly invokes *"décollation"*) rather than *"cou."* The poet's interest in capital punishment and sacrifice has been treated with unparalleled insight by Pierre Pachet in *Le premier venu. Essai sur la politique Baudelairienne* (Paris: Denoël, 1976). A discussion of his perspective exceeds the scope of this article, but my reading of "La corde" and of Baudelaire's politics as a self-sacrificial poetics is informed by and in dialogue with Pachet's reading of the poem (through Bataille's text on Manet) as an example of a "murder through negligence." Pachet examines how capital punishment, suicide, and conspiracy are privileged *topoi* in Baudelaire, intended to reveal and disrupt an increasingly conformist social order that coopts all individual thought. Yet I believe this profound political pessimism to be counterbalanced by Baudelaire's scrutiny of the structural homologies between poetry and politics, an ironic demystification and self-demystification that functions as its own species of *engagement*.

14. Louis Sébastien Mercier, *Le nouveau Paris* (Paris: Fuchs, 1789), vol. 3, 4. See Lynn Hunt's *The Family Romance of the French Revolution* (Berkeley and Los Angeles: University of California Press, 1992) for a discussion of the cannibalistic connotations of Mercier's description and, more generally of the psychosexual dimension of revolutionary symbolism and its rearticulation of the family as a paradigm for politics. My thanks to Susan Maslan for pointing out this passage.

His blood flows; they dip and dip the tip of a finger, a pen, a piece of paper; one person tastes it and says: "It's awfully salty!" An executioner
at the edge of the scaffold sells and distributes little packets of his hair;
people buy the string that once attached them, every one takes away a
little piece of his clothing, or a bloody vestige of this tragic scene. I saw
the entire population go by, arms linked, laughing and chatting famil-
iarly, as if returning from a celebration.

In this spectacular rite, a community is symbolically founded and nour-
ished by the distribution of its sovereign-victim's body. The cannibalistic imagery of Mercier's description, and the reference to the ribbon or
cordon tying the king's hair, are details that resonate powerfully with
the prospective circulation and consumption of the noose in "La corde."
Designated as *horrible et chère relique* [a horrible and cherished relic],
the noose will serve as an ironic substitute for the sacred body, ushering
in a community founded not on symbolic parricide, but rather, symbolic
infanticide, an anonymous community governed by the laws of commerce: "Et alors, soudainement, je compris pourquoi la mère tenait tant
à m'arracher la ficelle, et par quel *commerce* elle entendait se consoler"
[And I suddenly realized why the mother was so intent on snatching the
rope from me, and by what trade she intended to console herself].

Like many of his generation, Baudelaire was fascinated by the ritu-
alistic and sacrificial elements of the French Revolution, the spectacular reversibility of victim and executioner staged by the decapitation
of the king. Consider, for example, the following stanza from "Le voyage," which could provide its own *pendant* or gloss on Mercier's account of the bloody feast consecrating the king's execution:

> Le bourreau qui jouit, le martyre qui sanglote;
> La fête qu'assaisonne et parfume le sang;
> Le poison du pouvoir énervant le despote
> Et le peuple amoureux du fouet abrutissant (I:132).[15]

The ecstatic executioner, the sobbing martyr / The feat seasoned and
scented with blood / The poison of power irritating the despot / And
the mob in love with the deadening whip.

Extolling somewhat theatrically the festive carnage of the revolution,
such passages resurrect the violent origins of the postrevolutionary so-

15. A stanza to compare with Baudelaire's conflation of the bourgeoisie and the *peuple* in his description of the violence of the June days: "Les horreurs de juin. Folie du peuple et folie de la bourgeoisie. Amour naturel du crime" (I:679) [The horrors of the June
days. Madness of the mob and of the bourgeoisie. Natural love of crime.]

cial contract, a violence that has become clouded and diffused by the apparently benign mediocrity of Napoeon III and his authoritarian democracy.[16] The occluded brutality of the "lien social" is latent throughout "La corde," where the community, so conspicuously absent for most of the tale, virtually reconstitutes itself around the boy's dead body and seeks to appropriate the severed fragments of his noose, in a cannibalistic ritual reminiscent of the king's execution.

Baudelaire's dictum, "toute révolution a pour corollaire le massacre des innocents" [All revolutions have as corollary the massacre of innocent people] is an eloquent comment on the *price* of revolution and counter-revolution, and of the murderous rites of collective purification. Yet "La corde" also suggests that, unlike the bloody spectacles of revolution (the Terror, the June days), the violence particular to the postrevolutionary epoch is insidiously woven into the social fabric by the mercenary logic of *commerce*. Attesting to a crisis in representing the postrevolutionary collective as bound by the harmonious threads of *fraternité* and *concorde*, "La corde" points to the emergence of an order where the logic of the market, in service of superstition, fosters its own species of terror. A possession relinquished, if not sold, by his parents, figuratively consumed by the painter, his family and neighbors, the boy symbolically gestures toward the bodies and beings that suffer the price of new social modes of production and consumption. Both at the center and the margins of the relations enabled by his body, he is—significantly—barred from consumption. His "immoderate and excessive" tastes are forbidden and threatened with punishment. His suicide, then, is a powerful demystification of the underlying logic governing both aesthetic and social production. By staging himself as a *nature morte*, the boy literalizes his own reification, and unveils the latent violence of a community in which a person's body only acquires value through its *symbolic* circulation.[17]

16. The reference to "le peuple amoureux du fouet abrutissant" conjures up the poet's disillusionment with the overwhelming majority who supported, through plebiscite, legitimating Napoleon's *coup d'état:* "In short, before history and the French people, the great glory of Napoleon III will have been to prove that the first person to come along can govern a great nation by simply seizing the telegraph and the national press. Those who believe that such things can be achieved without the consent of the people are idiots, as are those who believe that glory can only find its basis in virtue. Dictators are the lackeys of the people—nothing more—a pathetic role indeed, and glory is but the product of one mind's adaptation to the nation's stupidity" (I:692).

17. In keeping with the spirit of the market, a body acquires value when it yields more than has been invested into it. As Baudelaire trenchantly says in his notebooks: "Le com-

Baudelaire fully grasped the consequences of revolutionary upheavals in the body politic for the living and vulnerable bodies within it. As a poet-dandy and an allegorist, he intimately knew such violence to be the material consequence of idealist systems imposing their form upon an embodied and differentiated social content. His provocative declaration, made in the early days of the abortive Second Republic, indicates a keen awareness of the human cost of revolutionary upheaval: "Lorsque Marat, cet homme doux, et Robespierre, cet homme propre, demandaient, celui-là trois-cent mille têtes, celui-ci, la permanence de la guillotine, ils obéissaient à l'inéluctable logique de leur système" [When Marat, that gentle man, and Robespierre, that unsullied man, requested, the one, three hundred thousand heads, and the other, the permanence of the guillotine, they were obeying the ineluctable logic of their system].[18] The poet's apodictic declarations about the bloody realities of revolution are more than the provocative *boutades* of an aesthete thrilling to the spectacle of history. They are unflinching, if sardonic, assessments of the price of revolution. Revolutionary utopianism, in its vision of a body politic as matter to be shaped into coherence and purified of undesirables, is almost always associated with sacrificial terror in Baudelaire's thought. For the revolutionary necessarily turns a blind eye to the human cost of transformation, to the bodies that were once attached to the three hundred thousand heads requested by Marat, that is to say, to *le fait réel*.

Perhaps even more unbearable than the spectacular despotism of the Terror for Baudelaire, however, was the headless, flabby despotism of the multitudes in postrevolutionary France. His outbursts against the formless hydra of democracy should not be dismissed as the histrionics of an aristocratic aesthete repudiating his dabbling in republican

---

merce, c'est le prêté-rendu, c'est le prêt avec le sous-entendu: *Rends moi plus que je ne te donne*" (I: 703, my italics) [Commerce is a loan returned, it is a loan with an implicit "Give me back more than I gave you]. "La corde" explores this implicit premise: the mother makes a profit off the death of her child; the painter's investment in his model(s) must have been amply repaid by his paintings, if his "business" keeps him out for several hours at a time. As for the neighbors who solicit the rope, their everlasting fortune will only cost them a few francs.

18. Claude Pichois et Jean Ziegler, *Baudelaire* (Paris: Julliard, 1987), 269. See also Baudelaire's sketch for a prospective prose poem: Poèmes en prose (pour la guerre civile): "Le canon tonnne . . . les membres volent, . . . des gémissements des victimes et des hurlements des sacrificateurs se font entendre . . . c'est l'humanité qui cherche le bonheur" (I: 371) [Prose poem (for a civil war): the canons thunder . . . limbs fly . . . we hear the groans of victims and the shrieks of the executioner . . . this is humanity in search of happiness].

politics.[19] His disgust at the United States—described as a shapeless monster—is telling in this regard. It betrays an obscure yet remarkably prescient sense of the violences underlying a decentered, commercial metropolis: "mais *Cela*, cette cohue de vendeurs et d'acheteurs, ce sans nom, ce monstre sans tête, ce déporté derrière l'Océan, État!" (II: 327) [but *That*, this mob of sellers and buyers, this no name, this headless monster, this deported thing behind the ocean, a State!]. A social field governed by the fluctuating rules of the market, politically mystified by an apparent diffusion of class antagonism, and in which "this mob" blindly collaborates with its own subjection—this also seems to have been Baudelaire's thumbnail sketch of the brave new world inaugurated by the Second Empire.

In his portrait of Théophile Gautier, Baudelaire proposes a curious parallel between the utopianism of revolutionary thought and the suffocating conformism of its failed aftermath. He blames this *tyrannie contradictoire* on the fact that France, and "le caractère utopique, communiste, alchimique, de tous ses cerveaux ne lui permet qu'une passion exclusive: celle des formules sociales. Ici, chacun veut ressembler à tout le monde, mais à condition que tout le monde lui ressemble" (II:125) [the utopian, communist, alchemical character of all its brains allows for only one passion: social formulas. Here, everyone wants to be like everyone else, but only if everyone else is like them]. The utopian attempt to alchemically transform the world to the measure of its abstract formulas is echoed in the majority's desire to contemplate and consume its flattering self-images in art. The revolutionary's will to purification thus finds its degraded correlative in the bourgeoisie's attempt to hold the multiplicity of its social and cultural environment in the strangling grip of its conformism. The violence of this passion for narcissistic self-replication is hauntingly conveyed throughout

19. Linda Orr has persuasively argued that Baudelaire's turn to violence in his poetry and notebooks is a vengeful and fruitless exorcism of his generation's past republicanism and its discursive debt to Robespierre, but also, more shamefully, to Proudhon and Michelet: "The Terror was wandering or erring in the nineteenth century in the form of these misreadings, as errors that produced this gooey mess, worse than the Terror itself, as far as Baudelaire was concerned. In fact he fantasized about resorting to his own terror as the only way of getting out of the twisted legacy of the Terror." *Headless History: Nineteenth-Century French Historiography of the Revolution* (Ithaca: Cornell University Press, 1990), 28. Again, I agree with the general thrust of Orr's argument, but point out that Baudelaire's ironic rewriting of that discourse deftly punctures its legitimacy in order both to critique the failure of republican idealism and to show how the misuses of its rhetorical legacy are precisely what blind people to the latent violence of their everyday practices, as the example of *commerce* suggests in "La corde."

Baudelaire's poetry. The usurping twin brother of "Le gâteau" or the malevolent, proliferating old men of "Les sept veillards," recover some of the disquiet occulted by the apparently benign cult of universal sameness.

"Non seulement je serais heureux d'être victime, mais je ne haïrais pas d'être bourreau—pour sentir la révolution de deux manières" (II:961) [Not only would I gladly be the victim, I would also not abhor being the executioner, in order to experience the Revolution both ways], announced Baudelaire toward the end of his life. In a sense, his vocation as poet locked him into this contradictory historical predicament long before he chose to embrace it. For the poet-dandy is at once the despotic figure *par excellence;* his sovereign imagination "executes" a recalcitrant and fragmentary reality in its image. And yet, as Walter Benjamin has shown, the poet-merchant is also at the mercy of the market's stranglehold. The hanging boy of "La corde," whose noose suggests voicelessness made visible, is a striking avatar for this predicament. An anterior version of the poem makes this parallel more explicit, for it concludes thus: "Un mètre de corde de pendu, à cent francs le décimètre, l'un dans l'autre, chacun payant selon leurs moyens, cela fait mille francs, un réel, un efficace soulagement pour cette pauvre mère" (I:339) [One meter of a hanged person's rope, at one hundred francs per decimeter, all in all, each paying according to his means, it comes to one thousand francs, a real, an efficient relief for this poor mother].[20] How could the fate of the noose, the appraisal and circulation of its fragments, not resonate with that of poetry and its circulation in the newspapers? As each decimeter of rope is worth one hundred francs, similarly, each line of Baudelaire's prose poems fetched roughly 0.15 francs apiece. The preface to *Le spleen de Paris* fully acknowledges that the prose poems emerge out of these new conditions for literature's production and consumption. Advertised as a corpus that can be hacked into pieces (or *tronçons*), the format of these poems is designed to provide "admirables commodités" for the writer, editor, and reader alike as the text passes through their hands: "Considérez, je

20. The parallel between the poet and the hanged (which gestures back to Villon) transforms the text into a symbolic scaffold, a "gibet symbolique où pendait mon image" ("Un voyage à Cythère"). For a political reading of "Un voyage à Cythère," which sees the "pauvre pendu muet" of the 1855 version as an allegory of the ritual killing of the Second Republic, see Richard Burton's *Baudelaire and the Second Republic: Writing and Revolution* (Oxford: Clarendon Press, New York: Oxford University Press, 1991), 312–19.

vous prie, quelles admirables commodités cette combinaison nous offre à tous, à vous, à moi et au lecteur. Nous pouvons couper où nous voulons" (I:275) [Consider what admirable commodity such a combination provides for all, for you, me and the reader. We may cut where we please]. A textual body cut up into fragments in order to facilitate its circulation, the strings of the poetic lyre on sale for a few francs apiece, such metaphors capture some of the violence of the market's logic, and of literature's paradoxical implication in it. Poetry has relinquished its hieratic autonomy. It is coopted and cut up by the demands of an urban consumer culture, victimized or prostituted by its readers' narcissistic investments. Yet, as Baudelaire also suggests throughout his *oeuvre*, art in its own way participates in the (dis)figuration of bodies, the capture and shaping of matter into symbolic form. Poetry's idealizing force resonates and even at points collaborates with the broader cultural logics of representation that violently imprint a mobile and differentiated social body. That Baudelaire was able to probe the depth and complexity of poetry's imbrication within shifting forms of violence speaks to his acutely ethical understanding of history. For to inhabit the oscillation between victim and executioner, alternatively and reciprocally, is to deeply understand the human cost of the revolutions—both spectacular and veiled—that unfold around us.[21]

It is impossible to impose neat, allegorical closure upon Baudelaire's poetry, and teasing out the possible historical significances of the poet's notorious ironies is risky business indeed. By applying pressure to the linguistic ambiguities of "La corde" and spinning out the political resonances of its imagery, I have tried to shed some light on the poet's prescient understanding of terror not as a historical event, but rather, as a force infiltrating every nerve of the postrevolutionary social body. The ritual public executions of the Terror exhibited the sacrifices that founded and consecrated a new social order. Besides sporadic resurgences that failed to bring about the republic, these purgative violences, Baudelaire suggests, sank underground. A diffuse force nourishing a decapitated social organism, one of terror's most insidious new faces is commerce. The illusions bred by commerce are as in-

21. "Car tout est à la fois queue et tête, alternativement et réciproquement" (I:275) [For everything is at once head and tail, alternately and reciprocally], Baudelaire says of his prose poems, suggesting that literary form both accommodates and disrupts contemporary ideological investments in the act of reading. I have attempted to suggest how this formal self-reflection productively challenges the commercialization of literature and, by extension, demystifies the commodification of bodies in the literary and social texts.

numerable as the relations between men and men, men and things, and men as things. It is perhaps Baudelaire's most enduring gift as a poet— one for which he dearly paid the price—that he did not attempt to tear this veil of illusions, but instead, illuminated from within the intricacy of its weave.

III. Alternative Negotiations

RICHARD TERDIMAN

Political Fictions: Revolutionary Deconstructions in Diderot

> Qu'il est facile de faire des contes!
> [It's so easy to make up stories!]
> —Diderot, *Jacques le fataliste*

This essay weaves its reflection around a series of pairings. *Body* and *story*. *Materiality* and *imagination*. *Fiction* and *lies*. *The Enlightenment* and *postmodernity*. These are the polarities that, refracted through Diderot, I hope may illuminate some questions at the heart of the volume of *Yale French Studies* on "Fragments of Revolution."

Diderot died in 1784 and never wrote about the Revolution. Necessarily we see him from the other side of this epochal event. How might we relate to him today? Modernity and postmodernity have regularly been dazzled by Diderot. We have seen our contemporary preoccupations uncannily anticipated in his reflections and representations. Any reader of *Jacques le fataliste* can recognize just how much the antic textual practices with which Diderot was experimenting in that novel foreshadow familiar postmodernist textual moves. Is this similarity a coincidence? I will claim the contrary. A double relation, of technical inheritance and of shared cultural problematic, links eighteenth-century reflection on "fiction" and "verisimilitude" to current worries about "representation," "language," and "textuality." My essay seeks to tell a story about the perplexities that occur when culture changes—particularly, about what happens when the changes in question involve a fundamental register through which people make sense of the world. In this case, the register in question is the functioning of *representation*. In our world of virtuality today, the capacity to deal with fictions seems intrinsic and indispensable to experience. But this was not always so. "Fiction" was once a problematic and controversial attainment. During that period of incipience, writers and readers wrestled

YFS 101, *Fragments of Revolution,* ed. Weber and Lay, © 2002 by Yale University.

with the forms of cognition and imagination that "fiction" proposed to make available to them. The most thoughtful of them even worried about what in culture might be *threatened* if "fiction" became an accustomed form of narrative practice and cultural imagination.

The first of the disparate and seemingly irreconcilable pairings that motivate my discussion is the one I call "body and story." In the aftermath of Saussure and Structuralism, what most people will initially notice about this pairing is the incommensurability that for a century now has made *representation* a central enigma in theoretical reflection. The lability that characterizes imagination and language-use collides with the dense materiality of the corporeal; the untrammeled "flight of fancy" contradicts the cumbrous inertia of the flesh. With the modes of their existence so disconnected, how do we get from things to words, or back to things again? The refractory nature of the task of fitting signifiers to referents—when reflection over the past century or so has underlined how radically little they have in common—defines modernity.

Mallarmé is a canonical theorist of this separation. According to one of his most celebrated images, we may write about palaces, but the stones to which our words refer will never fit between the pages of our books.[1] Mallarmé's figure projects the complication of our experience of extra-textual materiality. The map is never the territory; the language we use is always separate from what it intends to designate or describe. And in the movement from modernism to postmodernism, we have increasingly taken this separation not only as unbridgeable but as unrationalizable, even as meaningless. But if *words* don't simply refer to *things*, must we cut them off entirely from each other? We have tended to treat the rift as an unbridgeable chasm, as if no circulation or mediation were possible between these realms. Such a view—*"il n'y a pas de hors-texte"*—has become the foundation of the metatheory of "textuality" that has dominated the past few decades of literary and cultural theory.[2]

1. Mallarmé, *Oeuvres complètes*, ed. Henri Mondor and G. Jean-Aubry (Paris: Gallimard-Pléiade, 1945), 366. See Richard Terdiman, *Discourse/Counter-Discourse: The Theory and Practice of Symbolic Resistance in Nineteenth-Century France* (Ithaca, N.Y.: Cornell University Press, 1985), 288–94.

2. Derrida's italics. The dictum is from *De la grammatologie* (Paris: Minuit, 1967), 227 (English translation: *Of Grammatology*, trans. Gayatri C. Spivak [Baltimore: Johns Hopkins University Press, 1974], 158). Just before his celebrated apothegm, Derrida speaks of the "general propositions that we have elaborated above, as regards the absence of the referent or the transcendental signified" (ibid.). See also Derrida, *Dissemination*, trans. Bar-

In reaction to the uncompromising doctrine projected by this widely-held postmodern doxa, let me suggest what I want to argue in "Political Fictions." For more than a generation in cultural criticism and theory, we have explored the heady lability of language and of thought. The impulse to do so was well-founded, and we came by it honestly. It based itself in and it carried forward the project of liberation that, since the Enlightenment, has been a pervasive aspiration, in the European-American world at least. But in a kind of intellectual question-begging, this thinking about thinking has tended to project our aspirations for freedom into a reductive conception of thought itself. The issue—framed since Marx's resonant eleventh thesis on Feuerbach as the dialectic between *theory* and *practice*—is surely not new.

But modernity and, even more intransigeantly, postmodernity have scanted reflection on the constraints that make the realization of freedom arduous. Somewhat self-indulgently, they have privileged thought's autonomy over its mystifying but powerful fetters.[3] Here I want to examine the other side of a dialectic whose resonances sometimes seem nearly inaudible today. I want to contend that we need to return attention to what in thinking, language, and culture, remains *refractory*, despite self-congratulatory notions of the signifier's free play and the expansive dissemination of language. Today such a perspective has arguably become the unthought. But it was not so in the Enlightenment period that I want to pose as a cultural and intellectual counter-frame that can help us denaturalize fundamental assumptions of our own period. After two hundred years of an epochal effort to project and achieve *liberation*, let us try to imagine how we might recapture and retheorize the notion of *constraint*.

In what follows, I take Diderot's novel *La religieuse* as the testing point for my argument about fictionality and truth, about semiosis, materiality, and bodies. *La religieuse* is a hybrid, heteroclite, self-divided

bara Johnson (Chicago: University of Chicago Press, 1981), 328. Diderot comes close to such a linguistic absolutism in the *Salon de 1767*, 6e site, when he seems to argue that there is nothing but words; Diderot, *Oeuvres complètes*, ed. Herbert Dieckmann, Jean Fabre, Jacques Proust, and Jean Varloot, 25 vols. (Paris: Hermann, 1975–1986), 16, 217. Unless otherwise stated, texts by Diderot are cited from this edition (identified as *DFPV*).

3. Consider Terry Eagleton's condemnation: "It is . . . hard to see how this view [postmodernism] is not just another form of idealism, for which freedom resides in reading the world differently." Eagleton, *The Illusion of Postmodernism* (Oxford: Blackwell, 1996), 65. Compare Fredric R. Jameson, *Postmodernism or, The Cultural Logic of Late Capitalism* (Durham, N.C.: Duke University Press, 1991), 324: "From the postmodern side . . . the 'end of history' here simply means that anything goes."

text. It is made up of two discontinuous—one might almost think irreconcilable—parts. The novel is cast in the mode of memoir, as a first-
person autobiographical narrative supposedly composed by a runaway
nun named Suzanne Simonin. But Suzanne's account of her suffering
in forced claustral confinement does not stand alone. It has always been
accompanied by a second text in the form of a frame or preface, pur-
porting to explain the unusual circumstances in which the novel itself
came into being. The novel's "Preface" was originally composed not by
Diderot, but by his friend and collaborator Baron Grimm (*DFPV* 11: 15).
It was published in March 1770, ten years before the text of the novel.
Subsequent to its initial appearance in 1770, the preface was reworked
by Diderot himself for at least a decade. It then reappeared at the time
of the serial publication of Suzanne's purported autobiographical account—the novel we call *La religieuse* proper—from 1780 to 1782.

These two disparate components that make up the hybrid *La religieuse* were together the product of a hoax which the preface purports
to explain. In 1759, following financial reverses and an intensification
of his religious piety, the Marquis de Croismare, a member of Diderot's
and Grimm's circle, decided to leave the corruptions and expense of
Paris, and retire to his country estate in Normandy near Caen. Croismare's comrades in the capital missed him, and they sought to attract
him back to Paris. Beginning in early 1760, they devised a plot to do
so. They concocted a young woman, Suzanne Simonin, supposedly an
escaped nun, and contrived a poignant story concerning her plight.
Specifically, the fictive Suzanne implored the Marquis's assistance in
saving her from the authorities who, she claimed, were on her trail, supposedly seeking to arrest and return her to the nunnery from which she
had escaped. They hoped this story would intrigue Croismare and bring
him back to Paris.

Letters were sent to Croismare at his country estate in Caen, purportedly written by Suzanne and those who had given her asylum in
Paris, explaining her plight. Everything was organized with intricate
care—or guile, as we might rather put it. Croismare seems to have swallowed the story the conspirators had cooked up for him. His letters to
Paris concerning the matter (also published in the preface) were earnest
and solicitous, and he took particular pains to urge the greatest caution
to avoid exposing Suzanne's whereabouts to the authorities searching
for her. This specular projection by Diderot and his friends of a virtuality with no reality behind it, this double *mise-en-abyme* juggling literature and materiality, is diagnostic because of the limitless slippage

that seems possible once we are in a realm of substitution. We look for that which might be grounded, that which will not wantonly lend itself to exchange, replacement, simulacrum, and falsification. But in a world of language, this nostalgia for stability of meaning can never be fully satisfied. In this sense, we might think of the intricate deceptions of espionage as the radical antinomy of corporeality's stolid constancy. In intelligence work, *bodies are created to lie.* In fiction and theater, we know that we are being gulled. On the other hand, the corrosiveness of the spy world depends upon a unilateral violation of the representational—the social—contract. Bodies engaged in deception thus seek to produce a consciously-induced false consciousness. They so betray their *embodiedness,* they so want to achieve mendacity, that they decorporealize themselves and become nothing but signs, mere *figures* of bodies, with all the ambiguity that inheres in such entities.

This eerie flickering *between* materiality and language is what Diderot was trying out or trying on in *La religieuse.* Think, then, of the novel as an exploration of the freeing of language in a field of constraining bodies, an experiment not only with the liberating play of signifiers, but also, and crucially, with the constraining force of materiality. That dialectic can be veiled in the pure celebration of semioticity that various strands of poststructuralism have sought to promote or, at the other end of the reduction, in the false immediacies of naive realism. But compared with these polar truncations, Diderot wants to make the case *hard.* For this, bodies serve as a privileged ontology for, unlike meanings, they cannot be instantaneously superseded or made over. And unlike meanings, they can absolutely and consequentially *die.*[4]

Bodies are my code for designating this resistance to semiotization. We may think that everything is a sign. But some things carry their semioticity *resistantly,* unwillingly. They do not glide insouciantly into mutation, they rather seem captured in some ontological version of gravity. They do not float; they are not free; they seem borne *down* in a material enactment of the constraint that defines them as what they are, and that pulls them and the phenomenology of our experience with them in a direction *contrary* to that figured by language's lability.

4. In his seminar on *The Purloined Letter,* Lacan makes just this point in a thoughtful—if seemingly uncharacteristic—reflection on the refractoriness of bodies. He writes that the singular materiality of bodies arises from the fact that, unlike language-objects, they cannot survive dismembering. See Jacques Lacan, *Écrits I* (1966), cited by Anne Chamayou, *L'esprit de la lettre, XVIIIe siècle* (Paris: Presses universitaires de France, 1999), 68.

Language *requires* bodies. Materiality enters language fundamentally, as the quiddity of the signifier. Language needs bodies' grounding, needs the character of *being exacting* that bodies entail. But this dialectic isn't self-imposing for conceptualization; it is possible to lose track of it, whereupon these constraining modalities can float out of reach or out of mind. This is a liberation as poststructuralism often projects it; but it is also a loss.

Let us return to *La religieuse,* particularly to the text's metanarrative concerning its own history in the preface. It asserts itself as a mystification. Whether Diderot's hoax was meant to be on Croismare or on us (and we cannot ultimately tell), what *this* text was bringing into focus for Diderot was the realization that *no text can ever tell you whether it is veridical or not.* But if texts can hoax us, then *anyone* who relies on them is potentially the victim of their power—beginning with writers like Diderot himself. How could anyone be insulated from the uncertainty inherent in representations? The most unsettling element of the transaction arises when, in the face of a text's capacity for deception, we try to imagine how to separate the roles of perpetrator and victim, how to stabilize our own agency in using language without being used by it in our turn. This structure of potential reversal is a critical one because all cultures rely on tools—material or representational—to do their work. But such tools always bear the danger that their instrumentality can turn back against us. Any mediation between an agent and a task has the potential to take over determination of the relationship between them. This truth is unsettling. Such structures dominate our consciousness and our agency in ways that all of modernity has been seeking to comprehend.

What happens when real people are treated like characters in a fiction? Such a mutation locates the textual and social perplexity produced in and uncovered by *La religieuse.* That the world of representation and the world of reality are separable seems clear enough. But texts can make them intersect. Then something like an ontological category mistake arises—and because of it, an unsettling ethical and practical conundrum. For in any deception there is a risk of cruelty; in any fiction the potentiality of pain is inherent. *Representations can hurt.* But where and how does this performative capacity arise, where and how does it exercise its effects?

Modernism has so dissolved us into texts that the material or referential world seems simply to slip toward invisibility. Such denegation of the extra-textual is familiar. But it blinds us to aspects of the functioning of narrative to which Diderot and other writers in his period were finding themselves acutely attentive. Fictions interacted with these mechanisms and registered them. *But fictions also turned out to be located at the heart of the mechanisms themselves.* Their representations could not be sectioned off from what they represented.

This implication of the medium in its referent must have been discomfiting for an Enlightenment whose *political* interests lay in the use of texts as levers to press against reality. But when the supposed instrument for changing the world revealed itself as the heart of the mystery it was attempting to expose and rectify, then an uncanny re-situation of the problem imposed itself. To be sure, narratives are *not* just about narrative—particularly in the Enlightenment period. To begin with, *La religieuse* is a programmatically reformist text. A commitment to correct a set of particularly shocking abuses—royally-enforced incarceration in perpetuity for anyone having pronounced a monastic vow—frames the themes, setting, action, and narrative structure of the novel. But I want to argue that these textual characteristics cohere with the theoretical and conceptual preoccupations concerning language and narrative that are foregrounded in Diderot's fictions, and particularly in this one. As *La religieuse* constructs it, freedom is much more than an absence of confinement. Politics doesn't stop at the convent wall. And texts do not simply marshal reform in the juridical realm. Through the processes of representation and induced belief that they mediate, texts enfold the heart of the mechanism by which reality *resists* change. The world run by texts that has become familiar in our own period—not so much determined by as *living within* them—is coming into sight in these Enlightenment constructions of the social world.

In any case, *La religieuse* expands the field of politics beyond the theme of political and legal rights around which its narrative nominally turns, and connects it with a realm of social capacities and practices— the "literary"—that was still coming into focus in Diderot's time. The novel opens up this perception—of cultural inflections, of the centrality of its own mode within them—because in its exercise of narrative power it begins to perceive something about how *all* the elements and practices that determine social relationships, not simply those defined by the exactions of authority, are constituted.

Modern readings of *La religieuse* have generally and plausibly interpreted the successive convents in which Suzanne is confined as figures for Vincennes or the Bastille, and have construed the hierarchical rigidity of the ecclesiastical setting and its potentiality for violence as metonyms for Old Regime autocracy in general. But beyond such structures, what binds individuals and limits their freedom? If we imagine eliminating these more narrowly authoritarian irrationalities from social existence—as *La religieuse* does itself in its representation of Suzanne's stay at the convent of Longchamp under the virtuous rule of Madame de Moni—it is worth asking what this substitution of *humane* structures of power for cruel and irrational ones contributes to resolving the problem. The text projects a thought-experiment in enlightened rather than benighted administration. But it responds to this experiment in an unsettling way.

For Madame de Moni's inspiring benignity, while it softens the rigor of ecclesiastical incarceration, has a paradoxically malignant result. For Suzanne is manipulated more than anything else by her Mother Superior's kindness. By inducing her to pronounce her vows and accept the veil, the exceptionally virtuous Madame de Moni "ruins her" (as Suzanne herself puts it, 117). Can *La religieuse* then securely stabilize a distinction between a text like Madame de Moni's that is offered to sustain, and one that is offered to deceive? If not, what does the experience of such a mismatch between intention and consequence reveal about how language is coming to be perceived and practiced in this period?

Within a narrative, by virtue of the sensitivity that our writing and reading practices have institutionalized, any reference to *literature,* to the act or the effect of writing, seems automatically to foreground itself. Such representations form a constant metanarrative within any tale. But in *La religieuse* the textualization of such literary self-consciousness has a more focused and conjunctural meaning—and a more disruptive one. It reflects not simply literature's self-celebratory fascination with its own existence, but rather an ambivalent reaction to the inflection that in Diderot's period was progressively detaching narratives from real bodies, and transforming *deception* into *fiction*. In *La religieuse* the framing of the literary unsettles any easy ratification of fictional power, because fiction *worries* this text as much as it enables and sustains it. Then literature in its self-absorption does not so much self-affirm through such mirroring of its own existence as it self-questions and self-subverts.

So in diverse ways, some direct, some oblique, literature and writing find themselves identified within *La religieuse* as the heart of an ambiguous apparatus of deception. Through its reflections about narrative and fictionality, *La religieuse* reconceives a broad texture of linguistic and social forms and practices as in essence *political*—possessing the power to determine real lives and constrain real possibilities. Not only the constitution of state power and the exercise of disciplinary violence, but also the capacity of words and representations to order existence, become a focus of critique.

The notion and practice of *deception* is central to the reflections this novel registers concerning its moment and the functioning of its culture. Deception must be distinguished from fictionalizing if we are not to lose touch with the capacity for material consequence that is always deception's objective. In a deception, language remains intensely focused upon the willed production of authentic material outcomes. The problem of such consequentiality is fundamental and explicit in *La religieuse*. It is (according to the Preface) the basis of the text's existence to begin with. It is apparent in Suzanne's analysis of the omnipresent duplicity of convent life. The passages of the novel that analyze such hypocrisy offer a corrosive analysis of the material consequences of language's detachment from inner conviction. This analysis, however devastating, is familiar. But the congruence between the deception—the lie—stigmatized here and the one Diderot and his friends were practicing in their hoax of Croismare is astonishing. Reframed by the strange textual transaction that became *La religieuse*, hypocrisy plays the representation of the novel itself back into the space of bodies.

To be sure the consequences for the Marquis de Croismare, the mystification's nominal victim, were less dramatic than the novel represents them as being for the novices in the convent. Suzanne's account speaks of a distinctly graver outcome for the women systematically deceived by ecclesiastical authority. These delusive representations *drive them mad:*

> Il arriva un jour qu'il s'en échappa une de ces dernières de la cellule où on la tenait renfermée. Je la vis. . . . Je n'ai jamais rien vu de si hideux. Elle était échevelée et presque sans vêtement; elle traînait des chaînes de fer; ses yeux étaient égarés; elle s'arrachait les cheveux; elle se frappait la poitrine avec les poings; elle courait, elle hurlait; elle se chargeait elle-même et les autres des plus terribles imprécations; elle cherchait une fenêtre pour se précipiter. La frayeur me saisit, je tremblai de tous mes membres, je vis mon sort dans celui de cette infortunée. [92–93]

> It happened one day that one of these mad women escaped from the cell where she was locked up. I saw her. . . . I have never seen anything so hideous. She was completely disheveled and nearly naked; she was drag-

ging iron chains; her eyes were wild; she was tearing her hair; she was
striking her breast with her fists; she was running and screaming; she
was cursing herself and the others with the most terrible imprecations;
she was looking for a window to throw herself out of. Panic seized me,
my whole body was trembling, I saw my destiny in the fate of this unhappy creature. [My translation]

There is no doubt concerning Diderot's anger and revulsion at the suffering of the mad nun that he depicts through Suzanne's eyes.[5] The passage rightly takes its place in a long and passionate line of socially-
reformist representations. It aims at effectiveness, it wants intensely
to convince, it embodies a commitment to the material pragmatics of
texts. But how do we distinguish the etiology of this individual afflic-
tion, arising in the hypocrisy of the convent, from the narrative delu-
siveness of *La religieuse* itself? We could say that *La religieuse* risks
provoking in its textual situation the very derangement it describes in
its story. It practices precisely the lie, the mode of deception, that has
led the novel's unfortunate mad nun to her fate.

How easy it is to make up stories, as Diderot has written in *Jacques
le fataliste.* The truth is *one* because it is *constrained.* But once language detaches itself from its material anchor, from its connection to
inward conviction or outward reality, then constraint evaporates, and
all stories become possible.[6] In that sense fictions *need* to shuck off
bodies in order to unfold their capacity for invention. But the latter attainment is double-edged. The capacity for fiction doesn't come free.
Acting it out may entail the cost of an uncanny disorientation.

The novel is haunted by the embodiment of truth even as it launches
itself into the seeming identification of language with deception. Thus
the mad nun about whom Suzanne writes to Croismare bears in her af-
fliction, and as its cause, the marks of language—of narrative—in three
embedded senses. First, the hypocrisy to which she has been exposed,
the lies which she has systematically been told by the other nuns, clash
absolutely with her own experience of the convent. Such dissonance,
as R. D. Laing or Jacques Lacan would tell us, drives her crazy. Secondly,

5. Diderot's sister Angélique could have been the tortured nun described here. In
1748, at the age of 28, she died insane in the Ursuline convent in Langres (see *DFPV* 11:
92 n. 16).

6. The situation has precisely the same structure as the limitless transformation of
the contents of consciousness in the psychoanalytic paradigm according to Freud, once
the possibility of their mutation from the timeless registrations of the unconscious has
been admitted. See Richard Terdiman, *Present Past: Modernity and the Memory Crisis*
(Ithaca, N.Y.: Cornell University Press, 1993), 290–92.

the divergent and irreconcilable accounts of how the devil has taken hold of this mad woman delusively given to Suzanne by her *consoeurs* are entirely isomorphic with what Suzanne has been told from start to finish. They define the community's relation to the poor suffering woman, but they cannot be distinguished in their mode of deception. Thirdly, in a way that I believe we could have predicted based upon an analysis of the text's own systematic doubts concerning "writing," at the very center of the catalogue of lies quoted above we find a delusive castigation of *literature* itself as the cause of the nun's dementia: "she had read pernicious books which had corrupted her mind."[7]

We don't know the character of the books imagined to have been responsible for the mad nun's insanity. Were they theologically heretical, or only erotically novelistic? Whatever the case, what is active here is a canonical stigmatization of *pornography* as the cause of derangement. Pornography is *quintessentially embodied language*. It is *always* in touch with bodies.[8] This familiar critique then names the fundamental relation that *La religieuse* is working through and worrying about. For, to the extent that we keep the body at the center of our encounter with texts, then pornography stands as a limiting case of all writing. The question of representations and bodies that this designation evokes stands at the heart of Diderot's practice, and his interrogation, in *La religieuse*.

The only possible guarantor of any narrative is the pressure put upon it by some material referent, some extradiegetic reality to which it seeks to respond and in relation to which it measures its representation. Conversely, the eclipse of commitment to such referentiality leaves narrators free—but also adrift. This discovery is a systematic counterpart of the one that I argued precipitated out of the hoax of the Marquis de Croismare in *La religieuse*. The novel tracks down the lability that inheres in language, and the exemption from constraint that narrative constitutively grants to anyone who wishes to deploy it. But there are significant consequences of such franchise for the political

7. Then the classification of *La religieuse* itself under that category of damned and damning books only completes the imbrication of the contraries that a view more confident of the possibility of distinguishing verisimilitude from veracity would have sought, against the inner logic of the text itself, to insist upon.

8. See Jean-Marie Goulemot, *Forbidden Texts: Erotic Literature and its Readers in Eighteenth Century France*, trans. James Simpson (Philadelphia: University of Pennsylvania Press, 1994). The title of the original French edition (*Ces livres qu'on ne lit que d'une main*) foregrounds even more powerfully the characteristic of quintessential embodiment that defines pornography.

and social effectiveness of writing. An uncomfortable realization attends any revel celebrating the emancipation of narrative. It is that *truth suffers when texts are free.*

This realization about language's seeming exemption from fundamental material constraints would not be so troubling if we did not have our bodies to be concerned about. Then we could simply give ourselves over to unconstrained and merry play with the immateriality of texts. But whatever our contemporary romance with such a liberation from corporeality, Diderot worried intricately about bodies, and about the complication of *politics* that arise in their irreducible consequentiality. This is why bodies are thematized so insistently—by some accounts, so scandalously—in Diderot's own texts.

His *Encyclopédie* article "Jouissance" could be taken as an emblem of his thinking on these issues.[9] In its celebration of bodies and their physicality it captures a fundamental impulse in Enlightenment philosophical thought. From our point of view, the most resonant passage in Diderot's text may well be its striking representation of materialism's claims on understanding, and of reason's coordinate non-sovereignty:

> Un individu se présente-t-il à un individu de la même espèce & d'un sexe différent, le sentiment de tout autre besoin est suspendu; le coeur palpite; les membres tressaillent; des images voluptueuses errent dans le cerveau; des torrents d'esprits coulent dans les nerfs, les irritent, & vont se rendre au siège d'un nouveau sens qui se déclare & qui tourmente. La vue se trouble, le délire naît; la raison esclave de l'instinct se borne à le servir, & la nature est satisfaite. [*DFPV* 7: 576][10]

> When an individual meets another of the same species and of a different sex, all experience of any other want is suspended; the heart flutters; the limbs quiver; voluptuous images run through the brain; floods of humors run through the nerves, stimulate them, and end up in the seat of a new sense that manifests itself and torments us. Sight becomes distorted, delirium arises; reason the slave of instinct limits itself to serving the latter, and nature is satisfied. [My translation.]

9. As it recently has been by Georges Benrekassa, *Le langage des Lumières. Concepts et savoir de la langue* (Paris: Presses universitaires des France, 1995), ch. 5, which also reprints Diderot's text. See *DFPV* 7: 575–77.

10. The unexamined homophobia here is characteristic of Diderot's period, and (along with the reflexive traces of misogyny that often marked it) form one motivation for our contemporary resistance today to the Englightenment's claims and to its mode of understanding. Accepting the force of these criticisms, we need nonetheless to ask how much of Enlightenment fundamental insights would be undermined if these relics of intolerance were expunged.

This power of materiality to overwhelm cognition, of corporeality to submerge language, complicates any simple understanding of the Enlightenment's commitment to "rationality." For Diderot, rationality, however capital, is rooted in organic nature and in biology, which (according to this text) it serves as if with the "cunning of reason" that Hegel would later theorize. In *Philosophy and the Mirror of Nature*, Richard Rorty provocatively assets that "if the body had been easier to understand, nobody would have thought that we had a mind."[11] If we just could understand *bodies*, we might not be so obsessed with *understanding* itself. This perspective again urges on us the most careful attention to our own contemporary hypostasis of language's domination of social existence.

"Jouissance" seeks to reassess and advance the claims of materiality, so that the body is accorded due significance in the face of the political or theological subjections of a powerfully repressive state. But such a rebalancing in favor of the body is even more intensely at issue in *La religieuse*. Pain has the same capacity to overwhelm reason as pleasure does. So while the character of the experience at their centers is quite different in "Jouissance" and in *La religieuse*, the re-situation of rationality and of language, and the recalibration of their relationship to materiality, is revealingly parallel. But there are also complications in such a comparison. *La religieuse* worries particularly about bodies' capacities to withstand the force of representations, while sharing the commitment to materiality that in its more triumphalist mode "Jouissance" celebrates.

Recalling "Jouissance," we could say that in *La religieuse*, bodies and texts interact most intimately in *seduction*. Seduction happens when a text delusively seeks the control or the compliance of a body, when *in imitation of verisimilitude* it projects a false or constructed reality, believable but mendacious, *intended* to mislead. But that means that the theme of seduction foregrounds precisely the enigma of textuality about which Diderot worries in *La religieuse*.[12]

How, in the end, should we understand the problem of language and

11. Richard Rorty, *Philosophy and the Mirror of Nature* (Princeton: Princeton University Press, 1979), 239.

12. Not surprisingly, seduction is a theme that *La religieuse* itself proclaims and presses; indeed the word is prominent in Suzanne Simon's own lexicon (see *DFVP* 11: 91). Eve Kosofsky Sedgwick has provided the most careful treatment of "seduction" in relation to *La religieuse*, and is particularly attentive to the way the narrative draws us into the tale. My perspective here differs from hers. See Sedgwick, "The Privilege of Unknowing," *Genders* 1 (Spring 1988): 102–24.

textuality that Diderot worries in his narratives? Textuality engages us in what seems like a fruitless regress, a potentially endless series of reframings in which we seek a referential ground upon the basis of which we might distinguish the appearance of verisimilitude from the representation of truth. However naive it may seem in our period of postmodern orthodoxy, we can easily understand the impulse behind such a quest. For, despite the disdain for utility that we have inherited from nineteenth-century denunciations of middle-class ideology and practice, it would be hard to deny that language functions first of all to enable instrumental communication between concrete individuals in identifiable situations. It does not seem unreasonable to suppose that *all* signifying behavior retains some connection with, and is to some degree informed by, such primal linguistic and social determination in materiality, in a world of real bodies and real consequences.

So we look for bodies behind language. That is why the peculiar structure of the Croismare hoax—in which an intentionally delusive fictional narrative was devised by concretely identifiable people to produce overt behavioral effects in another real person—seemed to offer the opening to a register of factuality that might partially extricate us from the closure of disembodied language. This then might permit some perspective upon the disseminations and slippages of textuality that Diderot's text itself discovers in the course of its realization—as if astonished to find itself victimized by its own attempt to victimize. Unlike the case with our contemporary theories of textuality, the links between language and materiality projected by Diderot's narratives are not simply dissolved or abrogated. Rather they are diagnostically *complicated*. Indeed, Diderot bases his whole politics of discourse upon the notion that texts and materiality still contact and mutually determine each other.

There is another register of the mediatory relationship between materiality and language whose complications the Enlightenment worried about so persistently, and which might help us to renew our own arrested conceptualization of them. The developments in question surface in the relationship that mysteriously ties the seemingly disjunct worlds of socio-economy and literature. These worlds are *gendered*. Pocock makes the claim for the former realm:

> In the eighteenth-century debate over the new relations of polity to economy, production and exchange are regularly equated with the new ascendancy of the passions and the female principle. They are given a new role in history, which is to refine the passions; but there is a dan-

ger that they may render societies effeminate—a term whose recurrence ought not to be neglected.

A contrast in these terms between "patriot" and "man of commerce," between "virtue" and "politeness" or "refinement," emerges during the first half of the eighteenth century, with Montesquieu as . . . an authoritative exponent. [114][13]

In the literary sphere, the feminization of narrative is less a matter of metaphorical association than of genre, dramatis personae, tonal preoccupation, and theme. Men of letters were finding themselves impelled to imagine and to represent *women's* thoughts and perspectives. Of all the acts of fictionalizing, this cross-dressing may be the most consequential. For it willfully travesties, it programmatically alienates, one of the cardinal properties of identity. Its impropriety, then, might stand as the diagnostic sign of fiction.

In this light, let us consider the final words of Diderot's nun and of *La religieuse* itself: "Je suis une femme, peut-être un peu coquette, que sais-je? mais c'est naturellement et sans artifice" (288) [I am a woman, perhaps a bit coquettish, who can say—but naturally, not as a result of artifice]. This concluding text points to a perplexity that exceeds what the critical tradition has attended to. What did it mean for Diderot to write as a woman? We can imagine him composing this extraordinary conclusion in a mode that passes well beyond mere "coquetry"—a mode of antic, indeed extravagant antiphrasis. The hoax of Croismare began, I argued, in a will to explore the capacities of language to *mis*-represent, as a good-natured experiment with mendaciousness. So it should not surprise us to see the novel conclude with a particularly choice and bald-faced lie. But the protestation against "artifice" that Diderot chose to end with is nonetheless exquisite. Writing fiction always involves an act of *chutzpah*. But here we have its self-reflexive quintessentialization, a gratuitous lie about lying itself—mendaciousness squared.

13. On the rendering of these categories, see J.G.A. Pocock, *Virtue, Commerce, and History* (Cambridge: Cambridge University Press, 1985), 117–18. Pocock refers particularly to *Esprit des Lois*, Book 4, chap. 8. The relations of women to eighteenth-century fiction have been widely studied. See among many others Nancy Armstrong, *Desire and Domestic Fiction: A Political History of the Novel* (New York: Oxford University Press, 1987); Elizabeth H. Cook, *Epistolary Bodies: Gender and Genre in the Eighteenth-Century Republic of Letters* (Stanford: Stanford University Press, 1996); Mary A. Favret, *Romantic Correspondence: Women, Politics, and the Fiction of Letters* (Cambridge: Cambridge University Press, 1993); Catherine Gallagher, *Nobody's Story: The Vanishing Acts of Women Writers in the Marketplace, 1670–1820* (Berkeley: University of California Press, 1994); and Nancy K. Miller, *French Dressing: Women, Men and Ancien Régime Fiction* (New York: Routledge, 1995).

Nothing in the narrative can respond to this misrepresentation. Indeed, the enigma of textuality is that texts can *never* reliably or authoritatively guarantee their own veracity. Verisimilitude then comes to stand in as a kind of *pis-aller,* a learned next-best possibility, a bit like the way we learn to credit paper money as a substitute for specie. The advantages of such innovative representations are clear. But we ought not to bury or misrecognize their simultaneous ambiguity. I have been seeking to track the downside that, despite the liberatory play they authorized, I believe preoccupied Diderot in his fictions. This relay of increasing abstractions along the chain of signifiers makes it simplest to accept the flattening of all truth-claims into nothing more than neutral enactments of textuality itself, as we have frequently determined to do in our own period.

But Diderot was skeptical and troubled by such a capitulation to the ungroundable nonreferentiality of texts. For him, if representation was not answerable to materiality, then indispensable foundations of politics and reform simply risked evaporating. For all the energy he put, over so many decades, into promoting the transformation of his society—the elimination of irrationalities and the establishment of rights—he was uncomfortable with the telescoping of time and truth that fictional representation necessarily entails. Something within his projection of the world required accrediting the resistance of materiality and the refractoriness of time that it carries with it. This is one of the implications of his unremitting commitment to and exploration of materialist doctrine.

Materialism is assuredly no panacea. Two millennia of one of the most fundamental contentions in the history of philosophy, between diverse materialisms and whatever form of idealism we pose against them, demonstrate that no knock-down argument exists that in some unanswerable way could enforce materialism's claims. But we could understand Diderot's materialism as much simpler than an abstract philosophical doctrine. He projects materialism as an antidote to logomachy: as a constraint against the facility with which human beings manipulate language and make up stories—what in contemporary terms looks very much like the free play of signifiers. And he does so because such unimpeded compliance, such free play in language, gives us no traction against the constitutively refractory elements in our social, political, even biological existence. Whatever paradigm we use to model our experience, we need to capture and to communicate the fundamental *feel* of such resistant elements in lived reality.

We want to see the changes in the world we imagine, and indeed we want to see them soon. Yet the collapse of temporality into instantaneity that we have become familiar with in fictions places such reforms not nearer to hand, but makes them more distant, as the gap between language and the material world comes to seem increasingly unbridgeable. Imagination thus bears within itself an irreducible and inherent capacity for deception about its own functioning and utility. How do we make sense of this equivocation in the fundamental faculty with which we conceive of change and project the future? Today we are so immersed in the construction of these issues that has developed out of the Enlightenment discovery of them that we can hardly think that there ever appeared to be alternatives. But if imagination has been found insufficient, we might also seek to deploy its resources to re-imagine it itself. This, in any case, is what I have argued that Diderot, preoccupied in programmatic and fundamental ways with the efficacy of language in the alteration of the world, was seeking to explore in his narratives.

Words might seem capable of anything. But their freedom is never absolute. *Something always answers language.* Even as perversely mischievous a writer as Diderot was constantly constrained to register and react to the querulous independence of other subjectivities, even when the explicit objective of his text (as with his efforts to "manage" the Marquis de Croismare through the text of *La religieuse*) was to attempt to neutralize them. The pervasiveness of dialogue in Diderot's fictions radicalizes this structure of irreducible opposition and contention, and may indeed carry it as far toward representation of the irreducible *otherness* of social existence as anywhere in fiction.

A text always registers something outside its own limits. It is always driven or haunted by what exceeds it. The very urgency of its assertion makes no sense if there is no external and material world uncontainable within it with which it must contend, against which it is obliged to react. Dialogism is the fundamental ground of utterance. Ultimately, language imposes its irreducibly *collective* determinations upon any "individual" text. We wouldn't have language unless there were others to talk to, unless they had something to say that was different from what we have to say. No one controls discourse. This is the deep meaning of the uncanny reversal of instrumentality that I examined earlier, in which writers' textual tools seem to turn back against them to invert the control we imagine they exercise over their medium.

So our language can never escape bodies. The *others* are always materially there. Hence we are the text of our arrested attempt to textual-ize others. Then an agon like the one between narrator and reader that takes place so frequently in Diderot's narratives (particularly in *Jacques le fataliste*) stands as more than a waggish caricature manifesting the fears writers entertain concerning the querulousness of their increas-ingly invisible and even unimaginable audiences. In its very structure such a gambit represents the irrepressible force of the reversals of con-trol that are irreducible in language because, despite fantasies of au-thorial authority, language belongs to no one and speaks everyone.

What I am calling *materiality* is the structure of constraint that un-derlies such registrations of resistance, and that bears upon and against any text. It does so as a result of the irreducible *difference* that I have argued motivates every speech situation, every use of language—the uncontainable voices, practices, perspectives, and interests that, at the very moment the text may seek to incorporate and neutralize them, nonetheless explode its coherence and block any possibility of its au-tonomy or totalization. Texts represent many forms of alterity. But the fundamental difference projected by the constraints that frame textu-ality is the one that sets against each other the semiotic and the mate-rial registers of the world—the one that confronts bodies and stories.

Modernity sees the world as language. And remarkable insights about the world have arisen from our languaging of it. *But for model-ing the world's social and material processes, language offers an inad-equate paradigm.* When we use our seemingly weightless words to fig-ure the world's material density, a crucial mismatch occurs. Words assuredly are not the same as things. But what is the dimension of their difference? As I put it in *Present Past*, "language is compliant, things are resistant" (279). But that resistance constitutes our experience of reality, and language has trouble capturing it. We need to struggle against this paradigmatic disequilibrium if we are to draw the primor-dial weight of the world of real objects and real social existence into our representations, and express the refractoriness of materiality in the gossamer lability of words.

JENNIFER M. JONES

Personals and Politics: Courting *la citoyenne* in *Le courier de l'hymen**

In the 1770s a young man who was having difficulty finding a spouse decided to use the French journal *La feuille sans titre* [The Untitled Paper] to advertise for a wife.[1] After several issues in which he chronicled his travails and the responses he had received, he proposed an even more striking tactic for finding a wife: he would offer a lottery. All eligible women who wished to apply would pay a small sum and the winner would receive this money as her dowry. In the end, the editor confessed that the whole story was a fiction, a satire on modern marriage and courtship. The joke no doubt proved highly entertaining, for the editor referred to it in the next several issues. But just twenty years later, printed advertisements for spouses had moved from the realm of humor to reality. Beginning in 1791, a Parisian journal, *Le courier de l'hymen: Journal des dames* [Marriage Update: A Women's Newspaper], regularly began to publish personals ads such as the following:

> A widower, age 36, without children, who is a mercer by trade with a well-stocked boutique in a good quarter of Paris filled with all sorts of fabrics and other merchandise, desires to form a new marriage with a young woman of 22 to 26 years who comes from a good family, who is well brought up with good moral principles and who is accustomed to living among the better sort. He prefers sentiments to fortune.[2]

Le courier de l'hymen began publication at a moment when many French men and women believed that courtship needed to be funda-

*I am indebted to Margaret Waller for her research assistance and to the participants at the University of Pennsylvania French Cultural Studies seminar for their helpful criticism. Thanks, as always, to Chris Rasmussen for his careful reading of my work.

1. *La feuille sans titre* 271 (29 October 1777).

2. *Le courier de L'hymen* (24 April 1791), 76. All translations throughout this essay are my own.

YFS 101, *Fragments of Revolution*, ed. Weber and Lay, © 2002 by Yale University.

mentally reworked to reflect republican values: the aristocratic trappings of powder and wigs, body gestures, and verbal greetings needed
to be replaced by a style of courtship consonant with republican simplicity. The verbal antics and sartorial gestures of the *petit-maître* and
the *coquette* had to be reformed for greater transparency and sincerity.
Old Regime seduction needed to give way to unions based on *sensibilité* and economic security.

With the rise of new beliefs in the eighteenth century concerning
the importance of companionship and love in marriage, courtship had
begun to generate new kinds of anxieties for parents and elders and
heightened tension between parents and children. During a Revolution
that spoke the language of children freeing themselves from despotic
paternal rule, men and women in the early 1790s were occupied with
ushering in momentous changes in both the values and institution of
marriage.[3] Although historians can date and detail with great precision
the passage of new revolutionary laws regarding the secularization of
marriage and divorce, historians still know relatively little about the
ways in which transformations of laws affected individuals' subjective
feelings about marriage and the complicated mix of flirtatious seduction and economic calculation we call courtship. In a revolutionary culture in which the power of fathers, priests, and kings had all been de-
sacralized, how were young men and women to court?[4]

Le courier de l'hymen opens up some of these questions about the
connection between politics and personal life during the early years of
the Revolution: what do these advertisements and editorials reveal
about new forms and ideas of courtship? And, in what ways did journals such as *Le courier de l'hymen*, "court" *la citoyenne* [the female
citizen] by providing a particular interpretation of the Revolution for
women's consumption? *Le courier* offers a glimpse of both the ways in
which men and women courted within the pages of revolutionary press
and in which the revolutionary female press courted its female readers.
Through *Le courier*, literate female citizens—part of the emerging pub-

3. On the connection between family life and politics during the Revolution, see
Lynn Hunt, *The Family Romance of the French Revolution* (Berkeley: University of California Press, 1992.) See also Suzanne Desan's work on the connections between family
law, politics, and gender during the Revolution, "'War between Brothers and Sisters': Inheritance Law and Gender Politics in Revolutionary France," *French Historical Studies*
20/4 (Fall 1997).

4. For a comprehensive examination of revolutionary legislation on marriage, see
James Traer, *Marriage and the Family in Eighteenth-Century France* (Ithaca, NY: Cornell University Press, 1980).

lic sphere of print culture—were brought into and engaged with the revolutionary project of the reformation of manners and morals, a project particularly directed at women through the topics of courtship and marriage.

Recent work by scholars such as Sarah Maza has pointed to the growing importance in the second half of the eighteenth century of marriage as a symbol of a morally reformed society. From Greuze's paintings to Diderot's *drame bourgeois*, latter eighteenth-century culture emphasized that the happily married couple would regenerate society through its healthy progeny and its moral purity. From *philosophes* to physiocrats—from Rousseau to Turgot—those who wrote on luxury, depopulation, and the dangers of urban culture expressed fears that existing courtship practices would lead to seduction rather than marriage, and to decadence and depopulation instead of proper reproduction.[5]

The imaginative world of eighteenth-century fiction particularly highlighted the corruption of aristocratic courtship and marriage. But the sexual vulnerability (and desirability) of the single working woman was also amply noted in the writings of moralists as well as libertines, from Louis Sébastien Mercier to Rétif de la Bretonne. As historian Arlette Farge's work has shown, courtship was fraught with dangers for urban working women as well. Established social codes of courtship— gift giving, secret promises, and physical intimacies—seemed to be breaking down in the urban milieu of eighteenth-century Paris. Young women received mixed signals from suitors, were preyed upon by employers, and often ended up betrayed and pregnant.[6] Within the emerging middle class of office holders, merchants, and *bourgeois de Paris*, courtship conventions also changed dramatically as local lineage and close political and economic ties to a particular quarter gave way to broader social, political, and economic networks by the later eighteenth century.[7]

The new model of courtship offered by Rousseau's novels seemed to provide an answer to the problems of courtship, which were perceived to afflict men and women from a broad range of social backgrounds. In *La nouvelle Héloïse*, Julie's seduction by St. Preux and her

5. See Sarah Maza, *Private Lives and Public Affairs: The Causes Célèbres of Pre-revolutionary France* (Berkeley: University of California Press, 1993) and "Only Connect: Family Values in the Age of Sentiment: Introduction," *Eighteenth-Century Studies* 30/3 (1997), 207–12.

6. Arlette Farge, *Fragile Lives* (Cambridge: Harvard University Press, 1993).

7. See David Garrioch, *The Formation of the Parisian Bourgeoisie, 1690–1830* (Cambridge: Harvard University Press, 1996).

marriage to Wolmar suggest the possibility of happiness in marriage and the danger for women of sacrificing parental authority to pursue their own romantic desires. Likewise, in *Émile*, Émile's courtship of Sophie offers a model of a reformed courtship that combined personal fulfillment and marital joy with obedience to the wise counsel of parents.

In the best-selling romantic fictions of the second half of the eighteenth century, such as Rousseau's *Émile* and Bernardin de Saint-Pierre's *Paul et Virginie*, young lovers are "made for each other," raised from birth almost like brother and sister to become the perfectly matched pair, the happy couple.[8] But how were real men and women living in large cities like Paris to attain this newly instilled fictional desire for a soul-mate? How would they be able to tell a virtuous suitor from a dissipated *roué*, the woman of their dreams from the Old Regime nightmare of the pleasure-seeking, frivolous wife? They would do so by reading—by partaking of a new form of commercialized courtship found in the pages of a journal that appeared in Paris in 1791. In the pages of the *Le courier de l'hymen*, revolutionary print culture provided an answer to the personal and political question ushered in by the Revolution: without clerical and paternal authority, how would children without fathers find a mate?

Le courier de l'hymen was published within the context of a rapid expansion of the press between the summer of 1789 and the Constitution of September 1791. During this period the French press had unprecedented political freedom. Over three hundred new titles were published in Paris during 1790 and almost as many again during the first nine months of 1791.[9] A number of these works were addressed to women and pertained to women's issues. For example, *Les étrennes nationales des dames* demanded representation for women in the National Assembly, and the right to divorce and sexual liberty for women. Fashion journals such as the *Cabinet des modes* commented approvingly on the influence of the Revolution on both women and their fashions. Even some journals written by men and for men, such as *Le journal de la société* and *La bouche de fer*, advocated women's rights.

Le courier de l'hymen was edited by a man but addressed primarily to women and is believed to be the first journal devoted exclusively to

8. *The Family Romance*, 29–32.
9. Hugh Gough, *The Newspaper Press in the French Revolution* (London: Routledge, 1988).

personals advertisements in France.[10] *Le courier* was published twice a week between 30 January 1791 and 24 July 1791, with a subscription price of 24 *livres* per year in Paris and 30 *livres* in the provinces.[11] The editor claimed that its "motive most useful and of the most general interest" was to make known the intentions of all parents, young people, single people, and widows wishing either to find matches for their children, form new marriages, or to "follow the penchant of their heart." Those who wished to place or respond to an advertisement were to report to the editor's business office at 9, rue Serpente, where the editor would respond to "all honest propositions."

Although the advertisements placed in the journal were equally divided between advertisements for wives and husbands, from the outset the editor stated that the journal was "particularly devoted to women."[12] Not only would the journal help them find a husband, but it also offered to provide a public forum in which women could criticize husbands who were "too brutal to listen peacefully to their wife's complaints." Perhaps, the editors hoped, "an unjust husband, upon hearing the anonymous reproach, would correct his behavior while pretending not to recognize himself in the depiction." In addition, the journal covered all acts of the National Assembly relevant to "private society," reviewed new books dedicated to improving the happiness of spouses, and discussed plays, fashions, and *anecdotes piquantes.*"

Several Old Regime women's magazines had criticized contemporary marriages as unhappy and constraining for both husbands and wives. In 1787, for example, the premier fashion journal of its day, the *Cabinet des modes*, wrote:

> If you see a man and a woman in the same carriage, one silently staring out the right window and the other silently staring out the left window, you can say without ever being wrong: there is a husband and wife.[13]

Far from denigrating marital relations, however, *Le courier* was dedicated to the belief that marriages could and should be happy. These happy marriages were to be arranged through the "rational," enlightened publicity offered by print culture and were to be constituted on

10. For background on the journal see Evelyn Sullerot, *Histoire de la presse féminine en France, des origines à 1848* (Paris: Librairie Armand Colin, 1966).

11. Eight surviving issues can be found in the Bibliothèque Nationale.

12. *Le courier de l'hymen*, prospectus (1791).

13. *Cabinet des modes* [1787].

a progressive—even proto-feminist—basis. The journal pleaded for men's and women's right to divorce, hailed Condorcet's beliefs about women's equality with men, and supported women's education.

During the Revolution "the rights of women" could encompass many different and even paradoxical political positions.[14] The brand of feminism presented in *Le courier* did not clearly mark the political sympathies of the editor. In May 1791, a letter to the editor from a political club asked, "Monsieur, is your journal aristocratic or democratic? Our opinions are divided. Some say 'yes' and some say 'no.' Respond to us honestly." The editor, however, responded cagily, "My party is the truth. I am neither democratic nor aristocratic but follow the truth."[15] In fact, the anecdotes and editorial asides of the journal place the editor within the milieu of moderate revolutionaries. In one anecdote, the editor lampooned an elegantly attired *"demoiselle"* who refused to dance with a soldier at a party because "the national uniform gave her vapors."[16] In another passage the editor maintained that he was hostile to "Marat and to all those of a piece with him."[17] Throughout the pages of the journal the editor saluted "our good patriots."

The journal was filled with political asides, not only in the editorials, but also in the advertisements themselves. In May 1791, a thirty-three year old widow advertised that she wanted to meet a man in his late thirties who had "a strong and pronounced opinion on current affairs."[18] A man from the Antilles seeking a Parisian wife wrote that he wanted his prospective spouse to know that he had never abused his rights in order to subjugate his "mulattos or negresses." Although he boasted that he was a delegate of the National Assembly, he added that he did not care if his wife had strong opinions on political affairs as long as she did "not lean too far to the left or right and conserved *le juste milieu*."[19] A month later, a twenty-five year old woman responded to the delegate's ad:

> Forgotten in an Ursuline convent since the age of seven, I still don't want an American for a husband, even if he is a national deputy, if he was one of those who made 660,000 slaves pay with their liberty for the pleasures and opulence of 40,000 Europeans.[20]

14. See Joan Scott, *Only Paradoxes to Offer: French Feminists and the Rights of Man* (Cambridge: Harvard University Press, 1996), chapter 1.
15. *Le courier* (5 may 1791), 87.
16. *Le courier* (3 March 1791), 15.
17. *Le courier* (24 July 1791), 178.
18. *Le courier* (5 May 1791), 88.
19. *Le courier* (20 February 1791), 1.
20. *Le courier* (3 March 1791), 15.

Advertisements of this sort may have encouraged readers to consider that political sympathies might be as important in choosing a spouse as the amount of dowry or annual income, and to consider that political and marital virtue might walk hand in hand.

Not only in their attention to politics, but in other respects as well, *Le courier's* personals ads are quite different from the abbreviated ads found in daily papers and magazines today. Only one ad described the appearance of the advertiser; none specified desirable physical attributes for his or her spouse. Most of the advertisements, however, did state the man or woman's precise age and the desired age range for the prospective spouse. Most men sought wives ten to twenty years younger than themselves, with the age differential growing significantly as men aged. There were, however, a few exceptions such as a forty-six year old widower who sought marriage with "a widow who has a small, honest income, a sweet character, and who approaches my age."[21] Most women sought husbands who were four to six years older than themselves, again, with the age differential growing for older women.

Most of the advertisements furnished detailed information on the individual's profession, income, and property. In some advertisements men specified the size of the dowry they wished their wives to bring to the marriage. A twenty-eight year old man who hoped to set up his own mercer's shop wrote that he wanted to marry a woman his own age or younger who had a dowry equal to his own worth to invest in the store. A forty-two year old widow without children wrote that she had 1,800 *livres* in income and wished to marry a man with at least 3,000 *livres* in income. Many of the men and women who advertised came from a prosperous commercial milieu—grocers, mercers, and clothing merchants. They owned shops and collected rent. Men in this group advertised for wives with considerable dowries, worth 15,000 to 20,000 *livres*. At the top of the range, a twenty-six year old woman who wanted to set up a grocers or drapers shop wrote that she expected to be given a dowry of 80,000 *livres*. The women in this group sought husbands whose worth was comparable to their own. A thirty-two year old widow who owned a grocery store was looking for a husband worth at least 12,000 *livres*. A twenty-seven year old woman, who described herself as the head of a *magasin de modes* [clothing store], sought a husband worth 15,000 *livres*.

Other advertisements were submitted by teachers, lawyers, land-

21. *Le courier* (19 May 1791), 104.

owners, army officers, notaries, clerks, and small office holders. One man, two years after the Revolution had begun, still described himself as a "chevalier de Saint-Louis" but few gentlemen appeared in the pages of the journal. Another man, who described himself as "a former gentleman" looking for "a nobleman's daughter," wrote to suspend his ad, explaining that he would "prefer to remain single than to see his ad appear on the same sheet as that of his tailor."[22]

Although economic considerations were paramount, many men and women neglected to mention the economic status they desired in a spouse and focused their attention on other qualities. None of the advertisements expressed the desire to have children; but many advertisements did state quite frankly that they were looking for a partner who was not already tied down with children. Several advertisers mentioned that they were looking for a spouse who would be happy to live in the provinces or in a particular region. Other advertisements were filled with personal details. A sixty-four year old widower wrote that he was looking for a woman "with a sweet character and above all a taste for solitude."[23] A forty-two year old lawyer wrote that he desired to marry a girl from a good family who "had a knowledge of music and drawing."[24] But by far the most frequently requested qualities in wives and husbands were *"sensibilité"* (sensitivity) and *"douceur"* (sweetness). The advertisements were filled with requests for "sweet and sensitive" husbands or wives.

The presence in many of the advertisements of precise descriptions of property, professions, and income spoke to the importance of marriage as an economic relationship, while the addition of more personal and subjective desires spoke to newer values of companionship and intimacy in marriage. In a culture haunted by fears of Old Regime artifice and deception, the transparency of the descriptions seemed to offer a surer, more modern, and more republican form of courtship for those more interested in a moral marriage dedicated to virtuous reproduction rather than to aristocratic seduction. As the editor emphasized in his prospectus, "in order to respect the good morals which are the foundation of all society," he would "only receive decent requests which had marriage for their ultimate object."[25]

The new republican emphasis on equality and the transparency of

22. *Le courier* (24 February 1791), 6.
23. *Le courier* (24 April 1791), 76.
24. *Le courier* (20 February 1791), 2.
25. *Le courier*, prospectus.

moral character heightened fears that had long existed in early modern cities concerning artifice, duplicity, and seduction. With the overthrow of the existing social order and the abolition of ranks, orders, and distinguishing garb, the editor complained, who could be sure whom one was courting? In the second issue of the journal, the editor wrote an extended commentary on just this problem of social confusion of ranks in revolutionary Paris:

> It was perhaps easier to distinguish previously in France to which order in society a Frenchman belonged. Previously when one saw a man in a scarlet habit one could know, there is a canon who says the mass. Or, one could tell that underneath the wig and riding coat, there is an elegant chevalier off to a ball.
>
> But today, monk, soldier, and artisan all resemble each other. When one says now, "there goes a Jacobin," one doesn't know if it is a scholar or a former prince of the blood. . . . Even the Quakers haven't raised uniformity to such a high degree of perfection![26]

The editor touted his enterprise as an enlightened solution to this very problem—within the pages of his journal, names would be withheld, but one's true identity as a suitor (predicated on income, intentions, and moral character) would be revealed. As an antidote to the dangerous real world of courtship, the journal offered its readers an imaginary community of prospective spouses where virtue and honesty reigned.

Yet, if this was a world of honesty, the vision of sensitivity and sweetness being offered shared much with the imaginative world of late eighteenth-century fiction. And the act of reading these personal advertisements could just as easily take part in a tradition of the anonymous urban voyeur (à la Rétif de la Bretonne) as that of the authentic potential spouse. Far from offering a stable and unproblematic new mode of courtship, the personal advertisements of Le courier were a symptom of the very dangers of urban seduction they were trying to combat: voyeurism, anonymity, and veiled intentions.

Le courier offers an intriguing glimpse at the ways in which the complex entwining of the personal and the political during the Revolution helped give shape to an urban culture based on commercialization, spectacle, a new sense of imagined communities and perceived boundaries between individuals, the needs of families as collective groups and the needs of children as individuals, and the needs of the public and the imperative of private desires. As Lynn Hunt observes in

26. *Le courier* (24 February 1791), 5.

her reading of Sade's *Philosophy in the Boudoir,* when reduced to absurdity, the republican ideology of fraternity and transparency might render all women "public women" (i.e., prostitutes) and create a cult of violent, anti-social egoistic desire.[27] In a revolutionary culture that spawned both harsh new measures of policing the private lives of citizens in the name of "public safety" and new ways of piquing the erotic desires of private individuals through political pornography, a common voyeuristic delight blurred the boundaries between policing others and pleasuring oneself. Without succumbing to the extreme of either the police or the pornographer, the editor of *Le courier de l'hymen* nevertheless sold to his readers the anonymous urban experience of peering into others' lives.

Le courier points not only to the politicization of marriage and private life but to the emerging connections in the late eighteenth century between commercialization, print culture, and intimate experience. It takes part in an anonymous, distinctly urban experience of commerce and readership, an experience of seeing and *not* being seen, as it peers into shop windows, the private lives of the protagonists of novels, or the lives of potential spouses. The revolutionary personal advertisement fused not only the personal and the political, but the personal and the commercial, and the personal and the textual. That is, they provided a hybrid form that drew on elements of literary character sketches found in eighteenth-century novels and the commercial shorthand of the advertisement. More than prospective spouses, personal advertisements provided the private delight of imagining *others* courting.

No matter how many marriages were actually made through the pages of *Le courier,* the fiction of courtship was seductive in and of itself. The editor was only too aware of the voyeuristic delight that could be procured in his journal. As he candidly stated in his prospectus, "At a time when we are saddened by all sorts of complaints and lamentations by our journalists, women will not be upset to find at least one paper with a less somber tint than those that sadden them and which won't occupy them with tragic scenes. Our journal will try to provide them with an agreeable distraction, to bring the smile back to their lips, and to make them forget for a time all those serious ideas."

Even if the journal was intended, in part, to make women forget the "serious ideas" of revolutionary politics, the advertisements and editorials implicitly underscored the connection between the personal

27. *The Family Romance,* chapter 5.

and the political in revolutionary culture. In this culture, marriage was conceived of as profoundly political—personal marital happiness was the very basis for the moral regeneration of the nation. As the editor proclaimed in his opening issue, "We await the days that will be more propitious for marriage to enrich our pages with the names of our citizens who will come to pay their tribute to the nation and abandon the ranks of our *égoïstes célibataires* [selfish single people]."[28] By bringing the intimate search for a spouse into the public world of print journalism—by publicizing the "marriage plots" of dozens of ordinary men and women—the journal encouraged female readers to believe that, although they may not have marched on Versailles or attended the National Assembly, they too could be part of the revolutionary project.

The personal ads of *Le courier* help us to see the complex process by which individuals both made sense of their private lives in the context of revolutionary politics and made sense of the Revolution in deeply personal terms: as a young woman wrote to the journal, in a passage that blurs the boundaries between the personal and political in complex ways:

> It is very easy, monsieur, to find that the Revolution is going well when one loses nothing and gains liberty. But if you were a young woman, if you were twenty years old, if you had a father who couldn't give you a dowry, perhaps the Revolution would not seem to you the crown of happiness.[29]

Le courier de l'hymen flourished during a brief revolutionary moment when personal happiness and political revolution could be spoken in the same breath—when the distance between individualism and fraternity, between individual desire and the general will, seemed bridgeable. The journal was dedicated to the project not only of revolutionizing courtship but also of courting its female readership, hoping to convince them that both marriage and Revolution could indeed offer "the crown of happiness."

28. *Le courier* (20 February 1791), 1.
29. *Le courier* (20 February 1791), 3.

JEAN-MARIE ROULIN

Mothers in Revolution: Political Representations of Maternity in Nineteenth-Century France

If the nineteenth century is indeed the century of the Revolution, it is equally the moment when modern systems of historical understanding, whose major stages are marked by Hegel and Marx, were determined. The Historian's explanation, founded principally on economic and political causes, also leaves room for an anthropologic understanding of societies, one that escapes History's omnipotence. Freud's *Totem and Taboo* is certainly the best-known example of this possibility. Applying psychoanalytical causality to groups, Freud offers a model—a highly speculative one—for understanding the past that emerges more from anthropology than from mechanisms constructed by nineteenth-century historiography. More recently, Fredric Jameson, articulating Freud's and Marx's thoughts, brilliantly showed to what extent the family novel could intervene in grasping collective history,[1] and Lynn Hunt has used it as an instrument for understanding the French Revolution.[2] Fifty years before *Totem and Taboo*, Johann Jakob Bachofen,[3] a jurist by training, proposed a hypothesis of an original matricide, rather than that of the founding murder of the father. Thus, in *Das Mutterrecht, eine Untersuchung über die Gynekokratie der alten Welt nach ihrer religiösen und rechtlichen Natur* (1861), Bachofen

1. Fredric Jameson, *The Political Unconscious. Narrative as a Socially Symbolic Act* (Ithaca, New York: Cornell University Press, 1981).

2. Lynn Hunt, *The Family Romance of the French Revolution* (Berkeley/Los Angeles: University of California Press, 1992). Equally, Sartre, while remaining within the framework of a Marxist analysis, emphasized the importance of the study of the family, because it is what provides the child with the keys to deciphering social structures, mediation between the individual and the universal. See Jean-Paul Sartre, *Questions de méthode* (Paris: Gallimard, 1960), 82–85.

3. On this little-known thinker, see the chapter on him in Lionel Gossman's *Basel in the Age of Burckhardt* (Chicago and London: University of Chicago Press, 2000), 109–200.

YFS 101, *Fragments of Revolution*, ed. Weber and Lay, © 2002 by Yale University.

interprets *The Oresteia* as the sign of a revolution that topples the matriarchy in favor of the patriarchy. The matriarchy governed primitive societies: the memory of this matrifocal society has been repressed by modern societies. This work, eclipsed by Freud and the demon of paternity, has been little noted; nevertheless, Hélène Cixous has not overlooked it and Luce Irigaray pursues the idea that society is founded on an original matricide.[4] This paper will explore the pertinence of such an approach, and, working from selected examples, show how the mother and motherhood intervene in nineteenth-century representations of the Revolution.

It must first be noted that the mother and motherhood became the object of particular attention in society toward the end of the ancien régime, following a change in sensibilities in which Rousseau played an important role. In 1797, Louis-Sébastien Mercier observes that the city is populated by "a multitude of children nursed by their mothers. . . . For our Frenchwomen, maternity is becoming another degree of pleasure: all of them nurse, all find honor in being mothers."[5] This daily evidence of motherhood will inform political and historical representations.

David's paintings of History offer a particularly interesting example of the representation of the mother in the political arena between the end of the ancien régime and the Revolution. The women inhabiting his paintings are less objects of desire than figures of motherhood. "Le Serment des Horaces" ("The Oath of the Horatii") (1784) establishes an antithesis that David willingly and repeatedly explored: the opposition between the virile world of politics and private feminine space. In this particular case, the mother still only appears in the background of the composition.

In "Les Sabines" ("The Sabine Women") (1799), David did not choose the moment of the rape, the explosion of violence resulting from erotic desire and from rivalry in love, but rather the moment of reconciliation.[6] The woman is represented first as mother: the exposed breasts of the kneeling woman in the foreground are directed toward the children playing on the ground, and the composition's most elevated character is a babe held aloft in his mother's outstretched arms. Of course, the

---

4. "Sorties," in Catherine Clément and Hélène Cixous, *La jeune née* (Paris: UGE "10/18," 1975), 151. Luce Irigaray, "Le corps-à-corps avec la mère" (1980), in *Sexes et parentés* (Paris: Minuit, 1987), 23–26.

5. Louis-Sébastien Mercier, *Le nouveau Paris*, ed. J.-C Bonnet (Paris: Mercure de France, 1994), chapter 96, "Les mères sont nourrices," 438–39.

6. Lynn Hunt has shown how this painting demonstrates a reconciliation engendered by the women (167–169).

children represent the future to be built, but the mothers are the ones who, in drawing attention to the children, are the incarnation of reconciliation.

"Les Licteurs rapportant à Brutus les corps de ses fils" ("Lictors Bringing to Brutus the Bodies of his Sons"), painted for the 1789 Salon, took on a political resonance after the fact, opening the door to a variety of readings in a critical debate that divides art historians.[7] This painting does not seem to me to be an echo of a specific occurrence, of contemporary current events. Rather, I believe it offers a representation of a political imaginary and invites a double reading. On one level, it offers a scene of Roman virtue, a father meting out justice to his own sons, while the woman, a privileged figure of lamentation and pathos, incarnates the loss of private peace. The mother's and father's respective reactions reveal a radicalization of the separation of the spaces that belong to each sex. Within a neoclassical setting, incarnating the masculine political territory, Brutus is seated beneath a statue of Rome and leaning on a bas-relief representing the Roman she-wolf. The right part of the painting, reserved exclusively for the women, is separated by a Doric column; a wall-hanging closes the perspective and a cloth covers the table where a work basket sits. This object, associated more with genre painting than with historical painting, becomes a reference to a pastoral universe, one that will be disturbed by the irruption of political violence in the form of the bodies being carried in. The second level plays on the personality of Brutus, both founder of the republic and a man who has condemned his sons because they conspired to reinstate the Tarquinii—a man whose name is destined to reappear in roman history. In this way, the painting can be read as a metaphor for the revolution that, upon evicting the Tarquinii, inaugurates the republic. Yet, as I have noted, two female figures also appear in the space of the painting reserved for the political: the allegorical statue of Rome, the City, and the emblem of royalty, the she-wolf that nursed Romulus, the first king. It should be remembered that Brutus's sons' conspiracy was suggested to them by their mother's family. Thus, in establishing the republic, Brutus places himself under the patronage of the fatherland, Rome, but strikes out at an order placed under the sign of a she-wolf, and punishes his sons for having chosen the maternal side. Each of these acts takes the form of violence perpetrated against a matrilinear lineage: thus, the women's space cannot be reduced to a

7. See Antoine Schnapper's comments in *Jacques-Louis David, 1748–1825* (Paris: Réunion des Musées Nationaux, 1989), 196–200.

suitable place for the expression of sorrow, but, rather, represents the target of Brutus's political action. Other examples will support the hypothesis that political violence targets an order guaranteed by the mother.

As it is integrated into paintings inspired by Roman history, motherhood will come to contribute to the allegorical space of representations of political entities. With its appearance in Fénelon's *Télémaque* (1699), a text whose poetic importance equals its political importance, the "motherland" becomes an increasingly widespread notion during the Revolution. Thus, Maurice Agulhon has shown that motherhood is often one of the traits ascribed to *la Marianne* or to other allegories of the republic.[8] The most striking example undoubtedly dates from 1848, when a competition was held to designate a painting that would represent the republic. For this occasion, Honoré Daumier proposed a sketch strongly influenced by a Roman Grace: "La République nourrit ses enfants et les instruit" ("The Republic") (Fig. 1) represents a woman majestically seated with her three children, the first two each at a breast, and the third reading at her feet, so that education is added to her attributes.[9] Motherhood thus becomes a privileged symbol of the nation, the republic, or the homeland. Replacing the relationship of subject to King, it offers a twofold affective dimension: a nourishing and educating homeland like the one we find in Daumier. There are abundant examples in texts from this period, ranging from Michelet, for whom woman occupies an essential place: "When his own mother is lacking, a child must find a mother in his homeland,"[10] to Hugo: "My mother," says Enjolras in *Les misérables*, "is the Republic."[11]

This initial overview raises two issues. The first is related to the significance assigned to the mother, a figure of reconciliation in a pastoral universe where rivalry is abolished, and, in Luce Irigaray's view, a symbolic object of revolutionary violence. The second has to do with the means of signification itself: we pass from biological motherhood taken in its literal sense (Mercier) to motherhood's commitment in allegorical figures. Therein lies a semantic game on which fictional texts can widely play: from the mother as a character in the story to a variety of

8. Maurice Agulhon, *Marianne au combat. L'imagerie et la symbolique républicaines de 1789 à 1880* (Paris: Flammarion, 1979).

9. For more on this painting, see Henri Loyrette's commentary in *Honoré Daumier 1808–1879* (Paris: Réunion des Musées Nationaux, 1999), 244–58.

10. Jules Michelet, *Le peuple* (1846) (Paris: Marcel Didier, 1946), 91. For more on the mother in Michelet's work, see Thérèse Moreau, *Le Sang de l'histoire. Michelet et l'idée de la femme au XIXe siècle* (Paris: Flammarion, 1982), 175–200.

11. Victor Hugo, *Les misérables* (Paris: Gallimard "Pléiade," 1951), 690.

Figure 1. Honoré Daumier, *La République,* 1848. Oil on canvas. Musée d'Orsay, Paris.

symbolic representations of motherhood deployed throughout the text. The way this metaphoric process unfolds will also be examined here.

In many ways, *Lorenzaccio,* a drama published in 1834, offers a reflection on the July Revolution viewed through the prism of Florence in 1537. In the same movement in which he represents a tyrant's murder, Alfred de Musset also questions political language itself. In one of the play's most caustic dialogues, Lorenzo asks the painter Tebaldeo if he can paint Florence:

> *Tebaldeo:* Yes, my lord.
> *Lorenzo:* Why, then, can't you paint a courtesan, if you can paint an evil place?
> *Tebaldeo:* I have not yet been taught to speak this way of my mother.
> *Lorenzo:* What do you call your mother?
> *Tebaldeo:* Florence, my lord.
> *Lorenzo:* Then you are nothing but a bastard child, for your mother is nothing but a trollop.[12]

In this scene, Lorenzo exposes the metaphoric discourse of an artist who believes himself to be free in his acts and his inspiration. Among the elements in Tebaldeo's candid credo, the symbolization of the city as "mother" is highly charged, in language that is more characteristic of a citizen of revolutionary France than that of an artist of the Italian Renaissance. By pretending to be unaware of the meaning of the word "mother," Lorenzo unmasks the metaphor's founding analogy. This deconstruction of Tebaldeo's discourse does not show that the painter wishes to be outside of the political realm, but rather that he himself is, however unwittingly, a prisoner of its rhetoric. Through the taboo placed on the mother, he denies himself any critical discourse concerning the city.

However, this stripping away of an element of revolutionary rhetoric is accompanied in Musset's work by the construction of another myth. In fact, this metaphorical figure is countered by a mother in the literal sense, Marie Soderini. Musset gives her a role that she does not play in his principal source, Varchi's *Storia fiorentina,* placing her in Florence at the time of the duke's murder and making her his sister-in-law Catherine Ginori's companion. The space of her theatrical entrance (the banks of the Arno) and the tone of her first words situate her in a pastoral univers: "The sun is beginning to set. . . . Beneath the reeds, the frog rings its little crystal bell. All these evening harmonies are indeed a strange thing with the far-off noise of this city" (I, 6). In Florence itself, Marie incarnates the primitive and pure universe of Lorenzo's childhood in Caffagiuolo. In this way she is contrasted with Florence, the prostituted, perverted mother, and this opposition is un-

12. *Lorenzaccio,* Act II, scene 2.

derscored by the end of the scene, which closes with the curses of the exiles leaving Florence: "Farewell, Florence . . . , sterile mother, you who no longer have milk for your children. . . . Farewell, Florence, the bastard daughter. . . . Farewell, Florence! Cursed be the breasts of your women!" (I, 6).

Immediately we see that a strong antithesis is created: on the one hand, the metaphoric mother—a politicized and therefore a corrupted whore—and, on the other, a figure of purity, of a universe preceding the fall. While her rhetoric is not revealed in the play itself, Marie Soderini's character is defined through metonymy (the space she invokes) and by the metaphors she employs ("its little crystal bell"). She belongs to the universe of myth, which results from a construction of language just as much as Florence does. At one point in the play, however, Lorenzo wonders about this myth of maternal purity: "While pregnant with me, of what tiger did my mother dream? . . . From what wild womb, from what hairy embrace do I come? Was my father's ghost leading me, like Orestes, towards some new Aegisthus?" (IV, 3). The allusion to Aegisthus implies Clytemnestra's betrayal, mentioned in the monologue's opening sentence. More specifically in this text, Lorenzo evokes the mother's desire, which, as Irigaray has shown, is forbidden (Irigaray, 23).

Marie Soderini's purity and Florence's impurity are thus two conditions of the same figure, whose shared point is Lorenzo's conception and birth. The incarnation of the mother's desire and the site of her fall, he is called to make amends for her sins, to restore the mother's body, and to return her lost purity to her. As bait to lure Alexandre into the trap where he will be killed, Lorenzo chooses Catherine, his aunt, a replacement figure for the mother. This gesture replays the primal scene, but this time in order to conserve, or, better still, to restore maternal purity at the very instant when it would be lost. The expression of this purity passes through an image of nursing: "Well then! I have indeed committed many crimes, and if my life is ever on any judge's scale, on one side there may possibly be a mountain of tears; but perhaps on the other there will be a drop of pure milk fallen from Catherine's breast, and which will have fed decent children" (IV, 5). Making amends for the ontological and historical offense from which he was born: such could be Lorenzo's mission in a family scenario. It must be remembered that the image of nursing evokes the curses of the exiles, opening up this image of motherhood to political meaning. The dilemma posed by the two antithetical images of the mother—a corrupt prostitute within the city on the one hand, or a pure woman in a pastoral setting outside the city on the other—is not overcome. The duke's murder and Lorenzo's death will change nothing. Rather, as is evidenced by information delivered rapidly at the beginning of Act 5, it will be followed by the death of Marie Soderini, for which Lorenzo feels responsible: "That my mother might die from all this, that is what could happen" (IV, 9). Rebellion against the duke indirectly carries matricide along with it. Lorenzo's gesture is perhaps initially this: murder of the corrupted mother, of the whore, who is nevertheless inseparable from her mythic double, the innocent mother. Any entrance into History, then, is a fall from an idyllic universe from which violence and rivalry are absent. Any hope for the return to pastoral purity—for the city of Florence and her subject Lorenzo—passes through a murder that symbolically consecrates the mother's death. Through this matricide, Musset affirms the impossibility of the mother's innocence, because by his very presence the subject incarnates the mother's desire for the father, which cannot be erased.

   Lorenzaccio offers yet another image of the depraved mother in Florence. A scenario that justifies the revolutionary gesture is that of the mother who abandons her husband and children for another man. The treacherous Clytemnestra, like Hamlet's mother Gertrude, must be punished for her crime. In contrast to her arises the figure of Orestes, who often incarnates regret where one would instead expect the murderer of the father Oedipus. (Oedipus is invoked by Lorenzo as one of the models of his tyrannicide; and it was a name given to Robespierre in 1840 by E. Lairtullier in *Les femmes célèbres de 1789 à 1795*[13] (*Famous Women from 1789 to 1795*). He also appears in Hugo's work in the character of Gennaro who, in *Lucrèce Borgia*, kills a woman who he learns is his mother just after having stabbed her. Orestes is also the subject of a painting much commented upon at the 1800 Salon: "Les remords d'Oreste" (Orestes' Remorse) (Fig. 2), by Philippe-Auguste Hennequin, in which Orestes, holding Electra in his arms, pursued by the Furies, looks with terror at Clytemnestra's dead body, or, more specifically, at the dagger piercing her naked breast. Certainly, Orestes offers a very telling illustration of remorse: the Furies hounding him are more expressive than Oedipus's blind wanderings. But it is difficult to find a

13. E. Lairtullier, *Les femmes célèbres de 1789–1795* (Paris, 1840), volume I, 39.

PEINT PAR HENNEQUIN.

Dessiné par e Marchais.　　　Gravé à l'eau forte par Quéverdo.　　　Terminé par Pigeot.

LES REMORDS D'ORESTE.

Figure 2. Quéverdo, after Philippe-Auguste Hennequin, *Les remords d'Oreste* [n.d.]. Etching. Bibliothèque nationale, Paris.

clear and unambiguous meaning for this painting.[14] Irigaray's intuition offers a fruitful path for reading: "What appears in the most routine of daily acts, just as in the totality of our society and culture, is that the latter operates on an original matricide" (23). She links this idea to the fact that the law of the father does not forbid the desire for the mother, but rather the mother's own desire. One can therefore wonder if a recurring scenario that haunts the Revolution does not rely on the idea of the murder of a bad mother who desires an incestuous or forbidden object—the political enemy—who is replaced by the single mother devoted entirely to her children, as incarnated by the Republic: the body of Clytemnestra in Hennequin's painting, lying with a dagger in its breast, can be compared to Daumier's "La République."

Alexandre Dumas's *La Reine Margot* (*Queen Margot*) (1845) offers a good example of the bad mother in politics, presenting a portrait of Catherine de Medici as a blood-thirsty queen, in a rather lively historiographic tradition. This novel, conjuring up the wars of religion and the passage from the Valois to the Bourbon dynasty, can be described as an allusion to a controversial episode of French history as seen through the prism of the Revolution. The foreign queen, Catherine de Medici, foreshadows, more darkly indeed, the notorious depravity of Marie-Antoinette. On his death bed, Charles IX has this conversation with his mother:

> "And by what right, Madam, do you stay [at my death bed]?" asked Charles IX.
>
> "By a mother's right."
>
> "You are no more my mother, Madam, than the Duke of Alençon is my brother."
>
> "You are delirious, Sir," said Catherine; "since when is the one who gives life no longer the mother of the one who received it?"
>
> "From the moment, Madam, when this denatured mother takes back what she gave," answered Charles, wiping away the foam that had come to his mouth.[15]

14. See Jérémie Benoit's *Philippe-Auguste Hennequin 1762–1833* (Paris: Arthena, 1994), 55–57. In Anatole France's *Les Dieux ont soif* (*The Gods are Thirsty*) (1912), Evariste Gamelin, a painter seated on the Revolutionary Tribunal, is working on an "Oreste veillé par Electre sa soeur," inspired by Hennequin's painting. It is meaningful that Gamelin gives his characteristics to Orestes, a figure who symbolizes the revolutionary, at the time when the Queen's trial is taking place.

15. Alexandre Dumas, *La Reine Margot* (Paris: Le Livre de Poche, 1994), 598.

In this dialogue, Charles IX puts in place a maieutic system reminiscent of Musset to show that Catherine de Medici succeeded in breaking a bond that is, because its foundation is in nature, the most unbreakable: the corrupt mother destroys the motherhood within her. Punctuating this dialogue with a very concrete image, the foam coming from the king's mouth offers a metaphor for the rejection of his mother's milk. Thus it is Charles IX's wet nurse who becomes the holder of maternal rights, authorized to care for the dying man. Catherine, the bad, corrupt mother cannot incarnate the homeland, so Dumas makes her into a "Florentine," omitting the fact that she had arrived in France at the age of 14, the daughter of a French mother.

Responsible through her negligence for the murder of her son Charles IX, she directs her desire in a second perversion that alludes to accusations leveled against Marie-Antoinette, toward the Duke of Alençon: "Indeed, Catherine did prefer this son, either for his bravery, or rather for his beauty, because, in addition to the mother, the woman was present in Catherine" (401). Dumas thus describes her as more woman than mother, as she betrays the new nature that motherhood should have given her. From this moment on, she is nothing but a wicked stepmother for her subjects: the murder of a young page, Orthon (Chapter XLV), is both the foreshadowing of Charles IX's murder and a synecdoche for the way Catherine treats her subjects. In this scene, the two characters are described in terms of family, the "queen mother" opposite a "child" or a "poor boy," another metaphor for the relationship between Queen and subject. The page is murdered in the heart of the Louvre, in a secret passageway swallowed by a hidden dungeon whose trap door is operated by Catherine de Medici, and is engulfed in the "womb of the earth" (457). As the mistress of the Louvre, a castle worthy of a Gothic novel, she alone possesses all the keys, the keys to life and death. The melodramatic murder of the page establishes Catherine as a bad mother, infanticidal and all-powerful, swallowing up her children in the bosom of her home according to her political whim.

It is no surprise, then, that Dumas calls the Valois family "The Atrides" (Chapter XL), a generic name designating the fratricidal struggle opposing Henri d'Anjou and Charles IX, under the highly biased arbitration of Catherine de Medici. Orestes appears, but to qualify the friendship between La Mole and de Coconnas, "Orestes and Pylades" (Chapter XLIV). In "At the home of this family of Atrides" (437), Coconnas playfully describes himself as la Mole's Pylades. Yet these two friends, even though they are beheaded, do not figure at the heart of the historical intrigue, which is ultimately based on the rivalry between Catherine de Medici and Henri de Navarre. The novel's epilogue describes Henri's escape, just as it announces his return through foreshadowing. Henri is given Orestes's mission: dethroning a corrupt dynasty incarnated in the Queen, and replacing it with a new order, that of the Bourbons. This reading shows that the vision of changing dynasties or political regimes is haunted by the idea of a relation with the mother, replaying the original matricide which, for Bachofen and Irigaray, is the foundation of all society.

In addition to the debauched Florence, *Lorenzaccio* also offers the portrait of a mother representing a Florence idealized in the eyes of Tebaldeo and linked to a pastoral universe. Balzac's *Les Chouans* (*The Chouans*) and Hugo's *Quatrevingt-treize* (*Seventeen Ninety-three*) develop these images in a complex way. The fact that Balzac and Hugo, in what can be considered two of the most important novels written in France about the Revolution in the nineteenth century, choose the Vendée region rather than Paris as the main site of the action, undoubtedly stems from something central in the image of the Revolution.[16]

Les Chouans ou la Bretagne en 1799 (*The Chouans or Brittany in 1799*) (1834), came out in 1829 at the height of the historical novel's popularity in France, under the title *Le dernier Chouan ou la Bretagne en 1800* (*The Last Chouan or Brittany in 1800*). It takes place during the last powerful moments of the Chouan rebellions in 1799. Balzac introduces a love story in the midst of the tensions of the Revolution. A discourse on History[17] is woven into the story of the desire of the two protagonists, Marie de Verneuil and the Marquis de Montauran. Within this network, figures of motherhood again play a crucial role. It should be remembered that 1799 is the year of Balzac's own birth—a coincidence perhaps, but one linked to the thematics of endings and begin-

16. See Claudie Bernard, *Le Chouan romanesque. Balzac, Barbey d'Aurevilly, Hugo* (Paris: PUF, 1989).

17. The meeting of the love story and historical novel has been sufficiently commented since Lukács; in her introduction to *Les Chouans* (in Balzac, *La comédie humaine* [Paris: Gallimard "Pleiade," 1977], vol. 8, 859–96), Lucienne Frappier-Mazur shows the deep interdependence between the love intrigue and the representation of History in this novel. See also Pierre Barbéris, "Roman historique et roman d'amour. Lecture du *Dernier Chouan*," *Revue d'histoire littéraire de la France*, 75/2–3 (1975), 283–307.

nings,[18] as well as to motherhood, which, if not directly found in the plot, is present at a symbolic level.

The landscape is an essential element in this novel. The action takes place around Fougères. The description of the Couesnon valley, where the initial episode is set, endows the site of the action with feminine symbols: "From there, the officers discovered the entire expanse of this basin, as remarkable for its soil's prodigious fertility as for the variety of its aspects. From all sides, jagged mountains rise like an amphitheater, disguising their reddish sides beneath oak forests, and concealing small valleys filled with coolness along their slopes. . . . This green rug . . . locks away fertile secrets of beauty."[19] In his "Introduction to the First 1829 Edition," Balzac sees "one of the cradles of Chouannerie" (899) in the Fougères area. Now, the "cradle" metaphor comes up again in the description of the landscape itself (1113), and that of the "basin" even more frequently. The Fougères area is described in images of origins ("immense primeval forests," 918), even birth (Marie, coming into the area, "thought she was reborn," 1092). These original valleys are fraught with ambivalence: idyllic scenery and original violence. The Blue Soldier's first meeting with Brittany's forest begins with fascinated contemplation of the panorama and closes with slaughter. The landscape where at first sight images of fertility abound, turns out to be a deadly and sterile landscape due to the lack of civilization and commerce. In this way, Balzac calls into question the overly candid imagery of the pastoral scenery, such as it is represented by Lorenzo's mother, and origins. Here the space is not idyllic, but rather primitively savage and deadly. The constant comparisons with North American "Savages" echo Chateaubriand's perception of the American landscape in *Les Natchez* (*The Natchez*), a text published only in 1826: a place of origin, of pure nature, turns out to be a place of the fall and of death.[20]

The second network haunted by images of the mother is religion. The young Balzac is again marked by Chateaubriand, this time by *Le génie du Christianisme* (*The Genius of Christianity*), in which Chateaubriand accords a central place to Mary as a figure of mediation in a text

18. This novel, the first that Balzac signed with his own name, is also linked to the birth of the writer; see Anne-Marie Maron's remarks on the biographical context of the publication of this text in *Le fils prodige* (Paris: Nathan, 1993), 14–15, 98.

19. Balzac, *Les Chouans*, in *La comédie humaine* (Paris: Gallimard "Pléiade," 1977), vol. 8, 912.

20. See Jean-Marie Roulin, "Le paysage épique ou les voies de la renaissance," in J-C Berchet et Ph. Berthier, eds., *Chateaubriand. Le tremblement du temps*, (Toulouse: Presses Universitaires du Mirail, 1995), 19–39.

that sought to be a unifying force at the strategic moment of the pro-mulgation of the Concordat of 1801.[21] The influence on Balzac is evi-denced by the scene of the open-air mass, which evokes a primitive his-torical time ("the first times of Christianity," druids' stones serving as an altar, etc.), a time prior to symbolization: "Man here was only a fact and not a system, there was prayer, not religion" (1117). Parallel to phy-logenesis, elements of ontogenesis place this scene in a moment of child-hood: the Chouans are simultaneously "men and children" (1117). Ab-bot Gudin, in his sermon, makes himself the spokesman of Saint Anne d'Auray, who supposedly appeared to him. In the absence of the King in France, it is Saint Anne who inspires the Bretons in combat. She is described as the "aunt of God, as they say in Brittany" (1119)—"mother of God," Balzac had written, changing to "aunt" only for the 1845 Furne Edition (1797). An invisible figure, but one who is incarnated so to speak in the resurrection of a soldier with a remarkable name, Marie Lambrequin: Saint Anne gives birth to Marie. Nature's primitivism, the landscape metaphors, like the metaphor of the "basin," mix with the figures invoked to create a system that settles those present in a united community, plunged in a return to what Luce Irigaray designated as "wrestling with the mother."[22] This state is characterized by a type of naivete that is specific to youth—that of the "savage" and the child.

This scene is viewed through the eyes of another Marie, the third after Soldier Lambrequin and Saint Anne's daughter: Marie de Verneuil. This Marie is a perfect incarnation of the "type" as defined by Lukács, the character typified by an oxymoron—a virgin in soul and a whore in body, an aristocrat by relation (the Duke's illegitimate child) and re-publican by adoption—, sent away by Bonaparte at Fouché's behest. Within the love story, she is the rival of Madame du Gua, who is masked as the figure of a mother. She is the one who orchestrates the climax that leads to a birth. The climax is offered as both a resolution to the Balzacian family biographical imaginary and a symbolic system of His-

21. See especially the chapter "De l'incarnation." More generally, Christianity ap-pears here as a maternal religion: "the spirit of Christianity has a tender relationship with mothers' genius." (Génie du Christianisme [Paris: Gallimard "Pléiade," 1978], 664). On the emergence of the figure of Mary in the nineteenth century, see Stéphane Michaud, Muse et Madone. Visages de la femme de la Révolution française aux apparitions de Lourdes (Paris: Seuil, 1985), 17–78, and Georges Tavard, La Vierge Marie en France aux XVIIIe et XIXe siècles (Paris: Cerf, 1998).

22. The use of "wrestling" for the French "corps à corps" is taken from Gillian C. Gill's translation of Sexes et parentés, Sexes and Genealogies (New York: Columbia Uni-versity Press, 1993)—trans. note.

tory. During the nuptial mass, which echoes Abbot Gudin's mass through contrast, Marie reveals the name of her parents. Most importantly, she also reveals that her virginally named mother, Blanche de Castéran, had become an Abbess. After the wedding night, Marie once again dons the mask Madame du Gua had chosen for herself, and turns from a woman into a mother who sees the Marquis de Montauran as a child: "She turned and considered the sleeping Marquis, resting his head on his hands, the way children do. . . . 'Ah!' she said to herself quietly, 'he sleeps like a child!'" (1027). The fact that the Marquis—pushed by Francine and Marie acting as midwives—squeezes through a bull's eye window whose narrowness worries him ("I will never be able to pass through there!" [1208]), appears to be a metaphor for birth. A tragic birth, for Montauran is killed as soon as he sets foot outside of the room, a victim of Corentin's betrayal. From the point of view of Balzac's imaginary, he is killed by Hulot, a father figure, because of a betrayal instigated by the hated rival Corentin. From another point of view, it can be noted that the interior in this wedding night scene reflects the ancien régime: an altar has been built, the space belongs to the Marquis de Montauran, and a non-juring priest [a priest who has refused to take the oath of the new republic] blesses the couple; the exterior, the Brittany countryside, is the domain of the Republicans. The interior and exterior spaces evoke a political temporality, a past and a present dominated by Hulot and Corentin, an image of a countryside on the way to being conquered by the Revolutionary forces. It is truly the passage from the ancien régime to the republic, from 1799 Brittany to 1800 France that is symbolized here. The farewell to outdated monarchy—the King's absence, regression into primitivism—is described as a birth, ensured by Marie. Moreover, the death of this newborn manifests the impasse of a monarchy that relies on rural and regressive forces, and calls for a new conception of the monarchy, one that is respectful of the modern nation. Thus Corentin asks Hulot to transmit this message to his younger brother, his modern double: "If he wants to obey my last words, he will not bear arms against France, yet without ever abandoning the King's service" (1210). Establishing a difference between France and the republic, he prepares the way for a new course: attachment, not to the soil of the Vendée region, but rather to France as the fatherland, in order to reestablish a renewed monarchy.

Agulhon shows that *la Marianne* often bears characteristics of the Virgin Mary, as is evidenced by an extraordinary "Lettre à Marianne" (1856), Félix Pyat's republican *Ave Maria:* "Hail Marianne, full of strength, the people are with you, the fruit of thy womb, the republic is blessed!" (Agulhon, 164). This letter, written twenty years after *Les Chouans*, casts an interesting light on the figure of Marie de Verneuil, who is equally an image of the Virgin and the republic. Yet in contrast to Pyat's Marianne, she gives birth not to a republic, but to a new Royalism. Through this birthing, however, neither the mother nor the child will be saved. Donning Montauran's clothing, she sacrifices herself, but also appears with a new, final mask, perhaps the true one: she seems to abandon the republican ideal, unable to federate the various identities resulting from the Revolution, but does not indicate any future routes.

Quatrevingt-treize, published in 1873, develops a fictional account of the Vendée wars in a setting that brings to mind Hugo's family novel (his mother was from the Vendée and his father was a soldier). Motherhood appears clearly here as a central theme.[23] It is true that 1848, as Maurice Agulhon and Daumier's painting both show, placed a special accent on the republic's maternal dimension. Like in *Les Chouans*, the novel opens with a group of soldiers entering the wild brush of a dark forest at whose heart, "at the densest part of the thicket," says Hugo, "in a sort of hole in its branches, a sort of leafy room, half open like an alcove, a woman, Michelle Fléchard, was seated on the moss."[24] In a doubling-up of signs, the woman is discovered by a *vivandière* inside this feminized space; it turns out that she is a mother. Motherhood brutally interrupts the violence of the soldiers who were about to "open fire on her." In this way, the mother places herself outside the political realm. As far as she is concerned, neither a Blue Soldier nor a White Soldier killed her husband, rather, it was "a gunshot" (42). If she opposes the country to the fatherland, the land to the Law, it is less out of political conviction than from her inability to symbolize the fatherland. The essence of motherhood as it appears here is sacrifice, the sacrifice of bread that the starving Michelle Fléchard gives to her children.

23. See Victor Brombert, "Sentiment et violence chez Victor Hugo. L'exemple de *Quatrevingt-treize*," *CAIEF* 25 (1973): 251–267; Jeffrey Mehlman, *Revolution and Repetition. Marx/Hugo/Balzac* (Los Angeles/London: University of California Press, 1977), 56–58; and Sandy Petrey, *History in the Text: "Quatrevingt-treize" and the French Revolution* (Amsterdam: J. Benjammin B. V., 1980), 13–24. See also Guy Rosa's article "*Quatrevingt-treize* ou la critique du roman historique," *Revue d'histoire littéraire de la France*, 75/2–3 (1975): 329–343.

24. Victor Hugo, *Quatrevingt-treize* (Paris: Gallimard "Folio," 1979), 34. Here my analysis joins C. Bernard's as she describes the clearing as "alcove and womb" (174), a conjunction of eroticism and motherhood.

Faced with this rural model and its limitations, the soldiers claim paternal values and adopt the child: "the battalion will become the father" (45). In this manner, Hugo offers two opposing politics in familial terms. On the one hand, motherhood and reconciliation, likely to stop the civil violence, are characterized by sacrifice and lack of political consciousness, associated not with the home, but rather with nature, in what Sandy Petrey has called the pastoral discourse.[25] On the other, symbolic paternity is immediately characterized by its potential for violence, yet is still capable of commiseration and welcoming, as the act of adoption shows. A resolution to this alternative becomes apparent later in the text: there is no end to civil violence without an end to masculine domination and without the assumption of an instructive rather than a primitive motherhood. In this way, the prologue in the forest, where the mediating mother transforms the soldiers' violence into an act of adoption, announces the epilogue and the development of Hugo's thoughts in this novel.

Tellmarch, *tellus* and *mater*, marks a stage in this evolution: "In the presence of this suffering, this old man had a woman's thoughts. . . . In fact, it must be so charming to feel a small pink mouth drawing your soul from within your body, and who, with your life, makes its own" (287). But it is not merely a question of feeding, because this would mean remaining in Michelle Fléchard's pastoral and nearly animal ignorance. The instructive act is a way for Cimourdain to attain motherhood in his relationship with Gauvain: "The mind nurses; intelligence is a breast. An analogy exists between the wet nurse who gives her milk and the tutor who gives his thought" (157). Motherhood is thus defined once again by giving, where the transmission of knowledge is placed on the same level as that of food. Hugo emphasizes the materiality of this contact. Motherhood assures a physical relationship, while fatherhood implies an abstract operation. Gauvain extends this vision to social and political life: "The author being the starting point of authority, and authority being included in the author, there is no other authority than fatherhood; from there, the legitimacy of the queen-bee who creates her people, and who, being a mother, is queen; from there, the absurdity of the king-man who, not being the father, cannot be the master; from there, the republic. What is all this? It is family, it is humanity, it is revolution" (435). In this strange text, if paternal authority is legitimate when it is maternal, it is because there is

25. See chapter 3, "Pastoral and Historical Discourse," 35–50.

no author or legitimacy except in physical contact. Arguing with Cimourdain, Gauvain offers in opposition a matriarchal vision, listing the people to whom the child must be entrusted: "First to the father who engenders him, then to the mother who gives birth to him, then to the teacher who raises him, then to the city which makes him a man, then to the fatherland which is the supreme mother, then to humanity which is the foremother" (469). And when Cimourdain accuses him of forgetting God, he replies that God is at the end of this progression: "God opens himself; there is nothing else to do but enter" (470). Woman leads to God, who is described here as a kind of universal mother.

The climax shows that motherhood alone can save humanity. First in the Tourgue episode, in which the three children adopted by the soldiers are held prisoners, hostages of "the Ancester" Lantenac, Michelle Fléchard's animal howl will resolve the blocked situation. In fact, this cry leads Lantenac to free the children, breaking with the virile logic of violence, adopting a parental attitude, or better still, making a sacrifice of political ideal in favor of the family. The children's liberation is thus perceived as giving birth, and motherhood triumphs: "the victory of humanity over man. Humanity experienced through the inhuman. And by what means? The cradle" (429). This "cradle" contains the echo of the image of the babe raised above the melee by his mother in Les Sabines ("The Sabine Women"): a sign of the future, but also in Hugo's work a sign of man's new attitude toward the social group. The epilogue brings a conclusion to this journey. Visiting Gauvain in his prison, Cimourdain becomes a mother once again: "a mother watching her nursling sleep would not have a more tender and inexpressible gaze." Cimourdain's suicide after Gauvain's execution permits the final reconciliation of the mother's body: these two heroes become "two souls, tragic sisters" (482). Gauvain's death, and perhaps Cimourdain's as well, appears as a sacrifice, a value of motherhood. The path is also clearly marked: mother and cradle guarantee civil harmony, at the price of renouncing paternal violence. Still, motherhood has had to evolve: first represented as an isolated mother in a clearing in Brittany, it incarnates the country, before then becoming the foundation of the fatherland, of humanity even. This is the passage from a pastoral universe to a politicized vision of motherhood, where the mother is no longer only pure nature and life-giver, but also an educator. The child can then move from the primitive attachment to the mother's body to a symbolic attachment to the country's body, which has become the fatherland. Quatrevingt-treize imposes the primacy of the "wrestling" with the mother as a legitimization of the political tie: not only attachment to the land, but also support assured by education. In this respect, it realizes Daumier's dual goal: that of the mother/educator, in a vision at the heart of the Third Republic.

Two models arise from this overview: Clytemnestra with her breast pierced by Orestes's dagger, and Daumier's Republic, a rigid woman, absent from the world of desire, nourishing and protective, with her children living in peace in her shadow. These two figures are perhaps two stages of the same journey, the one suggested by Bachofen and Irigaray: revolution reactivates the idea of an original matricide. Moreover, making the mother into a symbol of the republic means doubly excluding the woman from the polis: in reducing her to either the virgin or the mother, she is kept at a distance from the order of desire and sexuality; under cover of elevation to allegory or metaphor she is refused political citizenship. Thus, a female totem is elaborated in her place—one that, in opposition to Freud, Bachofen had foreseen—, at once the memory of a murder and a guarantee of protection.

DARCY GRIMALDO GRIGSBY

Revolutionary Sons, White Fathers, and Creole Difference: Guillaume Guillon-Lethière's *Oath of the Ancestors* (1822)*

The scene is tearful (Fig. 1). Revolutionary soldiers swear their loyalty to France with a clamor of upraised swords. Some take leave of their wives and children. Guillaume Guillon-Lethière's picture of 1799 undoubtedly refers to—and rewrites—David's *Oath of the Horatii* (Fig. 2) exhibited fourteen years earlier. In both pictures, the fatherland is menaced and the brothers rally with arms held high on its behalf. In Lethière's painting, we see the pose of the *Horatii* reiterated (in reverse) in numerous vignettes: at center middleground, the fanning left hands of the soldiers who with their right hand lift spiking swords; at left foreground, the two men who extend a long sheathed sword and open hands towards the official on a step above them; at right, the rhyming, ornate soldiers (in uniforms designed by David), two of whom gesture to the ship while another momentarily advances from their lockstep in order to embrace his wife. As the latter detail suggests, Lethière's picture deviates from the *Horatii* in the prominence (and activity) accorded to France's female family members. It also deviates from David's picture in its absenting of the father. This, despite the fact that the painting is entitled *La patrie en danger* [The Fatherland in Danger].[1] Even in the

*I would like to thank Geneviève Marcel Capy, France's expert on Lethière and founder along with G.-Florent Laballe of the *Association des Amis de Lethière,* for her extraordinary generosity in sharing her knowledge and work with me. This article could not have been written without her scholarship. The *Oath of the Ancestors* is only available as an object of study for scholars outside Haiti because she and Laballe rediscovered it in the cathedral at Port-au-Prince in 1991 and succeeded in getting it restored by Musées de France conservators between 1995 and 1997. I also thank Jessica Dandona for her invaluable work as my research assistant in Paris, and Matthew Gerber, who is writing a dissertation on Revolutionary legislation on illegitimacy at U.C. Berkeley, for directing me to appropriate sources, including his own scholarship.
 1. Philippe Bordes, "*La patrie en danger* par Lethière et l'esprit militaire," *La revue du Louvre et des Musées de France* 4–5 (1986), 301–306. Of course, in its foregrounding

YFS 101, *Fragments of Revolution*, ed. Weber and Lay, © 2002 by Yale University.

Figure 1. Guillaume Guillon-Lethière, *The Fatherland in Danger*, 1799. Oil on canvas. Musée de la Révolution française, Vizille.

Figure 2. Jacques-Louis David, *Oath of the Horatii*, 1785. Oil on canvas. Musée du Louvre, Paris.

late days of the Republic, the land of the father is imagined as a land of citizens unified by a founding absence, the elimination of the King in 1792, as well as by a perpetual external threat: foreign enemies. Absent fathers and absent but imperiling enemies. Herein lay preconditions for revolutionary fraternity and self-sacrifice.

The liveliness and sheer competency of Lethière's picture distract us from the quandary of founding a nation upon absences, but the animation of the scene attests to the pictorial as well as political ramifications of parricide: the dispersal of loci of attention. Without the simple patriarchal structure of oath-taking in the *Horatii*, without a symbolic center, Lethière's sons swear allegiance to multiple substitutes; the magistrate on the step, for example, but most prominently, the immense, elevated female personification that presides—impassive and unmoved—over the scene of pathos. In Lethière's celebration of the French revolution, as in much revolutionary iconography, the "fatherland" to which men pledge loyalty is a woman rendered inanimate and monumental. But in order to take such an oath, the crowd of men at the picture's center must look over and beyond a thick wall of persons, representatives of the French polity of a different sort: the row of strangely diminutive, seated government officials, partly obscured in shadow; the brightly lit and oversized naked pink babies; and the large women who hold them aloft. The oath of France's soldiers must leap over these persons. Loyalty to France is presumably sworn on their behalf but also requires an overlooking. Lethière's picture is therefore not so unlike David's *Oath of the Horatii*. It recapitulates that devotion to *la patrie* entails sacrifice, or a refusal to privilege—in some cases, even to recognize—the competing claims that individuals, including family members, may embody.

Of course, the stone female personification is meant to be representative of France's collectivity, to encompass and incorporate those various interests, to make coherent and visually discrete what would otherwise remain heterogeneous (note that she incorporates, and in a sense reconciles, the mothers' gender and the deputies' pose). But Lethière, unlike David in 1785, seems to be drawn as much to multiplicity, to the compelling, confusing variety of a crowd of diverse persons, as he is to political, pictorial, and symbolic simplification. The crowd

---

of female protagonists, Lethière's painting of 1799 resembles David's *Intervention of the Sabines* of the same year. The latter painting, however, valorizes the ending rather than the perpetuation of war. Concerning David's *Sabines*, see my "Nudity *à la grecque* in 1799," *Art Bulletin* 80/2 (June 1998), 311–35.

imbues the picture with its vitality, movement, and narrative richness while the stone statue personifying France remains a place-marker within the painting, simply a (provisional) object of this particular act of oath-taking (as contingent and replaceable, it seems, as was Bailly on top of the table in David's *Oath of the Tennis Court* of 1791). For Lethière, what matters is the polity—its celebratory variety and improvised pageantry. He even tries to diversify those oddly passive French government officials seated in a row before the standing mothers; they are variably lit and posed (one turns his head to look up at the demonstrative mother behind him) and they vary in skin color. A black deputy sits at their center (Fig. 3). Such deputies of African descent had indeed sat in the revolutionary assemblies after Jean-Baptiste Belley, former military captain, had arrived as elected official from Saint-Domingue in 1794, and Lethière could very well have depicted Belley's replacement, the dashing young officer Étienne Mentor.[2]

Lethière's registration of the presence of colonial deputies of African descent in the revolutionary body politic is at once accurate, unusual among French paintings of the 1790s—Girodet's 1797 portrait of Belley stands as the other, better-known exception to the rule—and explicable because of his origins. Guillaume Lethière was born in the French colony of Guadeloupe.[3] The painter of *The Fatherland in Danger* was the illegitimate son of a French royal official, Pierre Guillon, and a black slave named Marie-Françoise "dite" Pepayë. Although he had lived in France since the age of fourteen—that is, for some twenty-five years in 1799—Lethière would have been known in Paris as a "man of color" or a *sang-mêlé* (mixed-blood) and also as a colonial or creole: a man, in other words, marked by racial difference as well as by birth in the colonies. He was nicknamed "l'Américain" by fellow artists. With everything to win and not much to lose, the politically disenfranchised "men of color" enthusiastically embraced the revolution of 1789. Their bid for political rights was especially threatening to those

2. On the politics of race during the Revolutionary period and on Belley's as well as Girodet's portrait, see my *Extremities: Painting Empire in Post-Revolutionary France* (New Haven and London: Yale University Press, 2002), Chapter 1.

3. On Lethière, see G. Florent Laballe and Geneviève Capy, *Guillaume Guillon Lethière. Peintre d'histoire 1760–1832* (Point-à-Pitre: Centre des Arts et de la Culture, 1991); Geneviève Madec-Capy, "Guillaume Guillon-Lethière, peintre d'histoire (1760–1832)," Thèse de Doctorat d'histoire de l'art, Université de Paris IV, 1997; and G. Florent Laballe and Geneviève Capy, *1848–1998. Cent cinquantenaire de l'abolition de l'esclavage. Le serment des ancêtres de Guillaume Guillon-Lethière* (Fort-Delgrès, Basse-Terre: n.p., 1998); Hans Naef, *Die Bildniszeichnungen von J.-A.-D.-Ingres* (Bern: Benteli Verlag, 1977) I, 403–20.

Figure 3. Guillaume Guillon-Lethière, detail of *The Fatherland in Danger*, 1799. Oil on canvas. Musée de la Révolution française, Vizille.

in favor of sustaining the colonial slave economy because many were educated, affluent, tax-paying landowners; some possessed slaves. Given their wealth, the only basis for their continued disenfranchisement was racial difference, a matter hotly debated in 1791 that led to a series of contradictory legislative decisions. It is worth stressing that free men of color, not black slaves, forced many (proslavery) Frenchmen to turn to race to legitimate the disenfranchisement of dark-skinned persons. The possibility that *sang-mêlés* could "pass" into the French polity of active citizens drew more rather than less attention to their differences.

Lethière responded to the revolution as did other "men of color." Twenty-nine years old in 1789, he became an ardent revolutionary patriot and would sustain his revolutionary politics until his death in 1832. His charisma, poise, and considerable talent must have contributed to successes achieved despite the reactionary politics of subsequent regimes (and despite his temper, which at one point led to the temporary closure of his studio after he killed an officer in a duel). Lethière's color, foreign birth, and Republicanism did not ultimately prevent him from receiving the highest honors on offer to painters during the Napoleonic Empire and Bourbon Restoration: Directorship of the Academy in Rome (from 1807–1816); membership in the Legion of Honor (in 1818); appointment to the Institute (in 1818); Professorship in the École des Beaux-Arts (in 1819). These successes are all the more remarkable given evidence that Louis XVIII may have been disinclined to honor him. The King refused to approve his first election to the Institute in 1816; significantly the monarch had also declined the nomination of another *sang-mêlé*, the composer Saint Georges, as Opera director (Florent-Laballe and Capy, 1991).

Traces of Lethière's difference are few in his paintings. Here clearly was an assimilated "man of color," integrated not only within France's official institutions but also within its artistic community, actual and pictured. He is included, for example, in Louis-Léopold Boilly's clubbish portrait of elegant artists gathered in Isabey's studio (Fig. 4). Tall and handsome, he stands wrapped in a cape at the picture's center; charismatic but not the least bit disruptive. Lethière was presumed by Boilly to belong, a presumption Lethière seems to have shared. And Lethière's pictures declare that belonging as well. The man who had visited David in prison[4] and who was repeatedly portrayed, along with his entire fam-

4. Lethière also testified against David when he was imprisoned after the fall of Robespierre; see J. L. Jules David, *Le peintre Louis David 1748–1825. Souvenirs et documents inédits* (Paris: Victor Havard, 1880), 221, 257–58, 285–87.

Figure 4. Louis-Léopold Boilly, *The Studio of Isabey*, 1798. Oil on canvas. Musée du Louvre, Paris.

Figure 5. Guillaume Guillon-Lethière, *Philoctetes on the Island of Lemnos,*
1798. Oil on canvas. Musée du Louvre, Paris.

ily, by his good friend Ingres, produced a series of respectable if unexcit-
ing neoclassical pictures over his career, often several years after the subjects had been painted by David and his students. David painted *Brutus*
in 1789; Lethière painted versions of *Brutus* in 1801 and 1811; Drouais
painted *Philoctetes* in 1788; Lethière painted versions of *Philoctetes* in
1788, 1795 and 1798 (Fig. 5). France's classical canon of exemplarity with
its cast of Greek and Roman heroes was his own. The black deputy in
The Fatherland in Danger is as outnumbered by heroic white protagonists in his oeuvre as he is within that painting.

There is one remarkable exception among Lethière's pictures, however, and it is another scene of revolutionary oath-taking, *Oath of the
Ancestors* (Fig. 6). The solitary painting within which Lethière chose

Figure 6. Guillaume Guillon-Lethière, *Oath of the Ancestors*, 1822. Oil on canvas. Palais national, Port-au-Prince, Haiti.

to inscribe his foreign birth—"né à Guadeloupe"—takes as its subject not the revolution in France but the revolution in another French colony in the West Indies, Saint-Domingue (present-day Haiti); the revolution, that is, that transformed France's most lucrative slave colony into the first independent nation created by slaves turned revolutionaries. The Haitian revolution was the black revolution that haunted France's white one; the black revolution that erupted as a consequence of France's white revolution but quickly exceeded its control; the black revolution that defeated Napoleon's troops in 1802 and culminated in the declaration of the independence of Haiti in 1804. White/Black: the Haitian revolution was racially polarized in ways that required that persons of color—those persons who were, to cite Werner Sollors, "neither black nor white yet both"—be subsumed under one rubric or another.[5] *Sang-mêlés* had to choose. That choice of alliance—in which racial allegiances and self-definitions could exist in tension with personal and economic interests—made persons of color the most unpredictable, potentially decisive constituency during the Haitian revolution. Swinging between strategic alliances with white colonists and with black rebels, men of color ultimately joined forces with the latter: this is the moment celebrated in Lethière's remarkable picture of 1822. The painting depicts the alliance between the mulatto officer Alexandre Pétion—significantly, in half black and half white—and the black slave leader Jean-Jacques Dessalines—all in black. The mulatto Pétion had chosen, along with his troops, to defect from Bonaparte's army in 1802.[6] The fact that the alliance of mulatto and black leaders ultimately led to their victory and the founding of the Haitian nation is signaled within the picture by the stele over which the two men swear their oath. It is inscribed with the words of the Haitian constitution: "L'union fait la force. Vivre libre ou mourir. Il n'y a de véritable liberté qu'avec la religion . . . les loix . . . La Constitution" (Union makes strength. To live free or to die. There is no true liberty except with religion . . . laws . . . The Constitution).

Significantly, Lethière, the Guadeloupean-born, Parisian painter "of color" made a picture called *Oath of the Ancestors*. The emphasis on ancestors suggests that the picture was a personal gesture of allegiance and familial affiliation, of descent and origins. Unlike his neoclassical pic-

5. Werner Sollors, *Neither Black nor White Yet Both: Thematic Explorations of Interracial Literature* (Oxford: Oxford University Press, 1997).

6. On the history of the Haitian revolution, see Thomas Madiou, *Histoire d'Haiti* (Port-au-Prince: Éditions Henri Deschamps, 1988).

tures, and unlike *The Fatherland in Danger, Oath of the Ancestors* was intended not for a French audience—it was never shown in Paris—but for a Haitian one. The painting was personally delivered by Lethière's son Lucien to Port-au-Prince where it still hangs. The son delivered the father's gesture toward their ancestors in 1823, two years before Charles X finally and punitively recognized the nation of Haiti in return for a crippling debt intended to compensate France for its losses. Lethière's painting of 1822 was therefore an act of recognition, a tribute, made in advance of the French nation and against the Restoration government and offered as a gift rather than as an incurred debt. Lucien's transport of the picture was a covert act, noted by a French "secret agent" in Port-au-Prince when the ship, aptly named the "Alliance," first arrived from France.[7]

Lethière, the Institute member, Legionnaire of Honor, École-des-Beaux-Arts professor, and former Director of the Roman Academy, was smuggling a representation of his ancestry out of France and into the nation that had successfully rebelled against it. The loss of Saint-Domingue was, even in 1822, a loss acutely felt by the French. The debates as to whether France should recognize Haiti fully betrayed a pervasive nostalgic and futile desire to return to a prerevolutionary colonial age when gold from slave labor piled high. *Oath of the Ancestors* was therefore a surreptitious revolutionary picture made in honor of another revolution won at France's expense. In this painting, Lethière aligned himself with the foreign enemies not figured in *The Fatherland in Danger*—the black and mulatto men who rebelled as soldiers rather than sitting decorously as deputies. In 1799 when *The Fatherland in Danger* was painted, in those late days of the Directory immediately prior to Bonaparte's seizure of power in a coup d'état, revolutionary France and revolutionary men of color were not necessarily at war, but they soon would be. *Oath of the Ancestors* depicts that later moment when French and Haitian interests were no longer reconcilable; when the brave young deputy Étienne Mentor was killed; when the patriot deputy Jean-Baptiste Belley was betrayed and died, like the black rebel leader Toussaint L'Ouverture, in a French prison. Lethière's painting bravely refuses to repress the war—the conflict— that brought Haiti into existence. Pétion and Dessalines stand on the chains of slavery in full military uniform and in the distance troops are visible and so too is the rising smoke. Slavery, the picture declares, was only abolished because of these Haitians' valor as military leaders, be-

7. Archives Nationales OM/CC/9a/52.

cause of their alliance, and because of their determination "to live free or to die."

Nevertheless, given its heroic circumstances as a clandestine gift to a repressed revolutionary past, Lethière's painting is, I feel, strange and heart-breaking. The heartbreak stems, of course, from the figure of God. The French patriarch missing from *The Fatherland in Danger* has not only returned but has returned more omnipotent than ever before: a billowing emanation of light surmounting the pyramidal composition (the word Jehovah written in Hebrew above his head). Blanched, symmetrical, white-haired, circled by an aureole of bright, icy blue drapery, the figure belongs to another coloristic and pictorial universe and leaves the persons and land below him dark and obscure, in shadowy earth tones. Indeed the white Godhead is depicted as the light source in the picture, illuminating the far edge of the platform on which Pétion and Dessalines stand and casting the foreground and the stele itself in deep shadow. Of course, this was the Restoration and, yes, the Haitian constitution referred to God and, yes, the picture would come to hang in the Cathedral at Port-au-Prince. But the intensely racialized politics of the Haitian revolution made the choice to include a figure of God impossibly compromising. What color could he be other than white? Was not Lethière a well-trained French painter who rightly turned to sanctioned precedents, among them, altarpieces like Guido Reni's in the Quirinal Chapel, pictures he would have known very well because of his long residence in Rome?

Lethière offered a gift of recognition to the Haitian people, but within his picture, he depicted that gift as the beneficent blessing of a white patriarchal Godhead. This clandestine, indeed rebellious, act by a man of color sadly reinscribed the ultimate authority of the white patriarch. Lethière's painting relied on the patronizing structure deployed in abolitionist imagery (Fig. 7) and recycled three years later in prints commemorating France's official recognition of Haiti: Charles X, hand raised, blessing a grateful personification of Haiti (Fig. 8). At least Lethière showed standing military men rather than kneeling, naked slaves or, still worse, in the prints of 1825, female personifications of the Americans. (Those latter commemorative images insidiously implied that France recognized an indigenous native people—America—rather than an African population that it had displaced and enslaved.) But the syntax of condescension in Lethière's picture and the prints is the same. Recognition is a gift, not an accomplishment; recognition represents benevolence toward a subordinate rather than surrender to a victor.

SOYEZ LIBRES ET CITOYENS.

Figure 7. Charles Boily after Pierre Rouvier, "Soyez libres et citoyens," frontispiece for B. Frossard, *La cause des esclaves nègres*, 1789. Engraving. Bibliothèque nationale, Paris.

Figure 8. Anon., "S. M. Charles X, le bien-aimé reconnaissant l'indépendance de St. Domingue," 1825. Engraving. Bibliothèque nationale, Paris.

Moreover, the Haitian revolution, this picture implies, remains in-complete without the recognition of the white French father. The al-liance between Pétion and Dessalines, the symmetry that makes their union as equals visible, requires their rhyming poses of attentive de-ferral to the third term. As in David's *Oath of the Horatii*, the brothers unite by responding identically to the patriarch who organizes them.

It is far too easy to account for and to dismiss the failures of Le-thière's picture. The templates offered by Franco-Italian pictorial tra-ditions made the representation of radical Haitian revolution diffi-cult and necessarily cobbled together. The very success of Lethière's assimilation as a French painter and citizen made his strange picture probable: half altarpiece, half revolutionary manifesto; half white, half black—like Pétion's uniform, like Lethière's colonial origins. But I would like to pause over the picture's weirdness, to delay its dismissal (or its celebration) as all that might have been possible. The strange-ness of the picture stems not only from its hybrid iconography but from the double gesture it enacts: *Oath of the Ancestors* is a picture point-ing back to the revolutionary birth of a black nation two decades ear-lier (1802–4), but also back to Lethière's colonial origins—to a prerev-olutionary past in the West Indies that the sixty-two year old painter had left behind in 1774, almost half a century earlier. Its retrospection is multiple: revolution and prerevolution; its geographical displace-ments are also: Haiti and Guadeloupe. But the picture is also a picture of 1822, of Bourbon Restoration, and of Paris. Why after all did Lethière paint *Oath of the Ancestors* in 1822, eighteen years after the founding of Haiti?

He did so partly because of recent events in Haiti. In 1811, the black leader Christophe had declared himself King Henry I and ruled the north with the lavish accoutrements of monarchy, while the "mixed-blood" President Pétion and his successor Boyer had sustained Repub-licanism in the south. Lethière sustains this opposition between black monarchical opulence and mulatto Republican simplicity in his juxta-position of the military uniforms of black leader Dessalines and mu-latto Pétion. In 1820, two years before Lethière painted his picture, the black monarch Christophe had died and the mulatto president Boyer had immediately declared the unification of northern and southern Haiti. 1820 thus marked the reintegration of (black and mulatto, north and south) Haiti as a Republic. Lethière, the ardent *sang-mêlé* revolu-tionary and republican, would have been pleased. In 1822, moreover, Boyer had temporarily seized control of the Spanish half of the island,

Santo-Domingo, uniting the entire island as the Republic of Haiti. 1822 was therefore an important date in Haiti's history as an autonomous Republican nation ruled by a mulatto president.

But Lethière's decision to paint *Oath of the Ancestors* in 1822 may also have stemmed from more personal events. Lethière had recently been forced, in Paris, to confront and to represent his Creole past as well as his racial identity. In fact, his difference and his origins had become a matter of public record. *Oath of the Ancestors* is signed "G. Guillon Le Thière, né à la Guadeloupe, An 1760, Paris, 1822, 7bre." Lethière thus inscribes the painting with both his origins and his picture's; his birth and, during the act of signing, his present. It is the name, "G. Guillon Lethière," that unifies and connects the dates, that makes the gap between 1760 and 1822 (and the space between Guadeloupe and Paris) continuous—a life. The name of this *sang-mêlé* painter was, however, as disjunctive a bricolage as his 1822 picture. At his birth, Lethière had been given a homonym of his father's withheld surname as his first name: not "Guillon" (fils) but, bastardized, "Guillaume." The name "Guillaume" was the extent to which the slave's son inherited a paternal name. Only fourteen years later, when his father brought him to France, was the future painter given a surname. France, not Guadeloupe, required a proper name, but it would not be his father's. In 1774, Pierre Guillon enrolled his illegitimate son Guillaume in art school and chose to call him "Le Tiers" because he was his third such "enfant naturel." Lethière's surname was therefore at once fabricated and a record of his position in his father's sequence of illegitimate children. The painter's name was produced by his illegitimacy and, at least for the son and the father, continued to signal it. The "Guillon" signed at the bottom of the *Oath of the Ancestors* marked, therefore, a later achievement: the legal recognition by Pierre Guillon of his illegitimate thirty-nine year old son in 1799, a recognition only made possible by recent revolutionary legislation of 12 Brumaire an II (1794) which attempted to extend equality before the law even to France's bastards. Pierre Guillon's recognition of Lethière also likely depended on the death of Guillon's two legitimate children—his lack, that is, of an heir to bear his name.[8] In 1799 Guillaume Lethière added Guillon to the name by which he was already well-known.

8. See Laurence Boudouard and Florence Bellivier, "Des droits pour les bâtards, l'enfant naturel dans les débats révolutionnaires," in Irène Thiry and Christian Biet, eds., *La famille, la loi, l'état de la Revolution au Code Civil* (Paris: Centre Georges Pompidou, 1989), 122–44.

Evidence suggests that the father and son were close despite the fact
that they lived most of their lives apart from one another. Their letters
indicate, for instance, that Guillon's legal recognition of Lethière was
an act they had long discussed and carefully considered. A letter of 1797
written by Guillon from Washington D.C. indicates what he believed
was at stake:

> This title announces to you my friend, the certainty of my paternity,
> the desire to transmit my name and my properties [*biens*] to he whom
> nature designates should possess them and who by his social virtues
> merits them as much as you do: for a long time, I have wanted to ren-
> der this justice if the exclusive laws of the ancien régime relative to
> your primitive condition had not taken the power away from me; and
> if those now repealing the former laws, and without a particular rule
> concerning this, had given me the power in a sensible fashion not sus-
> ceptible to contradictions; which I did not believe to be the case with
> the Code of Civil Laws of the new legislation. The first question that
> must be resolved immediately because the nullity of this application
> would engender incidents more prejudicial than profitable to your hap-
> piness, your satisfaction and your fortune, the objects of my paternal
> solicitude—is whether it is necessary to provide besides the name of
> the mother, her status, her condition at the time of the birth of her son,
> and if, an omission would lead to difficulties capable of rendering null
> the effects of the adoption [. . .and also] if the laws apply to an individ-
> ual over the age of 14 . . . Concerning [the condition of the mother], I
> fear as I said above that reticence on this subject will give birth to con-
> testations, [whether] well or badly founded, and that these would im-
> print [on you] the humiliation of publicity. From all of this comes the
> desire to know if the Code on adoption is made and promulgated and, if
> valid, whether it is possible to keep the secret [*garder le tacet*] con-
> cerning the status of the condition of she who brought you into the light
> of day. Finally what would be the real advantages you would derive from
> this?[9]

Guillon claimed that he had always wanted legally to recognize his illegitimate son. Lethière deserved to be recognized because he was indeed his son—nature designated him to be so—and because he was
worthy. But Guillon had not been able to do what he wished because of
the law (which deemed Lethière's status to be "primitive"). Now revolutionary legislation might permit the legal transmission of his name
and properties to his son, but the advantages of proceeding still might

9. Archives Nationales/476/AP/12; cited in Capy, 1997, 181–86; my translation.

not outweigh the risks, "the humiliation of publicity." Could the white father recognize his illegitimate son without exposing what he called "the secret"? Lethière's mother may have "brought him into the light of day" but she herself needed to remain in darkness. The question was whether Lethière's paternal origins could now come into the light of law while leaving his humiliating maternal origins obscure. Pierre Guillon's anxieties were not his alone. The revolutionary legislation and the debates it engendered repeated again and again that the illegitimacy in question was only that resulting from the sexual union of parents who were both free at the time of their child's birth.

Despite Guillon's concerns, Lethière would be legally recognized by his father in 1799. Nevertheless, twenty years later, Lethière's mother would become the subject of public inquiry. In 1819, when the painter was fifty-nine, his right to inherit Pierre Guillon's estate was contested in French court by a collateral relative. A man named Delpeyron claimed that he was Pierre Guillon's lawful heir, not because Guillaume Lethière's mother had been a slave, not because Guillaume Lethière was "mixed-blood," not because Guillaume Lethière was illegitimate—a bastard—but because he was an *"adulterin,"* the child of an adulterous liaison who was indeed excluded from the legislation concerning illegitimacy. Delpeyron's case pivoted on the contestation of Guillaume Lethière's date of birth and the fact that neither son nor father had produced a birth certificate in 1799. Because Pierre Guillon had been married in 1762, Delpeyron insisted Guillaume had not been born in 1760. He even produced a birth certificate for a boy named Guillaume born in 1765 to a "mulatta" named Marie-Jeanne (instead of Marie-Françoise). The fact that both mothers, in all likelihood both slaves, lacked surnames as did their sons—named only Guillaume—made Delpeyron's charges more difficult for Lethière and his lawyer to dismiss. To have only first names was to have less certain legal identities. Lethière was in a bind. He needed the recognition by Pierre Guillon that Delpeyron contested as illegal. He required, it seems, perpetual confirmation by his father, in this case, confirmation of his date of birth, in order to protect himself from the confiscation of his inheritance and the "humiliation of publicity." Short of that, he needed the sanction of France's courts.

He ultimately won the latter, but not without the publication in the *Gazette de France* and the *Moniteur universel* of his lawyer's statement. His story became public. Lethière's lawyer referred to the painter's origins and name as a "modest and naïve genealogy." Since Marie-

Jeanne was a mulatta, the lawyer needed to admit that Lethière's mother was black, not mulatta, but he would not say so explicitly. Instead he referred to her only as "a woman of color." The lawyer pointed out that while this fact might have clinched Delpeyron's case if Lethière had been born in Paris, such circumstances were "far from sufficient to establish a perfect identity" in Guadeloupe. There, women of color were as numerous as white women. The lawyer also admitted that if Pierre Guillon had given Lethière life alone, he may not have chosen to honor him with legitimacy. However,

> a lively and tender friendship united [father and son]; even absence itself could not alter their sympathy, an uninterrupted correspondence brought them proofs, across the oceans, of their mutual attachment. Pierre Guillon came to France; his son received him in his domicile at the Louvre; it was in this noble asylum, given by our Kings to the beaux-arts, that Letiers closed his father's eyes. Thus, Sirs, was purified the relationship whose origin was vicious.[10]

The lawyer's statement is deft and it is revealing. Neither Lethière's mother's blackness nor her status as slave are stated. The term "woman of color" leaves vague and unspecified her social and racial identity, although it makes clear that she was not white. Her identity, he underscores, was far from certain; in a fundamental way, it was insufficient. Instead, paternal affection plays an important role in the lawyer's defense and so too does Lethière's profession. The deathbed scene of filial piety occurs in the Louvre, the "noble asylum" of the arts given by the King to France's artists. Just as Pierre Guillon had recognized Lethière so too had Louis XVIII: the artist was a worthy son whose "vicious origins" were purified by his noble feeling and by the fact that his merit and his loyalty had been recognized, recognized by France's fathers.

"G. Guillon Le Thière, né à la Guadeloupe, An 1760, Paris, 1822, 7bre.": the signature on *Oath of the Ancestors* can be understood to serve as a legal document. The first name Guillaume, which had failed to distinguish Lethière from Marie-Jeanne's son of the same name, is truncated to "G." It was, one might argue, redundant with Guillon in any case and it is his father's surname that Lethière chooses to claim, along with his colonial birthplace, Guadeloupe and, just as significantly, his birthdate. G. Guillon Lethière, the third illegitimate son of Guillon, was born in 1760 in Guadeloupe not in 1765. He was illegiti-

---

10. *Gazette de France*, 28 February 1819; cited in Naef, 405–6; my translation.

mate but not *"adulterin."* His father's benificent act of recognition was legal and the painting implies, binding—the truth before God, the truth as if his Father was God. No wonder that the figure of Pétion is so much more animated and well-illuminated than Dessalines; the light of the Father brings him into light, the light of recognition in law as in history and as in pictures. This painting initiated by the unification of Haiti under a Republican mulatto president privileges the *sang-mêlé* over the opulently ornamented (read monarchical) black. This is not to minimize the alliance the picture expresses with Dessalines, the former black slave become rebel leader and founder of Haiti. This is a picture not just of a father and a son but also of revolutionary brothers. The problem is the difficulty in imagining from where and from whom Dessalines could come. God does not appear to be his father. The diagonal edge where black and white clouds meet at the picture's very center descends from God the Father towards Pétion, not towards Dessalines. The black military officer is cast in a more ambiguous, hushed shadow. His only possible parent is even less visible. She stands at the far right of the picture, behind the platform, arms upraised, holding directly before her a naked baby, like the women in *The Fatherland in Danger*, but she and her child are dark-skinned (Fig. 9). The black slave mother makes her appearance in Lethière's homage to his colonial past and to black revolution, but she is noticed only tangentially, late, and circuitously, when the viewer succeeds in turning away from the blinding light of the white patriarch and accustoms his/her eyes to the darkness.

Illegitimate sons and illegitimate revolutions required their father's recognition. The paradox is that they required it in order to sustain their autonomy in the world, as painters and as nations. And even under revolutionary law, illegitimate sons, like illegitimate nations, could not sue the patriarch for recognition. Instead, legitimacy and paternal lineage were gifts that needed, by law, to be freely given. French revolutionaries wanted to incorporate bastards into the body politic, but not to unleash paternity suits. Paternal recognition was a legal act that had to be initiated by the father, not the son, not the mother. Herein lay the structure reproduced in Lethière's picture of the founding of the Haitian nation. We witness the gift. To the deserving but not the demanding. We witness their legitimation. So far from revolution and yet legislated by it.

Paternity is, of course, a tenuous, uncertain relation. Perhaps this is why revolutionaries defined it as a gift, fundamentally an adoption.

Figure 9. Guillaume Guillon-Lethière, Detail of *Oath of the Ancestors,* 1822.
Oil on canvas. Palais National, Port-au-Prince, Haiti.

Biological paternity could be as easily disclaimed as claimed. By fathers, by mothers, or by sons. Paternity might be where one least expected it. Men of color may have been particularly alert to such questions as well as to their stakes. And they may have seen them in pictures where we see none. General Alexandre Dumas was Lethière's close friend and shared his circumstances. Two years Lethière's junior, Dumas was also born in the West Indies, in his case, Haiti, and he too was brought to France at the age of fourteen by a white French father who bore another name. General Dumas would die young, poor, injured by war, and betrayed by Bonaparte (who could not forgive him for abandoning Egypt), but his novelist son would frequent Lethière's fashionable salon throughout the Restoration, delighting in the painter's tafia from Guadeloupe as well as his attractive republican French mistress. In his *Mémoires*, the writer Alexandre Dumas would pay homage to the painter's generosity as well as his talent. And he would also rewrite, from the perspective of a man of color, Lethière's far-from-original neoclassical pictures. According to the novelist Dumas, Lethière's Philoctetes was none other than Dumas's beautiful, mortally wounded, Herculean father—a *sang-mêlé* who posed as an antique hero and "passed" so well that only son and painter could see him still. Brutus, the republican father who sacrificed his sons because they conspired against the republic, was also not what he seemed. Dumas recounts:

> The famous painter Lethière [was] author of *Brutus condemning his sons*, a heroism that always seemed to me a bit Spartan, until it was explained to me later by Ponsard's *Lucretia*. Monsieur Ponsard first revealed this great conjugal mystery, that the sons of Brutus were, not the sons of Brutus, but only the children of adultery: in having their heads cut off, Brutus did not sacrifice himself, he avenged himself![11]

Dumas shockingly rewrites the tale of the virtuous self-sacrifice of a republican patriarch. The very sacrifice of sons that made Brutus the most severe and patriotic republican is rescripted by the "mixed-blood" author as a form of self-interest and vengeance against his wife's adultery: "The sons of Brutus were, not the sons of Brutus." Nevertheless, in Dumas's lurid scenario, the sons could be recognized by Brutus as sons. And as sons they could also be killed by him. Ultimately, the father did not control paternity (Dumas's comma is devastating),

11. Alexandre Dumas, *Mes mémoires* (Paris, Gallimard, 1967), vol. 3, 14–15. The son of the General, the novelist Alexandre Dumas is known as Alexandre Dumas *père* to distinguish him from his son (the General's grandson) who also became a writer.

but he enjoyed the prerogative of choosing to recognize or not to recognize, to let live or to let die those he chose to claim as sons. Brutus
was the patriarch who wielded this control. Whether he was their biological father or not.

Sons, in turn, could choose revolution and also murder. Parricide
was enacted again and again in Haiti as well as in France. Or sons could
direct their longing for revolution and also for their fathers into their
art. They could imagine their fathers as Philoctetes and as God the Father, martyr fathers and deity fathers. Absences both. In the arts of
men of color, familial lineage was at stake but so too were absences
and compensatory recognitions. Looking back at the *Fatherland in
Danger*, it is worth noting that it is a picture not only of revolutionary
oath-taking but also of departures, of voyages, and of families separated by ships that take men elsewhere, away from wives, away from
mothers, away from children. In Lethière's life, he had been the revolutionary son who had entered France rather than left it, but his arrival
entailed leaving behind not only his slave mother but his French father. Lethière's departures and displacements were not easy ones nor
were they entirely predictable. The white father was in the colonies,
but the white fatherland was France where Lethière would reside for
58 of his 72 years.

In 1822, Lethière sent a gift back to his colonial past and to his father's, and he sent it with his twenty-one year old son who departed
from his father and his birth country to travel to Haiti. The small, shy,
fair boy pictured behind his French mother's skirt in Ingres' line drawing (Fig. 10) bravely defined himself as "a man of color"—the secret
agent in Port-au-Prince tells us so—and as his father's son, and returned
to the colonies of his father's birth. Lucien stayed in Haiti and married
a Haitian woman. He died only a few years later, leaving behind a young
daughter for whom Lethière would provide (as he provided for his el-
dest son Alexandre's children after his early death). Familial recognition and adoption were important acts in Lethière's history. While
Alexandre (possibly named after his friend General Dumas) would remain illegitimate, Lethière had married his younger son's mother only
months after his own father, Pierre Guillon, had finally legally adopted
him. For this creole man of color, the chain of lineage, of paternal succession, could not be taken for granted but needed to be made, by
French law—the law of the father, and of the fatherland, but also of the
revolution. Revolution, in Haiti as in France, could entail parricide, yet
it also promised recognition, incorporation, and adoption into the law-

Figure 10. Jean-Auguste-Dominique Ingres, *Madame Guillaume Guillon Lethière, née Marie-Joseph Vanzenne, and Her Son Lucien Lethière*, 1808. Graphite on paper. The Metropolitan Museum of Art, New York.

ful body politic. Those contradictory desires—for revolution, for parricide, and for paternal succession—could be inscribed, strangely and uncomfortably, in paintings like Lethière's where the expelled white father returns, but not as a man on the earth, and bestows his recognition upon his deserving dark-skinned sons.

Contributors

PETER BROOKS is Sterling Professor of Comparative Literature and French at Yale University. His most recent book is *Troubling Confessions: Speaking Guilt in Law and Literature.*

DAWN M. CORNELIO is Visiting Assistant Professor at Manchester College. Her research interests include the contemporary novel, translation, bilingual writers, and contemporary poetry. Her translations have appeared in *Poetry Magazine* and *Sites.*

DARCY GRIMALDO GRIGSBY is Associate Professor of History of Art at the University of California, Berkeley and author of *Extremities: Painting Empire in Post-Revolutionary France* (Yale University Press, 2002). She currently has two books in progress: *Creole Looking,* and *Colossal Empire, Colossal Engineering: France's Orientalism and its Modernity.*

JENNIFER M. JONES is Associate Professor of history at Rutgers University. Her research focuses on women in Old Regime France. She has written on French fashion culture (*Sexing La Mode: Gender, Fashion and Commercial Culture in Old Regime France,* forthcoming 2002) and is currently researching courtship and sociability in the Enlightenment.

HOWARD G. LAY is Assistant Professor of the History of Art at the University of Michigan. He has written on Degas, Seurat, the caricaturist André Gill, and the propagandist Émile Pouget. His book on oppositional visual practices in fin-de-siècle Paris, *Codes of Misconduct,* is forthcoming.

DARRIN M. MCMAHON is a Fellow in History at the Remarque Institute, New York University. He is the author of *Enemies of the Enlightenment: The French Counter-Enlightenment and the Making of Modernity* (New York: Oxford University Press, 2001), and the forthcoming *In Pursuit: A History of Happiness in the West* (New York: Grove-Atlantic Press).

ERIKA NAGINSKI is a junior fellow at the Society of Fellows, Harvard University, and an assistant professor in the Department of Architecture at MIT. She has written essays on Piranesi, on Riegl, and on drawing practices in the modern period. She is currently completing a book about sculpture at the end of the Enlightenment.

JEANNENE M. PRZYBLYSKI is Executive Director of the San Francisco Bureau of Urban Secrets, situated at the intersection of art, activism, and everyday life. She teaches art history and critical theory in the graduate programs at Mills College and the San Francisco Art Institute. Her book, *The Camera on the Barricades: Photography and the Paris Commune of 1871*, is forthcoming from the University of Minnesota Press.

JEAN-MARIE ROULIN, Assistant Professor at the University of Pennsylvania, is the author of *Chateaubriand, l'exil et la gloire. Du roman familial à l'identité littéraire* (Champion, 1994) and co-author of *Récits littéraires et romans populaires. Évolution des mentalités en Suisse romande au cours des cent dernières années* (L'âge d'homme, 1991). He has published numerous articles on the "Tournant des Lumières," French Romanticism, and on Swiss French Literature. He is currently working on a book on the epic in France from Voltaire to Chateaubriand.

DEBARATI SANYAL is Assistant Professor of French at the University of California, Berkeley. She has published articles in *Nineteenth-Century French Studies*, *Yale French Studies*, and *Representations* (forthcoming). She is completing a study on Baudelaire, violence, and poetry.

RICHARD TERDIMAN is Professor of Literature and the History of Consciousness at the University of California, Santa Cruz. He recently served as Visiting Professor in Romance Languages at Harvard University. His books include *Discourse/Counter-Discourse: The Theory and Practice of Symbolic Resistance in Nineteenth-Century France* (1985) and *Present Past: Modernity and the Memory Crisis* (1993). He is completing a book on the Enlightenment and poststructuralism: *Body and Story: Diderot Discovers Postmodernism*.

CAROLINE WEBER is Assistant Professor of Romance Languages at the University of Pennsylvania. Her forthcoming book is *Terror and Its Discontents: The Shadow of Totality in French Revolutionary Discourse* (Minneapolis: University of Minnesota Press).

Photo Credits

208. Réunion des Musées Nationaux.
209. Réunion des Musées Nationaux.
210. Réunion des Musées Nationaux.
214. Bibliothèque Nationale de France.
215. Bibliothèque Nationale de France.
222. Réunion des Musées Nationaux.
225. The Metropolitan Museum of Art, H. O. Havemeyer Collection, Bequest of Mrs. H. O. Havemeyer, 1929 (29.100.191).

The following issues are available through **Yale University Press,** Customer Service Department, P.O. Box 209040, New Haven, CT 06520-9040.

69 The Lesson of Paul de Man (1985) $17.00

73 Everyday Life (1987) $17.00

75 The Politics of Tradition: Placing Women in French Literature (1988) $17.00

Special Issue: After the Age of Suspicion: The French Novel Today (1989) $17.00

76 Autour de Racine: Studies in Intertextuality (1989) $17.00

77 Reading the Archive: On Texts and Institutions (1990) $17.00

78 On Bataille (1990) $17.00

79 Literature and the Ethical Question (1991) $17.00

Special Issue: Contexts: Style and Value in Medieval Art and Literature (1991) $17.00

80 Baroque Topographies: Literature/History/ Philosophy (1992 $17.00

81 On Leiris (1992) $17.00

82 Post /Colonial Conditions Vol. 1 (1993) $17.00

83 Post /Colonial Conditions Vol. 2 (1993) $17.00

84 Boundaries: Writing and Drawing (1993) $17.00

85 Discourses of Jewish Identity in 20th-Century France (1994) $17.00

86 Corps Mystique, Corps Sacré (1994) $17.00

87 Another Look, Another Woman (1995) $17.00

88 Depositions: Althusser, Balibar, Macherey (1995) $17.00

89 Drafts (1996) $17.00

90 Same Sex / Different Text? Gay and Lesbian Writing in French (1996) $17.00

91 Genet: In the Language of the Enemy (1997) $17.00

92 Exploring the Conversible World (1997) $17.00

93 The Place of Maurice Blanchot (1998) $17.00

94 Libertinage and Modernity (1999) $17.00

95 Rereading Allegory: Essays in Memory of Daniel Poirion (1999) $17.00

96 50 Years of *Yale French Studies*, Part I: 1948-1979 (1999) $17.00

97 50 Years of *Yale French Studies*, Part 2: 1980-1998 (2000) $17.00

98 The French Fifties (2000) $17.00

99 Jean-François Lyotard: Time and Judgment (2001) $17.00

100 France/USA: The Cultural Wars (2001) $17.00

Special subscription rates are available on a calendar-year basis (2 issues per year):
Individual subscriptions $26.00
Institutional subscriptions $30.00

ORDER FORM **Yale University Press,** P.O. Box 209040, New Haven, CT 06520-9040
I would like to purchase the following individual issues:

_____
_____

For individual issues, please add postage and handling:
Single issue, United States $2.75   Each additional issue $.50
Single issue, foreign countries $5.00   Each additional issue $1.00
Connecticut residents please add sales tax of 6%.

Payment of $_____ is enclosed (including sales tax if applicable).

MasterCard no. _____   Expiration date _____

VISA no. _____   Expiration date _____

Signature _____

SHIP TO _____

_____
_____

See the next page for ordering other back issues. Yale French Studies is also available through Xerox University Microfilms, 300 North Zeeb Road, Ann Arbor, MI 48106.

The following issues are still available through the **Yale French Studies Office**, P.O. Box 208251, New Haven, CT 06520-8251.

19/20 Contemporary Art $3.50	42 Zola $5.00	54 Mallarmé $5.00
33 Shakespeare $3.50	43 The Child's Part $5.00	61 Toward a Theory of Description $6.00
35 Sade $3.50	45 Language as Action $5.00	
39 Literature and Revolution $3.50	46 From Stage to Street $3.50	
	52 Graphesis $5.00	

Add for postage & handling

Single issue, United States $3.00 (Priority Mail)   Each additional issue $1.25
Single issue, United States $1.80 (Third Class)   Each additional issue $ .50
Single issue, foreign countries $2.50 (Book Rate)   Each additional issue $1.50

YALE FRENCH STUDIES, P.O. Box 208251, New Haven, Connecticut 06520-8251
A check made payable to YFS is enclosed. Please send me the following issue(s):

Issue no.   Title   Price

_____

_____

Postage & handling _____

Total _____

Name _____

Number/Street _____

City _____ State _____ Zip _____

- -

The following issues are now available through Periodicals Service Company, 11 Main Street, Germantown, N.Y. 12526, Phone: (518) 537-4700. Fax: (518) 537-5899.

1 Critical Bibliography of Existentialism	19/20 Contemporary Art
2 Modern Poets	21 Poetry Since the Liberation
3 Criticism & Creation	22 French Education
4 Literature & Ideas	23 Humor
5 The Modern Theatre	24 Midnight Novelists
6 France and World Literature	25 Albert Camus
7 André Gide	26 The Myth of Napoleon
8 What's Novel in the Novel	27 Women Writers
9 Symbolism	28 Rousseau
10 French-American Literature Relationships	29 The New Dramatists
11 Eros, Variations...	30 Sartre
12 God & the Writer	31 Surrealism
13 Romanticism Revisited	32 Paris in Literature
14 Motley: Today's French Theater	33 Shakespeare in France
15 Social & Political France	34 Proust
16 Foray through Existentialism	48 French Freud
17 The Art of the Cinema	51 Approaches to Medieval Romance
18 Passion & the Intellect, or Malraux	

36/37 Structuralism has been reprinted by Doubleday as an Anchor Book.
55/56 Literature and Psychoanalysis has been reprinted by Johns Hopkins University Press, and can be ordered through Customer Service, Johns Hopkins University Press, Baltimore, MD 21218.